Democracy and Moral Development

David L. Norton

UNIVERSITY OF CALIFORNIA PRESS

Berkeley / Los Angeles / London

University of California Press
Berkeley and Los Angeles, California

University of California Press, Ltd.
London, England

Copyright © 1991 by The Regents of the University of California

First Paperback Printing 1995

Library of Congress Cataloging-in-Publication Data

Norton, David L.
    Democracy and moral development / David L. Norton.
        p.   cm.
    Includes bibliographical references and index.
    ISBN 0-520-20348-8
    1. Political ethics—History.   2. Ethics, Comparative.   3. Ethics,
    Greek.   I. Title.
    JA79.N67 1991
    172—dc20   90-37723
                                                            CIP

Printed in the United States of America

1 2 3 4 5 6 7 8 9

For Mary

Contents

Preface

In the past decade, Anglo-American ethical theory has been showing signs of undergoing a sea-change. Though they remain as yet a minority, philosophers in growing numbers have been calling for the replacement of the modern mode of ethical theorizing by the very different mode that prevailed in classical Greece and Rome.[1]

The two modes of ethical theorizing are dramatically different because they begin with different fundamental questions. The fundamental question for modern moral theory is, What is the right thing to do in given moral situations? The corresponding question in classical ethical theory is, What is a good life for a human being? These disparate beginnings produce significant divergence both in the course of ethical inquiry and in the conduct of moral life.

What follows in the pages of this book is a treatise in political theory, yet it cannot be inattentive to ethics, for it is a treatise in political theory in the classical, not the modern mode, and in the classical mode ethics and politics are inseparable. An answer to the primary political question, What is good government?, is dependent upon an answer to the primary moral question, What is a good life for a human being?, which is in turn dependent upon an understanding of what a human being is. Good government is government that affords to the persons who comprise its constituency the requisite social conditions for leading the best lives possible. In the introduction that follows this preface we will set forth the eudaimonistic (classical Greek) understandings of what it is to be a human being and what it is to live a good life. I think the profundity of the ancient Greeks in the questions they posed and the answers they offered surpasses the modern understandings by which we live today. In chapter 1 we will seek the roots of the modern understandings, and identify their key deficiency, in the realpolitik of Machiavelli and Hobbes and the classical liberalism most notably of Locke. The rest of the book is an endeavor to set forth the social and political terms that are entailed by the eudaimonistic understanding of worthy, intrinsically rewarding living by persons, and to show how that understanding can be cultivated, and why it should be.

We may usefully preface what follows by saying a little more now about the contrast between modern and eudaimonistic ethics (with supplementation to follow at opportune places in subsequent chapters).

Eudaimonistic ethics is definitively identified by its preoccupation with the growth of moral character in individuals. To begin with the question "What is a worthy life for a human being?" is to be led immediately to problems of the development of moral character because any reasonable answer will include attributes that are not manifest in the beginnings of persons' lives, but are developmental outcomes. For example most of the moral virtues—such as wisdom, courage, temperance, justice—are not to be expected of children, but only of persons in later life, and only in the later life of persons in whom the requisite moral development occurs. In recognition of the focus of eudaimonistic ethics upon the development of moral character, I will classify it as "ethics of character."

By contrast ethics in the modern mode (since Hobbes) lends itself to classification as "ethics of rules." As noted above, its primary question is, What is the right thing to do in given moral situations? The established strategy is to formulate a supreme and universally applicable moral principle—such as Hobbes's natural right of self-preservation, Kant's categorical imperative, Bentham's "greatest happiness of the greatest number," Rawls's two principles of justice—together with criteria for distinguishing moral from nonmoral situations, criteria for recognizing relevantly different kinds of moral situations, and as far as practicable a complete list of rules for directly applying the supreme principle to different types of moral situations, or a list of rules of conduct representing the outcome of such application. Then moral conduct is the conduct that best accords with the applicable rules in given moral situations.

It must be noted that the disparity between the two modes is not "hard" but "soft," and in two senses. It is so, first, in the respect that historical exceptions are to be noted. There are character-ethicists in modernity—for example Nietzsche, Emerson, Thoreau, the Scottish "moral sense" school (notably Hutcheson, Hume, Adam Smith), James, Dewey, and including brilliant flashes in John Stuart Mill—but they are a distinct minority and had little effect against the dominant modern mode. And rules ethics was by no means unknown in the ancient world, but is recognizable there as the moribund residue of ethics of character.

Second, the modes are not mutually exclusive, but instead represent a difference in emphasis and understanding. Modern "rules ethics" cannot wholly ignore the development of moral character, for certain traits of developed character are needed if conduct is to accord with the appropriate rules. Conversely "character ethics" cannot escape the need of rules, conspicuously to regulate the conduct of persons who do not possess the requisite character development (until I wish to treat my neighbor fairly because of what he is and what I am, my conduct with respect to him must be governed by a rule of fairness). But this difference in emphasis, because it is pervasive, adds up to a radical transformation. Character ethics subordinates rules to the development of moral character and views them instrumentally with reference to that end; rules ethics attends to the development of moral character insofar as rule-abiding conduct requires it. A major difference is that character ethics demands of individuals a continuous moral growth—a "self-surpassing"—that is without upper limit so long as they live. By contrast rules ethics is minimalist, and in two senses.

First, it is minimalist in regarding many of the choice-making situations of ordinary life as nonmoral—for example, the choices of vocation and avocations to pursue, of friends to cultivate, of books to read. But if the development of character is the moral objective, it is obvious that these choices (for example) are moral, for they clearly influence such development.

We can capture the eudaimonist perspective by recognizing *the moral situation as the life of each individual,* within which nothing that appears is devoid of moral meaning.

Second, modern morality is minimalist by virtue of its understanding of rules as applicable uniformly to everyone under the requirements of "universalizability" and "impartiality." If what is right for anyone must be right for everyone in relevantly similar circumstances, then what is right must be such as can be recognized and acted upon by persons who possess very little in the way of developed moral character. Impartiality functions to preclude justification to persons who seek to evade the rules; but the cost is a moral minimalism that abandons elevated moral conduct. The typical modern way of handling moral conduct that in the least surpasses the minimum is by terming it "supererogatory," where this is understood as what is good to do but not bad not to do—that is, it is required of no one. This means that moral growth (beyond minimal rules-obedience) is required of no one. This eradicates the concept of *noblesse oblige* in its moral meaning, by which persons recognize that their responsibility for continuous moral growth is their responsibility for progressively more elevated moral conduct.

Presently in our country there is a mounting cry for "more integrity'" in business and public office. It is an expression of alarm at repeated exposure of deception and corruption in high places—Iran-Contra; Ivan Boesky and Michael Milken; E. F. Hutton; Skinner Peabody, Drexel Burnham; Bank of Credit and Commerce International (laundering drug profits); the General Electric, Wedtech, and Sundstrand contract scandals; the corruption-ridden practices in the Savings and Loan industry and in Housing and Urban Development. Apart from legal proceedings, the significant responses to date consist in a flurry of concern for the reformulation of professional codes of ethics, together with mounting endorsement of the introduction of courses of ethics in colleges of business, public administration, and the professions.

It deserves notice that these measures are rules resorts. As such they embody the presuppositions of rules-morality and leave untouched the deep problem of the development of the higher moral character that is requisite for worthy, responsible living. The disparity between disease and prescribed treatment is nowhere more striking than in a New York Times news story of July 13, 1988 that begins, "The Harvard Business School is expected to announce shortly that it will require entering MBA students to take a three-week course on business ethics." In eudaimonistic perspective, modern neglect of the development of moral character over four centuries has had the effect of trivializing the meanings of each of the moral virtues, while cutting them adrift from their foundations in moral development. In this light the Harvard Business School announcement is a *reductio ad absurdam* regarding the "integrity" that is wanting, but is proportionate to the modern, superficial understanding of this virtue. How and why this trivialization of the virtues came about will be the subject of chapter 1. The eudaimonistic understanding of the virtue of integrity will be offered in chapter 4, and chapters 3 and 4 will treat its foundations, its centrality to worthy living, its availability to all persons, and its cultivation.

Eudaimonistic political theory differs from modern political theory just as strikingly as eudaimonistic ethical theory differs from modern. It is not that each answers the basic questions differently, but that each begins with different basic questions. The reason this is so is that each starts with a different conception of human nature and individuality. That is where we will begin. The introduction sets forth the eudaimonistic understanding of human nature, individuality, and moral life; chapter 1 uncovers the roots of the corresponding modern conceptions. At bottom it is the question of how each of us conceives of himself or herself, and nothing that I provide in pages to follow is intended as coercive argumentation. Our self-conceptions are (if we have extricated ourselves from our conferred childhood identities, as self-responsible living in eudaimonistic perspective requires) our choice. If the eudaimonistic self-conception were to become prevalent, significant social changes would attend this transformation, and I have tried to indicate some of these. My ambition is to bring more light to the choice by explicating some of the important implications contained in the options.

In particular the introduction does not argumentatively defend eudaimonism but instead pictures it in a way that I hope enables the reader to experimentally adopt this perspective upon the world and himself or herself. Subsequent chapters offer, I trust, sufficient argumentation at appropriate places.

Acknowledgments

Although nothing that follows has appeared in print in its present form, some preliminary work on themes in the book has been read to various audiences and in a few cases published in essay form. In this connection I am indebted to the following sponsors of colloquia and symposia: the Department of Economics, University of Notre Dame; the Departments of Philosophy, Rice University and Texas A & M University; the Jones Graduate School of Administration, Rice University; the School of Management, Brigham Young University; the Fullerton Club and the Washington (D.C.) Philosophical Society. Related essays appear in Peter A. French, Theodore E. Uehling, Jr., and Howard K. Wettstein, eds., *Midwest Studies in Philosophy,* vol. 8: *Ethical Theory: Character and Virtue* (Notre Dame, Ind.: University of Notre Dame Press, 1988); N. Dale Wright, ed., *Papers on the Ethics of Administration* (Albany: State University of New York Press, 1988); Konstantin Kolenda, ed., *Organizations and Ethical Individualism* (New York: Praeger, 1988); Roger Skurski, ed., *New Directions in Economic Justice* (Notre Dame, Ind.: University of Notre Dame Press, 1983); and Maurice Wohlgelernter, ed., *History, Religion, and Spiritual Democracy: Essays in Honor of Joseph L. Blau* (New York: Columbia University Press, 1980).

One of the priceless benefits of academic life is the counsel and criticism that is generously forthcoming from dedicated colleagues. This book and I have gained immeasurably from conversation and correspondence with John H. Barcroft, Dayle M. Bethel, Anne Carson, Gilbert Harman, David Kirk Hart, John Kekes, Konstantin Kolenda,

Tibor Machan, George Mavrodes, Michael Oakeshott, Noel O' Sullivan, William G. Scott, Ellen K. Suckiel, Richard Taylor, Sanford G. Thatcher, Alan S. Waterman, and Stephen Worland. In several cases I am grateful as well for sustaining friendship.

The book has profited from the highly capable editorial attentions of Scott Mahler, editor in the humanities and fine arts, University of California Press, to whom I extend thanks.

My deepest debt, philosophical and personal, is to my wife, Mary Kille Norton, herself a philosopher. To the question that is sometimes put to us, "Do you talk philosophy at the dinner table?," our answer must be, *Nostra culpa*.

Introduction

What is the right thing to do in given moral situations? What is the best life for a human being? For the particular human being one is?

To entertain these questions is worthwhile only on the premise that human beings possess freedom of appropriate kind and measure. If what each of us shall do and become is without alternative, the notion of choice is illusory, and it is upon the opportunity to choose that the meaningfulness of the above questions depends. That most of us presuppose the reality of choice is evident in the conduct of our daily lives. We take seriously a host of decisions, ranging from such life-shaping ones as which vocation and avocations to pursue, and whether to marry, and whom, to the plethora of lesser choices that fill our days, such as whether to accept a particular social invitation or read a particular book. In this presupposition we are supported by moral philosophers, and a moral philosophy that denied it would be self-contradictory.

However, the experiment that this book represents rests upon the real opportunity of a more radical choice—the choice by human beings of the basic terms in which they conceive of themselves and accordingly conduct their lives—that is denied by many persons including some moral philosophers. I will not directly attempt to rebut their views, or defend by arguments the presence in persons of the opportunity to choose their self-conceptions. Instead, this introduction will seek to set forth the eudaimonistic conception of personhood in such a way that the reader can experimentally adopt it as his or her self-conception. Readers who are successful at this will have taken decisive steps toward answering for themselves the question of the possibility of choosing their self-conceptions—first, because the self as conceived eudaimonistically is very different from the modern conception of the self in which most of us have been conditioned, and second, because the experimentally adopted self-conception includes the opportunity of chosen self-conception, and moreover holds it to be every person's responsibility.

Our aim in this introduction, then, is to "get inside" the eudaimonistic conception of personhoood in order to see what it makes of our experience. For our initial access we will employ as our vehicle the ancient Greek myth of creation.

In the myth, the Deity fashions the earth and everything upon it by combining formless matter and immaterial forms and then assigns to a subordinate, Epimetheus, the work of distributing to the newly made creatures the attributes that will outfit them for survival. Obediently Epimetheus bestows upon the tiger its teeth and claws, upon the fox its wiliness, upon the fish its fins and gills, and so on down the list. But when Epimetheus arrives at the human being he discovers that his bag of attributes is empty, leaving this creature fatally naked and un-equipped for survival in the world. To the rescue comes Epimetheus's daring brother, Prometheus, who mounts to the heavens and steals from the gods their most precious possession, fire, by which to rectify the oversight of Epimetheus and outfit humankind for living in the world. But this "fire" is not to be understood as physical fire (for it has been identified—we rely here as did the Greeks upon Hesiod—as the gods' most precious possession; and had they need to keep warm, or cook their food, or smelt ores to make tools?). It is spiritual fire by which humanity is compensated; and this is nothing less than the power of creation, namely Eros.[1] With it humankind is equipped to complete the work left unfinished by the Deity and Epimetheus together, the work of fashioning itself.

All other beings unalterably are what they are by metaphysical necessity, but human beings lack metaphysical necessity thanks, in the mythical account, to Epimetheus' oversight. This lack is both humanity's freedom and its predicament. What Plato is symbolizing in his famous image of the human soul as chariot, charioteer, and two contrary-minded horses (*Phaedrus*) is that, distinctively, human being is problematic being; to be a human being is to be at bottom a problem to oneself, specifically an identity problem. It is the problem of deciding what to become and endeavoring to become it. The problem of deciding what to become is the problem of learning to recognize ideal goods and choosing among them which good to aim at as the goal of one's self-fulfilling and objectively worthy life. The problem of becoming the person one chooses to become is the problem of acquiring the resourcefulness and force of character to overcome external and internal obstacles.

Knowledge of ideal goods is wisdom and must be acquired by education, both formal and experiential. Knowledge of the particular ideal good that represents the fulfillment of the given individual is self-knowledge, which must be the paramount goal of education. Just as there are countless vocations that, though worthy, would not afford intrinsic rewards to a particular individual, so also with ideals of personhood. Self-knowledge begins in the discovery of the course of living (of which vocation is but a significant part) that affords intrinsic rewards to the particular individual. The Greek explanation of this relationship is framed in terms of innate potentialities within persons; the course of life that actualizes an individual's innate potentialities is experienced by him or her as intrinsically rewarding. It affords the kind of happiness or satisfaction that is peculiar to self-fulfilling conduct, for which the Greek term is *eudaimonia*. According to eudaimonism, persons innately possess not only potential excellences (the *aretai* that inhere in their ideal personhood, or *daimons*), but aspiration to actualize these excellences. In the definition proposed by Socrates, Plato, and Aristotle, human beings are "lovers of the good," seeking the completion that is denied them, in the myth, by Epimetheus's oversight.

Eudaimonia denotes both a condition and a feeling. It identifies the condition of living in truth to oneself, where the true self is one's daimon, and living in truth to it means discovering it—the self-discovery with which self-knowledge begins—and progressively actualizing it. As was noted above, the feeling can be termed happiness, but it is the distinctive happiness that attends self-fulfilling conduct. It is not, for example, the "happiness" of net desire-gratification, for people who lack self-knowledge will desire for themselves the wrong (dysdaimonic) things and experience pleasure nonetheless at the gratification of such desires. Nor is eudaimonia-as-feeling the proper aim of living, in the Greek view (which is to say that eudaimonism is not a form of hedonism). The proper aim is worthy living of a particular kind, realizing the particular values that constitute the individual's daimon. Eudaimonia is the necessary condition of such a life. As a feeling, it is the confirming sign that one is on the right course, the self-actualizing course. One is living in truth to oneself.[2]

And what of evil? In the Greek account, no one deliberately seeks evil, for to desire something it is psychologically necessary for a rational being—a being that has an idea of what it desires—to believe it good. The knowledge of what is truly good is wisdom and must be painstakingly acquired. Meanwhile the bad or evil may be mistaken for the good, and mistakenly sought. And it may be achieved, for while the innate potentialities of persons are good and not otherwise, nevertheless all persons are full of possibilities other than their potentialities, including possibilities for every kind of evil conduct. As here conceived, then, the task is that of education in the good, with special attention to self-knowledge, and accordingly moral education is the backbone of Greek pedagogy. To cite a modern example, Emerson's admonition, "Trust thyself" is warranted by the potential worth that is within every person innately, but to his words must be added the developmental imperative, "and strive to make yourself trustworthy."

Profound as it is, the ancient Greek account of evil leaves untouched the evil will, understood as the deliberate ambition to destroy goodness. For this reason the Greek account required supplementation and gained it in Friedrich Nietzsche's theory of *ressentiment*.[3] Nietzsche analyzes the evil will as a reactive phenomenon resulting from thwarting or frustration of innate aspiration to the good by obstacles in the world or in the self. Instead of simply giving up, some stronger-willed persons respond to thwarting by resolving to avenge themselves. Nietzsche perceives in ressentiment a virulent psychological corrosive that, when it gains foothold, can work within to transform the thematic motivation of a life from good to evil intent. (Plato's analysis of envy moves in this direction, but stops short of the evil will.)

But the contingency of the ressentiment response is demonstrated by countless persons who meet with comparable obstacles and frustrations but are not diverted from their aspiration to worthy living. The eudaimonistic strategy adopted by Nietzsche is to strengthen the good will to meet the adversity, both without and within, that it will certainly encounter. In their variety of ways, all of Nietzsche's writings are teachings in the cultivation in the self of the resourcefulness that worthy living requires, thereby to resist the temptation to ressentiment. Comparable dedication to the same purpose is evident in the writings of Henry Thoreau, whose thought remarkably parallels Nietzsche's in deep respects. Both Nietzsche and Thoreau recognize that the absence in human beings of metaphysical necessity must be compensated for by a necessity that requires to be self-supplied. Because it is the product of the will of the individual, and not conversely, it is termed moral necessity. Persons in whom it is lacking are described by Thoreau as "thrown off the track by every nutshell and mosquito's wing that falls on the rails."[4]

Recently John Kekes has sought to rectify what he perceives as the inadequacy of the eudaimonistic theory of evil by presenting an extended account of "unchosen" evils.[5] He holds that in its most pervasive form, the evil that humans do is attributable neither to evil will, nor to the ignorance that mistakes for good what is in fact evil. He argues that most evil is unchosen, and most unchosen evil results from the enactment by persons of the character and habits of conduct that were formed in them in childhood. Such enactment is not chosen because the character and habits of conduct were not chosen; they were formed in the dependent child by social influences.

But this is precisely why Socrates advised that "The unexamined life is not worth living." Thanks to the necessary socialization of children, the unexamined life is the thoughtless perpetuation of a conferred identity. It is not one's own life, and it defaults upon the moral responsibility of the individual to discover and actualize his or her distinctive innate potentialities for objective worth. The place for self-discovery is subsequent to childhood: it requires that a person bring the terms of his or her conferred identity to reflective awareness, as the first step toward the formation of the identity that he or she will bear in adulthood.

In summary, I think Kekes's valuable account of unchosen evil is mistakenly offered by him as a corrective to the Greek account. In fact he explicates the Greek "evil as ignorance" thesis, with special reference to ignorance of self. And the correctives he proposes are recognizable as implementations of the Greek imperative, "Know thyself."

According to eudaimonism, high moral character should as far as possible live by its own inherent self-demands, which measurably surpass the requirements of conventional morality. But because high moral character is a developmental outcome, external regulations are required for persons who have not attained it. The regulations, we propose, are of three kinds.

First, conduct is required to be generally law-abiding in the interest of social order. At the same time the intended outcome of self-directed living provides a criterion for distinguishing good laws from bad: laws must as far as possible conduce to, and not obstruct, the development of moral character. The second constraint is the universalizability-principle: each individual's chosen course of self-actualization must respect others' chosen courses. At this level of generality, universalizability does not suppress individuation by legislating uniform conduct in similar circumstances. Finally, chosen courses of life must hold reasonable prospect of issuing in objective values, recognizable as values by (some) others who are themselves leading objectively worthy lives. This is forecasting, and makes sound sense of the seemingly occult "prophesy" that Plato esteems in the *Phaedrus*.

In addition to the above-indicated modification in its theory of evil, Greek eudaimonism requires to be modified in the direction of open-endedness. The teleology of Aristotle, in particular, invites an understanding in which all human beings who live as they should are bound to converge on a single form of life, namely a life centering in the rational activity of detached contemplation. This has been termed by W. F. R. Hardie the "dominant end" interpretation of Aristotle, and Hardie initiated ongoing scholarly debate[6] by contrasting it with an "inclusive end" interpretation, according to which the use of reason serves to organize the lives of individuals so as to achieve their differing aims. My intent here is not to enter into the debate over the correct understanding of Aristotle, but rather to indicate that a eudaimonism that is viable today must be open-ended, recognizing a multiplicity of kinds of self-actualizing lives directed toward a multiplicity of ends. The varieties of value that can be actualized by human beings is unmeasured if not measureless, and it signifies innumerable possibilities for self-actualizing, objectively worthy living. Theoretical reduction of this variety to one or a few kinds is conspicuously Procrustean.

In the interest of deepened understanding, we may usefully speak now of what eudaimonism is not.

In the first place it is not an elitist theory, though it was indeed elitist in its Greek presentation and has sometimes subsequently received elitist formulation. Eudaimonism is coupled with democratic equality in the presupposition that to be a person is to be invested innately with potential excellence: all persons are alike values-bearers. This presupposition requires theoretical acknowledgment of the varieties of human value, as noted just above, and will be vindicated by training in the recognition and appreciation of this variety. Such training is the corrective to the parochialism that attends the human fatality of commencing life in a particular place at a particular time. The Aristotelian contention, on the "dominant end" interpretation, that abstract reasoning is the universal end of human life is inherently elitist because it favors those who by the "natural lottery" of birth are endowed with exceptional intelligence. But few will argue that the capacity to love, for example, or the virtues of fidelity, compassion, and integrity, are closely correlated with native intelligence, and by extension neither is worthy living of many kinds. In sum, connection between eudaimonism and elitism is historical and contingent, not logical and necessary.

Next, eudaimonism is not a form of egoism. It posits as the native motivation of persons the desire (Eros) to live a worthy life. The worth that is aspired to is objective worth, which is to say it is of worth, not solely or primarily to the individual who actualizes it, but also to (some) other persons—specifically to such others as can recognize, appreciate, and utilize the distinctive kind of worth that the given individual manifests. The music of Beethoven, for example, has enriched the lives of thousands of persons and may be supposed to have been intended by Beethoven to enrich lives other than his own. To be sure, most worthy lives find far fewer appreciators. Eudaimonism is not an invitation to court fame. But the terms are no less applicable: we want to be of worth to others, beginning in most cases with those we love. Critics who recognize that eudaimonism is not a morality of altruism have sometimes concluded that therefore it is a form of egoism ("long-range," "prudential," etc.), but this conclusion follows only on the supposition that conduct and intentions must be either altruistic or egoistic. This is a modern disjunction that eudaimonism denies. The objectively worthy life, as is its intention, will be of worth alike to others and to its agent.

Third, while eudaimonism is a variety of moral individualism, unlike some forms of individualism it does not conceive of individuals as "atomic," that is, as inherently asocial entities. Atomic individuality is associated with modern social contract theory, the classical forms of which hold that individuals antedate society and agree to associate by something resembling explicit or tacit contract. On this understanding their essential nature as individuals is what it is before they agree to the terms of the contract. It is presocial, prepolitical, and unaffected at bottom by the terms of association. Social relations are conventional and contingent, affecting individuals "externally" but not "internally." By contrast eudaimonism recognizes persons as inherently social beings from the beginnings of their lives to the end but contends that the appropriate form of association undergoes transformation. As dependent beings, persons in the beginning of their lives are social products, receiving not merely material necessities but their very identities from the adult community. The principle of association is the essential uniformity of associates, usually expressed in terms of basic needs. Subsequent moral development leads to self-identification and autonomous, self-directed living, but is associative as an interdependence based in a division of labor with respect to realization of values. The self-fulfilling life of each person requires more values than he or she personally realizes and is dependent upon others for these values. The principle of this form of association is the complementarity of perfected differences. Accordingly the meaning of "autonomy," if the term is to be applicable, must be consistent with interdependence. As we will use the term it means, not total self-sufficiency, but determining for oneself what one's contributions to others should be and what use to make of the values provided by the self-fulfilling lives of others. To follow the lead of another person in a matter he or she understands better than we is not a lapse from autonomy into heteronomy but a mark of wisdom.

"Individualism" has lately been under mounting attack by communitarians for allegedly precluding social relations that are essential to the well-being of persons. In chapter 6 we will argue that eudaimonistic individualism entails community and offer a description of that community. The typical error of current communitarian attacks is their failure to recognize distinctions among kinds of individualism.[7]

Finally, eudaimonism is not ethical subjectivism. It is true that it exhibits great concern for the subject—the self of each person—for example, by insisting upon the importance of self-knowledge and self-development. But the self is here conceived as a task, a piece of work, namely the work of self-actualization. And self-actualization is the progressive objectivizing of subjectivity, *ex*-pressing it into the world. This recognition exposes as a fallacy the modern use of "objective" and "subjective" as mutually exclusive categories. Every human impulse is subjective in its origin and objective in its intentional outcome, and because its outcome is within it implicitly from its inception, there is nothing in personhood that is "merely subjective," that is, subjective in the exclusive sense. Narcissism (with which individualism is sometimes charged) is a pathology that tries to amputate from subjectivity its objective issue. It is real enough, and was a propensity of some romantic individualisms that judged experience by the occasions it affords for the refinement of the individual's sensibilities. But the supposition that individualism is narcissistic subjectivism represents (again) a failure to recognize divergent kinds of individualism. For eudaimonistic individualism, it is the responsibility of persons to actualize objective value in the world.

From the foregoing conceptualization of individuality and worthy living, politics—understood as the art or science of government—arises at three points.

First, the mature, self-responsible, self-actualizing individual is self-governing, and this self-government requires strategies, techniques, and acquired, organized skills. In short it is obliged to be an art or science. This self-government is for eudaimonism the paradigm of good government, and the primary purpose of good collective government is to generalize the opportunity and the occasions of it among the constituency. In the development of individuals it is preceded by two stages of life—childhood and adolescence—which in differing measure as yet lack the capacity for self-government in the above meaning and therefore require to be externally governed in the manner appropriate to each. We propose that the form of government appropriate to childhood is unilateral authority, and the form appropriate to adolescence is collective self-government. In each case the paramount criterion of good government is that its exercise shall facilitate further development in the governed. Thus a unilateral authority, for example, that works to perpetuate or increase the dependence of its subjects thereby attests to its own illegitimacy. Similarly a collective self-government that fails to contribute to increasing capacity for individual self-government in its constituents is in default of its function.

The second point of origin of politics in the foregoing picture is recognizable in the fact that, as a developmental outcome, self-directed individuality has preconditions, some of which cannot be self-supplied by individuals. If persons are morally responsible for self-discovery and self-actualization, then by the logic that "ought" implies "ought to be able to," they are entitled to these necessary preconditions.* Here are persons' primary moral rights. Where the conditions are such as cannot be self-supplied by individuals, responsibility for provision is (we will argue) social. In cases of universal entitlement to necessary, non-self-suppliable conditions (e.g., of children to an appropriate education), responsibility for supply is not a community option and requires to be institutionalized by the state. In this limited respect the state is required to be what Michael Oakeshott identifies as a corporate enterprise association[8]—that is, an association organized to achieve specified ends—and politics is management of this enterprise. But what is thus

---

*This is a modification of my original attempt to derive rights by "ought implies can," for which I am indebted to Gilbert Harman and George Mavrodes. Refinements will be offered in chapter 5.

provided to persons is not "benefits" or "satisfactions" but conditions of the exercise of individual responsibility.

Because an extended society includes persons at all stages of development, there can be no prospect of the state "withering away." But it would be erroneous to suppose that external government is eliminable for the third stage of development—the stage of autonomous, self-directed living—considered alone. This is because in this stage autonomy, although manifest, is a growing but imperfect capacity. Therefore the social principle of the third stage, the principle of the complementarity of perfected differences, can never be more than imperfectly manifested through the initiatives of individuals, and requires institutional supplementation. There can be no utopian reliance on an "invisible hand" of complementarity to protect rights, settle disputed claims, enforce the law, defend the nation, and so forth.

The third point of origin is the requirement of social order. But politics neither invents nor merely imposes order, for achievement of order depends upon enlistment of volition and can only within limits condition the volitions on which it depends. In Oakeshott's words, "Government . . . does not begin with a vision of another, different and better world, but with the observation of the self-government practiced even by men of passion in the conduct of their enterprises."[9] In the worst state the principles of order are calculated to serve the ends of evil-doers; in the best state they are principles of self-discipline that worthy persons have recognized and adopted as conditions of self-actualization; in intermediate states they are principles that preclude the worst but are unconnected to the best, and by resting with minimally acceptable conduct contribute to what Mill perceived as "the general tendency of things throughout the world . . . to render mediocrity the ascendant power among mankind."[10]

Our primary theoretical problem in what follows presents itself as the horns of a dilemma. On one side lies the recognition that "morality cannot be legislated," because law can regulate conduct but not motives. On the other side lies the recognition by Greek eudaimonists that worthy living by individuals requires a conducive social context. An opening between the horns begins to appear upon examination of the Greek recognition.

In the first place it is not impossible for given individuals to demand more of themselves than prevailing conceptions of acceptable moral conduct include, but such persons will be too rare to make an appreciable difference. It is in the problem of *generalizing* self-actualizing living with its inner requirement for continuous moral growth that the need for a conducive social context arises. If, as eudaimonism contends, all persons possess innate incentive toward worthy living, a "conducive social context" becomes one that provides opportunity to all associates to discover and live by their innate moral incentive. John Dewey speaks on these lines when he says that, "Democracy has many meanings, but if it has a moral meaning, it is found in resolving that the supreme test of all political institutions and industrial arrangements shall be the contribution they make to the all-around growth of every member of society."[11] But given that the contributions to growth that Dewey speaks of refer to the growth of individuals that is dependent upon their own initiatives, the first concern of a eudaimonistic society must be to afford to individuals the types of experience that will engage these initiatives. This is "self-discovery," and we shall address it directly in chapter 3. By the inner logic of development the place for it is adolescence, and a conducive social context will recognize this developmental work of adolescence and supply its conditions. Because it as yet lacks self-knowledge and the strength of character that is built upon it, adolescence is highly vulnerable to misdirection, and the advisement is acute, "What is honored in a country will be cultivated there" (Pericles).

Next we will inquire into how and why the problem of self-knowledge came to be abandoned, and the aspiration to moral excellence eclipsed, in the modern conception of the self.

CHAPTER ONE

Classical Liberalism:
Individuality Recovered But Misdirected

As heirs of the classical liberal tradition, we are conditioned in its posited values of freedom, formal equality, instrumental rationality, voluntary association, and consensual government, all of which lie in the modern conception of individuality. Our thesis is that the historical explication of the implications of this conception of individuality, although confirming the soundness of some of its aspects, has also revealed serious deficiencies. In this chapter we will focus upon what we propose as the most serious deficiency—the nondevelopmental character of individuality in the modern conception. We will consider the profound sense in which the modern conception of individuality *is* nondevelopmental (it obviously incorporates some kinds of development), and question how and why it came thus to be conceived; why, as thus conceived, it took hold as the prevalent self-conception of individuals; and what its harmful consequences have been and are. All of this requires of us a historical investigation of the roots of modern individuality. But our central concern in this book is for persons and their situations in the present. We will work our way back to the present and argue for a reconceptualization of individuality that retains certain of the gains of classical liberalism but eliminates what the historical analysis discloses to be its central deficiency. Subsequent chapters will take up the question of how the revised conception of individuality can be made the operative self-conception.

We can find the heart of the modern conception of individuality by looking to the notion of perpetual social and historical progress that it spawned. To see why progressivism followed from the modern conception of individuality but not from the Hellenic Greek conception is to uncover a central difference between the two conceptions. For Socrates, Plato, and Aristotle, personhood is essentially moral, centering in values, virtues, and responsibilities. It is individualized in the twofold sense: (1) that the primary agency for values-realization is the initiative of each individual, and (2) that the values to be realized differ among individuals, and therefore must not be obscured in our minds by the eudaimonists' insistence upon the inherently social and political nature of individuality. They were not introducing the modern sociological claim that persons are, necessarily, from the beginning of their lives to the end, products of social conditioning. They were observing, rather, that because individuals differ from one another in the values they realize, and each needs other values additional to those he or she personally realizes, worthy living requires the continuous and complementary interrelationships of value that association and citizenship provide. The conception of the polis, then, is that of an institutionalized social organization designed to afford maximum realization of values by individuals, as well as optimal utilization of the values realized.

In this light our problem may be framed in the following terms. The growth of citizens, understood by eudaimonists as the moral development toward worthy living, is clearly a "progress," and a continuous progress terminating only in death. Why then did it not generate conceptions of social and historical progress? It is true that Hellenic Greece was heir to the archaic conception of history as cyclical and therefore unprogressive. Thus Aristotle says that the measure of time is motion, and "regular circular motion is above all else the measure, because this is the best known. . . . This is also why time is thought to be the motion of the sphere, viz., because the other movements are measured by this, and time by this movement. This also explains the common saying that human affairs form a circle, and that there is a circle in all other things that have a natural movement and coming into being and passing away."[1]

But instead of answering our question, this reposes it in the form: why did not the eudaimonistic notion of worthy living as continuous moral growth vanquish the archaic representation of history as cyclical and unprogressive? And the answer is that Greek moral theory developed in an aristocratic social context. In this entrenched context, Plato, Aristotle, and especially Socrates went far toward universalizing virtues across class distinctions; nevertheless the aristocratic idea prevailed (with Plato's and Aristotle's clear endorsement) of a changeless class structure that was as a whole unprogressive.

By contrast modernity's conception of individuality democratized the opportunity of limitless growth, thereby fitting the social whole into the idea of progress, while at the same time tapping a vast reservoir of stored energy that swept away the lingering influence of the ancient cyclical conception of history. But to achieve this democratization modernity was obliged to drastically alter the kind of growth with which "progress" was identified. It is this change that will be our focus in the present chapter.

It was the democratization of unleashed individual initiative that gave to historical progress the appearance, first of possibility, and subsequently (e.g., in Hegel, Marx, Comte, Spencer, and their respective followers) of inevitability. But what is now clear in retrospect is that modern progressivism had little to do with moral life and worthy living, centering rather in such matters as geographical exploration, the development of markets, the growth of technology and its material fruits—all conceived extramorally. Yet morality was not simply outrun or pushed to the sidelines by these dynamic influences. Rather, the influences were set in motion by a prior effect, termed an "intellectual revolution" by J. G. A. Pocock[2] and an "astounding transformation" by A. O. Hirschman.[3] The name of this revolution is realpolitik, and what it revolutionized was the Western understanding of moral development. Its most influential writers were Machiavelli, Bacon, and Hobbes.

Each of these men, by his insistence on clear-sighted attention to facts (Machiavelli's "*verita effetuale,*" Bacon's "mean particulars," Hobbes's "unvarnished facts") has been credited as a father of modern science. This has warrant but is apt to obscure the nature of their instigatory efforts. What was needed in preparation for modern natural and social science was a moral revolution that recalled the attention of human beings from the heavens and redirected it to the earth. This was accomplished by Machiavelli through, first, the secularizing of politics, and then the politicizing of morality. But we can see more clearly what was required in the case of natural science and will begin with a brief consideration of the preparatory work of Francis Bacon.

There is no mistaking Bacon's admonitory tone in his *Novum Organum*, as for example in the famous passage, "With regard to the Meanness or even the Filthiness of particulars, for which (as Pliny observes) an apology is requisite, such subjects are no less worthy of admission into Natural History than the most magnificent and costly;

nor do they at all pollute Natural History, for the Sun enters alike palace and privy, and is not thereby polluted."[4] Bacon is here struggling for the right to attend carefully to the mundane empirical facts before every person's eyes—a right that had to be wrested from the transcendental-eschatological tenet of Christianity that the mundane world was worthy of attention only for clues it might provide to the mind and will of God, and against the preoccupation of Aristotelian teleology with the ideal ends toward which processes of change in the natural world are directed. On both views it is at least beneath the dignity of the high-minded, and may discredit their high-mindedness, to take seriously, for its own sake and without transcendental redemption, the world of change and transitoriness. Bacon clearly saw that to overcome this valuation was prerequisite to the inception of empirical-experimental investigation on a significant scale, and he undertook to accomplish it: "In short, we may reply to those who despise any part of Natural History as being Vulgar, Mean, or Subtile and useless in its origin, in the words of a Poor Woman to a haughty Prince who had rejected her petition, as unworthy and beneath the dignity of his Majesty: Then cease to reign; for it is quite certain that the empire of Nature can neither be obtained nor administered by one who refuses to pay attention to such matters as being poor and too minute."[5]

The deep connection between this groundwork of Bacon's and the mission of Machiavelli lies in the problem of disorder and order. More specifically, given that the world and human experience are implicated in change and disorder and require stabilization through the introduction of order, what are the sources from which the order can be drawn? Before we look for the correspondence between Bacon and Machiavelli we must pause to appreciate the circumstances in their time that gave to the problem of order its urgency, namely the extreme disorder that attended the breakdown of medieval institutions.

In his great work on the rise of individuality in the Italian Renaissance, Jacob Burckhardt describes Florence as "in a chronic state of violence" compounded by "the rule of the nobility, the tyrannies, the struggles of the middle class with the proletariat, limited and unlimited democracy, pseudo-democracy, the primacy of a single house, the theocracy of Savonarola, and the mixed forms of government which prepared the way for the Medicean despotism." The states of the church "swarmed with petty tyrants." In "great bacchanalian outbreaks of military ambition" adventurers who could command troops, or condottiere, became rulers or henchmen of rulers, and Burckhardt describes relations between governments and their condottiere as "thoroughly immoral."[6]

Concerning himself with the quality of life of ordinary persons in the period, Johan Huizinga says it was "so violent and motley . . . that it bore the mixed smell of blood and roses"; it had a "tone of extravagant passion," and "a general feeling of impending calamity hangs over all"; everywhere "perpetual danger" and "continuous insecurity" prevail. He observes that "the custom of princes, in the fifteenth century, frequently to seek counsel in political matters from ecstatic preachers and great visionaries, maintained a kind of religious tension in state affairs which at any moment might manifest itself in decisions of a totally unexpected character."[7]

Describing the breakdown of the Florentine Republic between the first period of Medici rule and the second (the time in which Machiavelli wrote *Il Principe*), J. G. A. Pocock makes a telling association: "It is a Hobbesian world in which men pursue their own ends without regard to any structure of law . . . and that by which they pursue their ends is power, so defined that each man's power constitutes a threat to every other's."[8]

To Machiavelli the prevalence of political disorder demonstrated the hopeless inadequacy of previously relied-upon sources of order, that is, Christianity and Aristotelian teleology. Correspondingly these same sources were vigorously renounced by Bacon: "For we regard all the systems of Philosophy hitherto received or imagined, as so many plays brought out and performed, creating fictitious and theatrical Worlds."[9] And he contends that "our only remaining hope and salvation is to begin the whole labour of the Mind again; not leaving it to itself, but directing it perpetually from the very first, and attaining our end as it were by mechanical aid."[10]

In the last citation Bacon sounds a pervasive theme of realpolitik in the idea that the human enterprise must begin afresh and *de novo*, disregarding the past as a repository of errors that the "new men" shall avoid. Here realpolitik introduces the antitraditionalism that carries over into classical liberalism as rejection of the "tyranny of tradition." Only by the rejection of the past was Hobbes able to claim that "civil philosophy [is] no older . . . than my own book *De Cive*,"[11] and it is to the notion of de novo rebeginning that Locke's *Second Treatise on Government* owes its strikingly ahistorical character, as remarked, for example, by Peter Laslett.[12] Presently a leading criticism of classical liberalism comes from traditionalists who contend that it is without tradition other than its own antitraditionalism, by which it divests individuals of the extended "narrative" in which the narratives of their lives must be embedded in order to have meaning. Our own differing view on this matter will be offered in chapter 6.

What unites Machiavelli and Bacon is their revolutionary resolve to reject transcendent sources of order and uncover principles of order in immanent sources. By "transcendent" we mean here sources of order external to—beyond and above—the material that requires to be ordered, and by "immanent" we mean principles lying within this material. The full significance of this redirection of attention and inquiry is captured by John Dewey in *The Quest for Certainty*.

In a broad view, Dewey observes that humankind has employed two basic strategies in its search for security and an adequate measure of control over its own destiny. The first is the attempt to transcend the problematic existential situation with its inherent uncertainties, in the envisagement of changeless reality and eternal truths in a region beyond the mundane world, to be attained by Platonic dialectic, Aristotelian contemplation, or Christian grace. To those who have confidence in their ability to reach these goals, the transcendental solution doubtless can afford some measure of serenity, but its besetting deficiency, in Dewey's words, is that "it does not change the existential situation in the least."[13]

The alternative strategy is that of immanence. It consists in immersion in the contingencies of situations, leading to effective intervention through growing familiarity with regularities in their workings and interconnections. Whereas the transcendental strategy affords compensation to humankind for the disorder of the human situation, the strategy of immanence provides means to achieve order.

Machiavelli employed the categories of Greco-Roman thought that suffused the Florentine and Venetian republics as well as the Milanese imperium of his time. Accordingly he employed the term *"fortuna"* for disordered matter, and *"virtu"* for immaterial form. Then in the "typical motif of the Renaissance" (Garin),[14] *virtu vince fortuna*, the meaning is that matter is ordered by the infusion of form.

In the same way that Machiavelli perpetuated the "mirror for princes" genre but radically departed from its traditional content, so he perpetuated the *virtu vince fortuna* motif but with astonishing transformation of its meaning. The "form" by which "matter" was to be ordered lay not in a transcendent world, but in the "matter" itself. Here begins what Pocock calls Machiavelli's "drastic experiment in secularization." He engages in establishing that "civic virtue and the *vivere civile* may . . . develop entirely in the dimension of contingency, without the intervention of timeless agencies."[15] And to do so—here is the focus of this chapter—he must profoundly reconceptualize *virtu*.

The reasons for Machiavelli's "drastic experiment" are not far to seek, and in them only just below the surface we may learn why modernity has in the final analysis run on rails laid down by Machiavelli and Hobbes. Machiavelli and Hobbes together effected the secularization of politics and the politicization of morality. For our expression of the realpolitik insight on which they acted, John Stuart Mill's famous statement is unsurpassed: "Governments must be made for human beings as they are or as they are capable of speedily becoming."[16] By the politicization of morality in Machiavelli and Hobbes this becomes "moral philosophy must be made for human beings as they are or as they are capable of speedily becoming."

Machiavelli's drastic experiment was motivated by the failure of transcendental sources of order. As described above by Burckhardt, Huizinga, and Pocock, the extreme disorder of quattrocento Italy was graphic evidence of the failure of the ordering strategies of both Christian soteriology and Aristotelian teleology. To the philosophical mind of Machiavelli, less preoccupied with local circumstances and working at a higher level of generality than the minds of such of his notable contemporaries as Guicciardini and Botero, it was the source from which order was to be sought that was the key. Transcendental sources of order lay too far beyond human beings "as they are"; the "new realism" must be founded in immanent sources, sources available to everyone because they are *in* everyone. In his words, "The gulf between how one should live and how one does live is so wide that a man who neglects what is actually done for what should be done learns the way to self-destruction rather than self-preservation."[17] Machiavelli sought principles of order in fortuna itself—the mundane world of flux and transitoriness—and at the same time endeavored to disarm Christianity and Aristotelian ethics by secularizing both.

Whether or not it was the business of Christianity to regulate civil affairs had been a matter for intensive debate since at least the time of Augustine. As background to Machiavelli, William of Ockham had insisted on sharp distinction between the spheres of ecclesiastical and secular authority, and his arguments entered the mainstream of late scholastic political theory through Jean Gerson and the conciliar movement.[18] More radical still was the heretical contention by Marsiglio of Padua that all coercive power is secular by definition, effectively expelling the Church from political affairs.[19] What Pocock terms the "subversive" thinking of Machiavelli retains the earthly work of the Church, but yokes it to the secular interests of civic life. By itself, Christianity corrupts civic life by teaching "as man's highest good humility, abnegation, and contempt for mundane things," thereby rendering human beings weak and dependent, and delivering them "as a prey to the wicked."[20] Premising something akin to Emile Durkheim's theory of "collective representations"[21]—that the shared beliefs of a community require to be embodied in concrete symbols and repeatedly enacted rituals—Machiavelli assigns to Christianity the function of ceremonially reinforcing civic virtue. In short he secularizes Christianity by rendering it instrumental to civic ends.

But our central interest in Machiavelli and realpolitik lies in the "secularization" of Aristotelian ethics, which amounts to a radical transformation of the meaning of virtue that gave to modernity one of its definitive characteristics—its moral minimalism.

In Pocock's wording, Machiavelli "enters the realm of moral ambiguity" by making use of the polysemy that attended the term "virtue."[22] To the Greek eudaimonists, *arete* connoted moral excellence based in commitment to the actualization, conservation, and defense of certain objective values, and implying strength of character. To the ancient Romans, *virtus* connoted the strength to "deal effectively and nobly with whatever fortune might send."[23] In Christianity under the influence especially of Augustine and Boethius, virtue becomes purity, understood as absence of defilement by the world, and submission to Fortune, which is now understood as Providence.[24]

"Virtue" in Machiavelli retains the idea of strength in the Roman meaning, but undermines the Greek idea of objective goodness by associating strength with effectiveness and expediency. In Pocock's words, "*Virtu* took on the double meaning of the instruments of power, such as arms, and the personal qualities needed to wield these instruments."[25]

Il Principe is of course addressed to the "new prince" and the virtue in question is the prince's virtue, understood as just indicated. But Pocock observes that Machiavelli's *Discoursi* are yet more morally subversive than *Il Principe*. The reason is that in the *Discoursi*, the opportunistic virtue of the prince is generalized as citizen virtue.

We have spoken of "moral minimalism" as a definitive characteristic of modern life, and Hobbes is no less instrumental in establishing it than Machiavelli, but we have now in Machiavelli arrived at its point of inception, and it is important to recognize it as such.

What modern moral thought and conduct are "minimal" by contrast to is classical Greek and Roman moral thought and conduct, whose fullest and soundest understanding appears in the eudaimonism of Socrates, Plato, and Aristotle. Against this, modern morality is typically minimalist in two deep respects. First, it is minimalist in respect to the kinds of situations that count as moral. Modernity works with a threefold classification of actions from the standpoint of moral meaning: right actions, wrong actions, and morally indifferent actions. For eudaimonistic theory, all human conduct without exception has moral meaning, and the relevant distinctions are first, of course, between right and wrong actions, and second, between acts of maximal moral meaning and acts of minimal moral meaning. For its part, modern morality distinguishes moral situations from nonmoral ones. This distinction gives leave to whole disciplines to pitch their camp on nonmoral turf, as for example modern science has done on the basis of the fact-value distinction. But for eudaimonism there are no nonmoral situations for human beings, though to be sure some situations have lesser moral import than others. In this first respect, then, modern moral theory is minimalist by virtue of its constriction of the scope of morality to but some kinds of situations and some kinds of choices.

But it is the second respect in which modern morality is typically minimalist that Machiavelli has just introduced. It is minimalist in that it requires of persons very little in the way of developed moral character. It cannot require much in the way of developed moral character because it enlists morality alongside law for the preservation of social order. Social order requires the observation by (almost) everyone of rules that are understood and acknowledged as authoritative by (almost) everyone. This means that the rules must be very simple and straightforward, and acting in accordance with them must require very little in the way of developed moral character, for as more is required, the numbers of persons possessing the requisite development diminish. As J. O. Urmson has put it, "If we are to exact basic duties like debts, and censure failure, such duties must be, in ordinary circumstances, within the capacity of the ordinary man. It would be silly for us to say to ourselves, our children, and our fellow men, 'This and that you and everyone else must do,' if the acts in question are such that manifestly but few could bring themselves to do them, though we may ourselves resolve to try to be of that few."[26]

For Machiavelli, Aristotelian ethics was unworkable because it made excessive demands, requiring developed moral character that few persons possessed; it was therefore unsuited to persons "as they are or as they are capable of speedily becoming." For this reason it was perceived by Machiavelli as no less "transcendental" than Christianity, though in a different sense. We must look to the special sense in which the term is applicable to Aristotelian ethics from a realpolitik standpoint.

Metaphysically, the dualism that supports Christian transcendentalism finds no counterpart in Aristotle. Whereas the perfection to which human beings shall aspire according to Christianity is beyond the mundane world and incommensurable with it, according to Aristotelian metaphysics (as distinguished from Platonic) all perfections are indwelling in mundane things. This is a doctrine not of transcendence but of immanence.

But Machiavelli's focus is not upon Aristotelian metaphysics but upon Aristotelian ethics and the politics that is its civic context and expression. And the feature of Aristotelian ethics that Machiavelli took to be decisive is that its lofty aims (presented by Aristotle as the "intellectual" virtues) are without motivational connection to persons at the lowest levels of moral development. To introduce an indispensable term, Aristotle—like Plato and Socrates—employed the conception of *stages* of moral development. Within each stage moral growth is continuous, but between stages lie discontinuities that must be bridged by a "leap." The effect of this is that later stages of moral development are "transcendental" with respect to prior stages. They represent different perspectival worlds, which the individual at a prior stage cannot inhabit, and to which he is unconnected motivationally.

Aristotle, for example, offers three stages of moral development, which may be termed the "economic" stage, the stage of "moral virtues," and the stage of "intellectual virtues." The "transcendence" in this conception lies in the fact that the term "virtue" has its own meaning in each stage, which to a person in a given stage obstructs recognition of the meanings of the term in higher stages. These higher meanings transcend his conception of the world and himself. Plato's stages of development are immortalized as the famous "ladder of love" (*Symposium* 210), which begins with self-love, moves to love of a singular other person, then to more persons, then to humankind, thereafter to human institutions that embody forms of goodness, then to the Forms themselves, and finally to the ultimate Form, the Form of the Good, in which all good (and therefore loveable) things participate. Here again, "transcendence" resides in the fact that as love ascends from stage to stage it changes, not merely its primary object, but its nature as love. Accordingly what a person at a lower stage of development means by love is very different from what love means at higher stages, and the meaning it has for him obstructs his access to alternative meanings. It is implicated in a coherent world of meanings, the whole of which will be shaken by entertaining a key concept—in this case love—in an alternative meaning. And so for all key moral terms, such as honesty, courage, justice. So in particular for the *prudence* upon which realpolitik, by its emphasis, will oblige us to focus in due course.

Because the moral meanings of later stages of development are inaccessible (by ordinary means) to persons at lower stages, these higher moral meanings cannot enlist the initiatives of such persons. Accordingly a moral philosophy designed for persons "as they are or as they are capable of speedily becoming" must disregard higher meanings in favor of lower, and this is what realpolitik did.

If we now turn to the masses of ordinary persons as they were perceived by realpolitik we find a strikingly unattractive portrait. In *Il Principe*, for example, Machiavelli offers the advice that "One can make this generalization about men: they are ungrateful, fickle, liars and deceivers, they shun danger and are greedy for profit."[27] The opening words of the *Discorsi* speak of "the envy inherent in man's nature," and the work is built upon the supposition that "in constituting and legislating for a commonwealth it must needs be taken for granted that all men are wicked and that they will always give vent to the malignity that is in their minds when opportunity offers."[28] Guiccardini is if anything more unflattering, leading Henry Osborne Taylor to describe him as "a matchless observer of the concrete human fact," much less likely than Machiavelli to allow his observations "to be deflected to the constructive uses of his thought."[29] But it remained for Giovanni Botero to make explicit what was left implicit and sometimes disguised in Machiavelli and Guiccardini, namely that theirs was a description of humankind, applicable to the prince no less than to his subjects. In his treatise of 1589, *The Reason of State*, Botero says for example, "it should be taken for certain that in the decisions made by princes, interest will always override every other argument; and therefore he who treats with princes should put no trust in friendship, kinship, treaty nor any other tie which has no basis in interest."[30]

But two further modifications remained to be made before the realpolitik conception of human nature became the predominant modern conception, and Hobbes unerringly accomplished both of them.

First, the realpolitik conception required to be transformed from a description of subjects to princes, and princes to whoever dealt with them, to each person's self-conception. And second, the idea of "interest" had to be concretized and narrowed if it was to be efficacious, for that persons act on their interests is useful knowledge only if we can know what their interests are. Hobbes accomplished both modifications by the single stroke of rendering "interest" as "self-interest," directed first to self-preservation and additionally to "felicity." But before turning to Hobbes's moral egoism we must elucidate a step further the Machiavellian transformation of Aristotle.

In Aristotle's description of moral development, we have given the term "economic" to the stage prior to the moral virtues. It is a stage preoccupied with personal security and the acquisition of material goods,[31] and for Aristotle it contains no virtues. But Machiavelli perceived it as the stage in which all or most persons of his time were in fact lodged, and he used what we have previously seen to be the polysemia of the term "virtue" to invest the stage with virtues, reconceived as personal qualities that render individuals effective in pursuing their interests. Seeking immanent principles of order in fortuna itself, Machiavelli found one of them in the dissolution to which, following the morphology of Polybius and his fellow Stoics, Machiavelli held that all cultures are susceptible. But this required to be complemented by a principle of generation, and Machiavelli found it in individual ambition. The effect, as Pocock notes, was to transform fortuna into the two opposing tendencies of corruption and ambition, the latter now termed "virtu." Not only does this constitute the politicization of virtue, but it confines the conception of moral life to what Aristotle regarded as the first, premoral stage of individual development. It is minimalist in the decisive respect that the only development it acknowledges is development in the economistic terms of the first stage: a person becomes more effective at pursuing his interests, but what he perceives as his interests does not undergo significant alteration.

The same constriction is evident in Hobbes *vis a vis* Plato on the theme of love. As previously noted, for Plato the first stage in the development of love is self-love, but this self-love is by no means preclusive of love of others, being instead the precondition of it. The maturing of self-love entails continuous growth in the understanding of the self as the participant in an expanding world of values together with persons and institutions that are responsible for those values. By contrast Hobbes's moral egoism understands self-love in only the contracted, exclusive sense with which Plato's ladder begins, in which persons are basically rivals.

Modernity's moral minimalism, then, is rooted in what we referred to at the outset as its nondevelopmental conception of individuality. It indeed allows for development within the stage it recognizes—such a development as is represented by the accumulation of power, money, or fame, for example, together with increase in the requisite skills—but it recognizes no further stages of growth. In Hobbes's statement, "I put for a general inclination of all mankind a perpetual and restless desire of power after power that ceases only in death,"[32] no transformation of aim is evident, or intended. It is a forerunner of Bentham's "quantity of pleasure being equal, pushpin is as good as poetry,"[33] which Mill valiantly but unsuccessfully sought to overturn by his qualitative distinction among pleasures—a conception that establishes stages of moral development.

And we are now able to see that beneath what is often cited as a resemblance between eudaimonism and realpolitik—the enlistment by both of prudence in behalf of morality—lies a severe disparity. Citing the resemblance, Gregory Kavka, for example, says that "the basic theme of Part II (of *Leviathan*) is that the requirements of morality and the claims of self-interest can be generally reconciled. This theme has a venerable history, being clearly discernible in Western moral thought at least as far back as Plato."[34] But to leave the matter thus is seriously misleading, for no sooner is the parallel invoked than it discloses a fundamental discrepancy. In Plato and Aristotle the prudent self grows to meet ever-higher moral requirements; in Hobbes, the meaning of morality is diminished to the terms of an undeveloped prudential egoism. It is true that nothing in Hobbes prevents any person from expecting of herself progressively higher moral conduct; but such expectations are entirely a subjective affair. Hobbesian moral egoism is devoid of the moral responsibility for moral growth that is the backbone of eudaimonism.

And while by the logic of his language nothing in Hobbes prevents anyone from elevating her moral expectations of herself, Hobbes calculatedly undermines such enterprises by his assault on higher moral expectations and conduct as hypocritically disguised egoism. Therefore, while it is true, as Kavka says, that Hobbes's subjectivist definitions of good and evil—"Whatsoever is the object of any man's appetite or desire, that is it which he for his part calleth *good:* and the object of his hate and aversion *evil*"—do not entail psychological egoism, it is mistaken of Kavka (following Gert and McNeilly on this point) to offer this in support of the contention that "psychological Egoism does *no work* in Hobbes's moral and political theories."[35] The subjective definitions place no limit on what states of affairs may be objects of appetite or desire, but by collaterally discrediting apparently nonegoistic desires as disguised egoism, the combined effect is to leave nothing but egoistic desires. The "work" that this accomplishes is the constriction of moral life to what eudaimonism regards as but the first stage in the moral development of individuals— the cornerstone of modern moral minimalism.

Pity and charity are defined by Hobbes egoistically in *Human Nature*;[36] free gifts are so defined in *Leviathan,* where he also says that the family is held together by "natural lust," that people fulfill their obligations principally out of fear, and that "no man giveth, but with intention of good to himself . . ."[37] And it is of course in *Leviathan* that we find such sustained reductions of classical-medieval virtues as: "To give great gifts to a man is to honor him, because it is buying of protection and acknowledging of power. To give little gifts is to dishonor, because it is but alms, and signifies an opinion of the need of small helps. . . . To give way or place to another in any commodity is to honor, being a confession of greater power. . . . To speak to another with consideration, to appear before him with decency and humility, is to honor him, as signs of fear to offend. . . . Nor does it alter the case of honor whether an action, so it be great and difficult and consequently a sign of much power, be just or unjust, for honor consists only in the opinion of power."[38]

We have identified the mistake of several Hobbesian commentators in holding that psychological egoism "does no work" in Hobbes's moral and political theories. It does the decisive work of grounding modern moral minimalism in its aspect of constricting moral life to just its first stage as moral life was conceived by Greek eudaimonists and their Roman successors. In the terms of Richard Taylor it exchanges an "ethics of aspiration" for an "ethics of duty."[39] And that the duties in question are minimally conceived is evident in what Kavka terms Hobbes's "Copper Rule." The term has reference to the two-part structure of Hobbes's "laws of nature," or basic moral rules. Each law has a main clause that requires conduct of a traditionally moral kind, and a second clause that releases the agent from the specified conduct if others are not behaving in accordance with the rule. Thus, for example, Hobbes's second law reads: "That a man be willing, *when others are so too,* . . . to lay down this right to all things; and be contented with so much liberty against other men, as he would allow other men against himself"[40] (emphasis added).

Kavka commends the "Copper Rule" as against the Golden Rule because it avoids the latter's unilateralism, and he suggests as a rough summary of the former: "Do unto others as they do unto you."[41] And it is doubtless the case, as Kavka believes, that the Copper Rule is more realistic. This is of course consistent with the intent of realpolitik. But has Kavka recognized what moral content is excluded by Hobbes's qualifying clauses?

To show what moral content is locked out I will begin by rephrasing Kavka's rough summary of the Copper Rule to read, "Do unto others as *you think* they do unto you, or would do unto you if they could." Now, it is entirely possible to suppose that others deal with us perfidiously, or would if they could (that is, if their own power or position rendered them invulnerable to us). And in this case the Copper Rule justifies us in manipulative, exploitative, treacherous conduct toward them. My leave to revise Kavka's phrasing of the Copper Rule is supplied by the characterizations of human beings by Machiavelli and Hobbes, as for example, "they are ungrateful, fickle, liars and deceivers," and purportedly worthy human conduct (in the traditional sense) as hypocritically disguised egoism. This tells us that others will exploit us to their own advantage if they can, and the Copper Rule endorses us in similarly exploitative conduct toward others.

In short, the Copper Rule works to reduce moral conduct to the lowest common denominator, which is the conduct of persons in whom very little or no moral development has occurred. This has two important effects. It works to eliminate moral exemplars in a community or society (as Hobbes has already sought to do more directly by exposing them as disguised egoists). The significance here can scarcely be overestimated: as an affair of practice and practical reason, moral life is encouraged far more by example than by precept, and where examples are utterly lacking, precepts are rendered empty and void. Quite simply, practical precepts that are not practiced are not precepts. To put the matter concretely: persons who pursue their own moral development require within the circle of their acquaintance mentors, that is, one or more other persons who surpass them in respect to level of moral development, from whose example much about further moral development can be learned, and by whose example further moral development is encouraged.

Second, character growth in a human being is a form of self-transcendence involving the persistent venturing beyond one's prior self. In one's relations with others this means that one's own striving for moral growth is a continual striving for improvement upon those relations, which is to say it continually endeavors to go beyond those relations in their prior terms. The conclusion to be drawn is that moral growth is *dependent upon unilaterality,* and a moral philosophy that dispenses with unilaterality (as Kavka commends Hobbes's Copper Rule for doing) dispenses with moral growth, endorsing moral minimalism. In sum, *reciprocity* is not and cannot be the model of *moral* relations. For example, to expect reciprocity as the condition of, and the motivation for, giving a gift, is to strip one's gift-giving of the virtue of generosity. Even more conspicuous is the matter of our indebtedness to prior generations for our cultural inheritance: on the reciprocity-model we are expected to give in kind to those from whom we have received. The fact that in this case those from whom we have received no longer exist has led moral philosophers who theorize on the reciprocity-model to conclude that the notion of indebtedness to past generations is incoherent. But on the contrary, they are mistaken to theorize morality on a reciprocity-model. Granted that moral life involves not only giving but also receiving, what eudaimonism provides is a model of collaterality: we repay our debt to prior generations by endeavoring to provide as well or better for future generations as past generations have provided for us.

The true home of the reciprocity-model is economics, and we shall shortly consider the significance of this point. Our next order of business, however, is to entertain an argument by Kavka that Hobbesian morality, although offering no actual inducements to moral development in individuals, nevertheless makes room for it. In regard to our thesis that realpolitik built into modernity a moral minimalism (whereby, for example, the conscience of the contemporary businessman is in truth satisfied by the profits of his company, though he may be obliged to pay lip-service to "higher values"), it would be enough to show that the moral development that was held to be every individual's moral responsibility by classical Greek and Roman thought is ignored by realpolitik. But the actual case is that realpolitik not merely ignored individual moral development, but offered a conception of morality that precluded it. We can show this by considering Kavka's thesis to the contrary.

Kavka argues that Hobbes was a "Predominant," "nonmaximizing" "Rule-Egoist." Whether he is correct in the "nonmaximizing" and "rule" characterizations is not presently in question, and I will address myself only to "predominance" and what Kavka perceives to be an implication of it.

Kavka defines Predominant Egoism "in its most general form" as the doctrine that "self-interested motives tend to take precedence over non-self-interested motives in determining human action."[42] Because Kavka's express intention is to offer a revisionist Hobbesism for current use, it is important to note that Kavka is ascribing Predominant Egoism to Hobbes himself. On this interpretation Hobbes's moral doctrine accommodates "altruistic" motives, and Kavka specifies three such accommodations:

In many cases, overall self-interest and altruism will agree in the course of action they recommend, and the latter will add an increment of motivational force. In other situations, altruistic concerns may break a tie, or near tie, between different self-interested motives pointing toward different courses of action. And even when overridden by self-interest, altruistic motives may inhibit or delay action, motivate a search for new alternatives that serve both selfish and altruistic ends of the agent, and so on.[43]

But it is on what Kavka contends is yet a fourth accommodation of altruistic motives by Hobbes's theory that our attention centers, for here Kavka describes a two-stage model of moral development in individuals in which Predominant Egoism is confined to the first stage and is (i.e., can be) succeeded by Predominant Altruism:

Predominant Egoism, then, is the doctrine that self-interest tends to be overriding in people's motivational structures . . . at least until they have reached a stable and satisfactory level of well-being and security. Adding this restriction allows for the possibility that many, most, or even all people would be largely altruistic (or otherwise non-self-interested) if they were well-off enough in the present and expected to continue to be so in the future.

And Kavka assimilates this to Abraham Maslow's two-stage model of "deficiency needs" and "being needs," in which sufficiency of satisfaction of the former introduces and shifts priority to the latter.[44]

The problem with this as the presentation of an implication of Hobbes's moral theory is that Hobbes expressly precludes the ascent to the second stage by contending that sufficiency cannot be achieved in the first stage. He says of the "restless desire for power after power" that it "ceaseth only in death," not that it ceases (or transforms) with the attainment of a sufficiency of power. "And the cause of this," Hobbes continues, "is not always that a man hopes for a more intensive delight, than he has already attained to; or that he cannot be content with a moderate power; but because he cannot assure the power and means to live well, which he hath at present, without the acquistion of more."[45]

In short, as a person becomes better off he is an increasingly attractive target for powerful predators, against whom he requires yet more power.

Nor will Kavka's developmental model serve as revisionist Hobbesism that can still with warrant be termed "Hobbesian." It violates what Kavka himself recognizes as the deepest intent of Hobbes's moral philosophy, namely that of investing moral life with the motivation that prudence furnishes. It does so because Kavka unquestioningly relies upon the modern "altruism-egoism" bifurcation that was rejected alike by Hobbes and Greek eudaimonism. The Greeks furnished motivation for the loftiest moral conduct by demonstrating its worth, not solely for other persons, but also for the agent. Thus for Aristotle the best person "assigns to himself the things that are noblest and best," and these are justice, temperance, and other virtues, by his possession of which he benefits others, but also himself.[46] Aristotle thus denies the egoism-altruism disjunction by conflating self-interest and other-interest in the contention that the good that the self seeks is objective, that is, good for all. But Aristotle differs from Hobbes in recognizing that this conception of the self's good requires extended moral self-development. Hobbes rejects eudaimonism out of his realpolitik resolve to redesign moral theory for "human beings as they are or as they are capable of speedily becoming." Accordingly he relies on very little in the way of moral development in individuals and reconciles prudence and morality by moralizing selfish interests. If one accepts the egoism-altruism bifurcation, defining self-interest as preclusive of other-interest and conversely (Kavka expressly says that altruism is "non-self-interested"), and then presents altruism as a stage of moral life, one theorizes in direct opposition to Hobbes by conceiving of (a stage of) moral life that is devoid of prudential motivation. This is what Kavka does.

In Hobbes's conception, moral life in civil association is a matter from beginning to end of the selfish acquisition of material goods and power, with such concessions to others as are necessary to the selfish enterprise. For Hobbes there are no upper limits to the intelligent pursuit of material goods and power, no limit beyond which more of these things is recognized as debilitating to persons who continue to pursue them. This epitomizes the loss to modernity of the Greek counsel of *sophrosune,* or "proportion," according to which too much of most kinds of goods is as debilitating as too little. Without the recognition that some amount of material goods and power constitutes a sufficiency, moral life becomes a one-stage affair, because it is the possession of such goods in sufficiency that opens the individual to the recognition of quite different kinds of goods.

The notion of sufficiency in material goods and power makes no appearance in Hobbes because the wolf is always at the door. Behind civil association is the state of nature, to which civil association is ever in danger of reverting, and in which life is "solitary, poor, nasty, brutish, and short."[47] Hobbes's moral theory restricts moral life to the first level of development by representing it as incessantly liable to fall into the pit below.

We have addressed realpolitik's derivation of morality from politics—its "politicization of virtue"; now we must take note of its next step, consisting in the derivation of politics and morality alike from economics.

In Locke, classical liberalism's central purpose is to enfranchise the individual against the sovereignties of church and state. Its basic weapon in this endeavor is its doctrine of individual rights, but this doctrine requires as its complement a ready and reliable reservoir of individual initiative. This is so because rights are conceived negatively by classical liberalism, as protective of individual initiatives, and are gratuitous without the latter. To be effective the initiatives in question must be preexisting ones and not hypothetical initiatives that might (or might not) be engendered in the course of time by education, changes in social conditions, and so forth. Moreover, in keeping with the realpolitik resolve to rely upon immanent sources of order, the initiatives must be inherently orderly, at least implicitly, and if merely implicitly, then rapidly capable of becoming explicitly so.

These conditions were astutely perceived to be met by economic initiatives—the desire for material gain—and economics arose as the study of their inherent principles of order, or "laws." Classical liberalism did not have to seek them or valorize them because by the time of Locke that work had been done. Hobbes was a contributor to it as we have just noted. Its accomplishment is the "astounding transformation" documented by A. O. Hirschman. It is the beginning of what Louis Dumont identifies as the "decisive shift that distinguishes the modern civilization from all others and that corresponds to the primacy of the economic view in our ideological universe."[48]

The first step consisted in transforming the meaning of the traditional notion of natural law. To medievalists natural law was God's will made available to man as the analogue of divine law. But "by the seventeenth century," in the words of R. H. Tawney, "a significant revolution had taken place. 'Nature' had come to connote, not divine ordinance, but human appetites, and natural rights were invoked by the individualism of the age as a reason why self-interest should be given full play."[49]

But in self-interest per se it is not possible to find the order that politics requires, thanks to the diversity of interests covered by the term. The religionist's interest in salvation is self-interest, as was the preoccupation of civic humanists with honor and reputation. So likewise for the desire to acquire a skill of any kind, or to acquire knowledge through formal study, or to acquire a cultivated taste. If we suppose all persons to be acting on self-interest, nevertheless little regularization and predictability of conduct follows, thanks to the amplitude and elasticity of the concept. Accordingly realpolitik sought a predominant interest to which other interests are subordinate—and found it in economic interest. We saw it singled out in Machiavelli's description of the prince's subjects: ". . . they shun danger and are greedy for profit." As Hirschman documents,

> By the early eighteenth century we find Shaftesbury defining interest as the "desire of those conveniencies, by which we are well provided for, and maintained," and speaking of the "possession of wealth" as "that passion which is esteemed particularly interesting." Hume similarly uses the terms "passion of interest" or the "interested affection" as synonyms for the "avidity of acquiring goods and possessions" or the "love of gain."[50]

When Adam Smith (we speak of the Smith of the incomparably influential *Wealth of Nations* and not the Smith of *A Theory of the Moral Sentiments;* prima facie disparities between the two have long presented scholars with the problem of "the two Smiths") identifies economic interests as "the most vulgar and the most obvious,"[51] it is important to understand that he is not condemning them but commending them for their implicit orderliness by contrast to other "passions." Their "vulgarity" and "obviousness" attest to their universality, strength, and reliability. The insight that Smith here shares with his realpolitik predecessors is: be he king or commoner, statesman, businessman, freeholder or wage-laborer, insofar as a person acts on his *economic* interests, his conduct becomes predictable, and social order finds its immanent foundations.

The primary obstacle, of course, is that desire for material gain was deprecated by classical and medieval morality and religion if it exceeded strict limits. By abandoning upper limits, realpolitik endorsed what was recognizably not proportionate desire for material well-being but avarice, and churches rang with denunciations of avarice and usury to the time of the commercial revolution of the sixteenth century and beyond.

In this setting the valorization of the ambition of limitless material gain required special measures. And these measures were forthcoming. The "astonishing transformation" begins in Machiavelli's famous dictum that "reprehensible actions may be justified by their effects, and that when the effect is good . . . it always justifies the action."[52] It proceeds to the case for the civilizing influence of commerce, for example, in Montesquieu: ". . . it is almost a general rule that wherever the ways of man are gentle there is commerce; and wherever there is commerce, there the ways of men are gentle."[53] And it culminates in the doctrine of the invisible hand, together with the valorization of the "love of gain" by Puritanism that has been classically delineated by Max Weber and R. H. Tawney.[54] In the words of the subtitle of Bernard de Mandeville's *Fable of the Bees,* the doctrine of the invisible hand contended that "Private Vice is Publick Benefit." Together with Mandeville, variants of it are found in Pascal, Locke, Montesquieu, and Vico, but the most famous formulation is Adam Smith's contention that the "wealth of nations" is achieved, not by express design, but as the unintended consequence of exclusively self-interested striving for material gain by individuals. This of course becomes for Smith, as it had been for Mandeville,[55] the leading argument for *laissez-faire.* Self-seeking on the part of individuals will in society so interact with and check itself as to be for the benefit of the social whole, whereas unnecessary state interference will distort the delicate balance.[56] To be sure, neither Smith nor Mandeville are exponents of pure laissez-faire or the wholly undisturbed invisible hand. Mandeville, for example, calls upon "dextrous Management" of a "skilful Politician" to facilitate the workings of the invisible hand,[57] and Smith recognized entrenched resistance to the "system of natural liberty" requiring political action against privileged interests that, because such correctives could not be entirely successful, made the expectation of total free trade in Great Britain "as absurd as to expect that an Oceana or Utopia should ever be established in it."[58] But these considerations do not diminish the success of the invisible hand doctrine at moralizing material acquisitiveness.

Adam Smith's *A Theory of the Moral Sentiments* is another story. It is a cornerstone of the Scottish "moral sense" school of ethical theory that opposes the unrestricted sway of egoism in Hobbes and Mandeville by positing, together with "self-love," an instinctive "sympathy" for others and offering this as the basis of moral life. The disparity between this account of moral motivation and the motivations that are operative in *Wealth of Nations* has faced scholars with the problem of "the two Smiths," but it need not be considered here, for the Scottish moral sense school was ineffective against prevailing modern moral minimalism at reopening the self-conception of individuals to the recognition of higher levels in the development of moral character. The "economisticization" of morality was at the same time the moralizing of material gain, and armed with the conviction of its own righteousness this motive swept all before it. But also the Scottish moral sense school, by accepting the modern premise that morality, in partnership with law, is responsible for social order, precluded to itself the use of moral motives and understandings that (almost) all persons could not be presumed presently to possess and act upon. It thereby precluded to itself the higher moral motives and understandings that most persons cannot be presumed to yet have at any given time and place because they are developmental outcomes, requiring to be striven for.

A cornerstone of modern moral minimalism is the criterion of universalizability, understood as the principle that what is right for anyone to do in given circumstances is the same for everyone in relevantly similar circumstances. So understood, universalizability is a leveling device, for "everyone" inevitably includes persons of minimal moral development, from whom only minimal moral conduct can be expected, and it is supposed that only such conduct can be universalized. We will return to this theme.

Our thesis is that modern "progress" has been narrowly channeled by the valorization of economic initiatives at the expense of other "interests" in a historical movement originating in realpolitik. But realpolitik antedates classical liberalism, and it is to classical liberalism that our present-day self-conceptions are most directly indebted. Accordingly we now turn to the problem of the self-conception promulgated by John Locke. What we are interested in appears in sharp relief in the divergent understandings of Locke offered by C. B. MacPherson and such of his critics as Richard Ashcraft.

MacPherson attributes a major share of responsibility for modernity's reductive, economistic human self-conception to Locke. At first sight Locke's moral meliorism seems well removed from the endorsement of avarice as moral motivation, but MacPherson argues that on closer scrutiny such endorsement becomes apparent.

Locke famously identifies personhood with proprietorship understood as exclusive ownership, that is, with private property. Initially, Locke appears to set upper limits of two and perhaps three sorts to ownership of material goods. First is the proviso that a person may appropriate only so much as will leave "enough, and as good, for others."[59] Second, there is a "spoilage" proviso that limits ownership to "as much as anyone can make use of to any advantage of life before it spoils."[60] Finally, Locke at points appears to limit ownership to what a person can acquire with his own labor, for it is originally a person's body that is his exclusive property, and this property is extended by "mixing" one's body with materials provided by nature, that is, by labor.[61]

In his well-known and frequently disputed argument, MacPherson contends that for Locke, all three limits to material acquisition are nullified by the appearance of money. It nullifies the spoilage limitation for, in Locke's words, "gold and silver . . . may be hoarded up without injury to anyone, these metals not spoiling or decaying in the hands of the possessor."[62] The restriction to what a person can acquire with his own labor is lifted both by the opportunity to purchase the labor of others—that is, by the transformation of labor into a commodity—and by the earning power of money itself in the form of capital.[63] Concerning the proviso that "enough, and as good, be left for others," Locke contends that consequent upon the introduction of money,

he who appropriates land to himself by his labor does not lessen but increase the common stock of mankind; for the provisions serving to the support of human life produced by one acre of enclosed and cultivated land are—to speak much within compass—ten times more than those that are yielded by an acre of land of an equal richness lying waste in common. And therefore he that incloses land, and has a greater plenty of the conveniences of life from ten acres than he could have from a hundred left to nature, may truly be said to give ninety acres to mankind.[64]

This last is scarcely rivaled as a testimonial of faith in the invisible hand. It conveys the assurance that for those to whom not enough and as good *land* is left over, there will be better *living*. As MacPherson says,

This assumes, of course, that the increase in the whole product will be distributed to the benefit, or at least not to the loss, of those left without enough land. Locke makes this assumption. Even the landless day-laborer gets a bare subsistence. And a bare subsistence, at the standard prevailing in a country where all the land is appropriated and fully used, is better than the standard of any member of a society where the land is not appropriated and fully worked: "a King of a large and fruitful Territory there [Locke is speaking of the 'several nations of the *Americans*'] feeds, lodges, and is clad worse than a day Labourer in *England*."[65]

On the strength of Locke's endorsement of the invisible hand and commodity labor, and his removal of limits to material acquisition,

MacPherson pairs Locke with Hobbes as jointly responsible for the modern conception of progress, individual and social, as "infinite utilities maximization." Thus the economic preoccupation that theorists from Socrates to Maslow have regarded as the first stage of development is hypostatized as the whole of development, individual and social.

Vigorous opposition to this thesis of MacPherson appears, for notable examples, in the Lockean scholarship of James Tully, John Dunn, and Richard Ashcraft.[66] On the matter at issue it will suffice to consider Ashcraft, with the intention that our findings shall apply also to Tully and Dunn.

Ashcraft undertakes to refute MacPherson's claim that "Locke identifies reason with the propensity to accumulate capital," or in MacPherson's words that Locke assumes "unlimited accumulation" to be "the essence of rationality."[67] His argument is that beneath the individualism that is evident both in Locke's state of nature and his state of civil association lies a communitarianism to which the supervening individualisms remain bound. "It is true that, according to Locke, individuals have a right to their own person to which no one else can claim a right,"[68] but we must recognize that in Locke's view rights are bound in service to responsibilities: "The general point I am making is that, instead of focusing upon the declarative, naturalistic language of rights, we view Locke's discussion of property in terms of the intentional language of divinely instituted obligations. . . . This means that Lockean natural rights are always the active fulfillment of duties owed to God."[69]

According to Locke the "Fundamental Law of Nature" is "that all [persons], as much as may be, should be preserved."[70] As human preservation is not secured by nature unaided, man is obliged by the law of nature to labor for his preservation; thus Locke insists that "God, when he gave the world in common to all mankind, commanded man also to labour."[71] But in view of God's intention that all human beings should survive, the object of the labor of individuals must be the benefit, not of themselves merely, but as Ashcraft observes, "the common life of all."[72]

This understanding divorces Locke from Hobbesian psychological egoism and is certainly thus far correct. In his lectures on natural law, Locke denied that it was based on self-interest. Instead, natural law is based in and intended to preserve "the common life of man with man," and incorporates the virtues of "justice, friendship, and generosity."[73]

To this point Locke appears to defy MacPherson's interpretation, and on Ashcraft's (clearly correct) contention that for Locke, all subsequent developments remain bound by natural law and the derivative responsibility of human beings to labor for the common good, MacPherson may seem to be refuted—until we look to Locke's case for how the good of all is to be secured.

Locke says that although God gave the world to human beings in common and for their common benefit, "it cannot be supposed he meant it should always remain common and uncultivated." On the contrary, He has given the earth to "the use of the industrious and rational" individual whose "labour was to be his title to it."[74] So the common benefit introduces private property, and what happens next we have seen in the citations from Locke that were used in our consideration of MacPherson's case. By an invisible hand argument, Locke holds that accumulation of working property benefits all, for "He who appropriates land to himself by his labour, does not lessen but increase the common stock of mankind," and if the day laborer in England does not appreciate his advantage it is because he lacks acquaintance with the circumstances of (in Locke's example) American Indians.

At the same time the introduction of money has afforded opportunity for the accumulation of wealth that is not subject to Locke's "spoilage" condition, "these metals not spoiling or decaying in the hands of the possessor."[75] From this Locke draws the further conclusion that "gold and silver . . . may be hoarded up without injury to anyone."[76] According to Locke, the invention of money as the medium of exchange, is not a necessity of subsistence but a necessity for trade, and "the chief end of trade is riches and power."[77] As Ashcraft notes, the accumulation of money and the property attributable to money cannot in Locke find a natural rights justification, because for Locke "the Deity's purposes extend no further than what is necessary for the preservation of mankind [i.e., subsistence], which is the declared general objective of natural law."[78] But it can and does receive conventional rights justification, first because according to Locke it is "without injury to anyone," and second because the industrious use of money benefits others; that is, Locke's invisible hand argument is applied by him to the accumulation of capital.[79] As Ashcraft notes, Locke had "more than a small dose of skepticism concerning the increase of human virtue 'in proportion to the increase in wealth.' "[80] In particular, he recognized that concentration of wealth can lead to empire and tyranny; but he believed that this could be counteracted by replacing simple monarchy by balance of powers in government.[81]

Our conclusion is that although Locke indeed conceived the "Law of

Nature" as obligating persons to work for the common good at the level of subsistence, he represented unlimited material acquisition as consistent with working for the common good. MacPherson's conclusion that for Locke, unlimited material acquisition is the essence of rationality, appears to be invalidated by the recognition, correctly insisted upon by Ashcraft, that Lockean rationality is morally obligated to serve the Law of Nature. But by his invisible hand argument, together with his assessment of the consequences of the introduction of money, Locke leaves room (at least) for an understanding of unlimited material acquisition that obeys the Law of Nature.

We have sought to show that, prior to Locke, material acquisitiveness found strong and unequivocal support in realpolitik. In this setting Locke's thought certainly softened the harsh outlines of the realpolitik portrait of humankind, but it did nothing to check or redirect the unleashed initiatives.

Earlier we noted that the realpolitik conception of human beings was highly unflattering—"ungrateful, fickle, liars and deceivers," and so forth. Why were human beings ready to accept such a conception as their self-conception? Why especially, when Hobbes himself observes that all people wish to think well of themselves, and will "rate themselves at the highest value they can"?[82] The answer is that acceptance of the self-portrait afforded to persons the prospect of fulfilling themselves in the mode endorsed by the portrait—material prosperity—while at the same time the opportunity of such prosperity was appearing to an extent never before witnessed, thanks to the commercial revolution of the sixteenth century, following the opening of the New World. The prospect of "every man a merchant" beckoned and spurred the ascension of the bourgeoisie. As Tawney says, "When mankind is faced with the choice between exhilarating activities and piety imprisoned in a shriveled mass of dessicated formulae, it will choose the former, though the energy be brutal and the intelligence narrow."[83]

Nor was Machiavelli mistaken to rely heavily upon envy. For we may be sure that the denunciations of avarice and usury that rang from late medieval and early Renaissance churches had certain unintended effects. The vast majority of the faithful who heard them were persons to whom straitened circumstances afforded no least opportunity of gaining by either avarice or usury, but were instead their victims. What the subsequent direction of modernity indicates is that such practices as selling at extortionist prices, lending at exhorbitant rates of interest, and rack-renting produced in their victims not merely righteous indignation but envy. Machiavelli's ontologization of envy, like Hobbes's ontologization of selfishness, effectively justifies persons in acting upon it, even to the point of installing it as their pervasive and thematic motivation. For in this case to live on the basis of envy (or selfishness) is but to do as everyone else does—and indeed, without the hypocrisy and self-deception by which the "high-minded" disguise their conduct.

By ontologizing self-interest defined economistically, modernity narrowed human aspirations to suit the emerging opportunities. Moral minimalism resulted from the eradication from modern consciousness of the recognition of higher levels of moral development. It also resulted from the modern constriction of morality to but a sector of life. To the modern understanding an individual in the course of his or her life *encounters* moral problems among problems of other kinds. In the eudaimonistic understanding every person *is* a moral problem. The difference is dramatic. In the modern understanding most of the choices that an individual makes, including choice of vocation, of avocations, of friends to cultivate, of books to read, are nonmoral. Indeed, John Stuart Mill in his utilitarian voice says that "ninety-nine hundredths of all our actions are done from other [than moral] motives, and rightly so done if the rule of duty does not condemn them."[84] But if the development of moral character is the basic moral imperative, it is obvious that the choices just named are moral choices because they influence such development.

Modernity's zoning of morality affords to entire disciplines the opportunity to pitch their tents on nonmoral turf. "Pure" science did so on the basis of the purported fact-value disjunction; and business management has done so on the bridge of the science of economics. The prevailing spirit of management theory and practice is succinctly captured by management scholar Neil W. Chamberlain:

Employees are being paid to produce, not to make themselves into better people. Corporations are purchasing employee time to make a return on it, not investing in employees to enrich their lives. Employees are human capital, and when capital is hired or leased, the objective is not to embellish it for its own sake but to use it for financial advantage.[85]

The modern rise to predominance of both science and business appears to be accounted for on the basis of powerful innate human incentives—the love of truth on one side, and the desire for material gain on the other. But if our account of the formation of the modern sensibility is reasonably accurate, the following consideration must be added. The effect of modern moral minimalism is to afford to moral life little space for the aspiration that is a definitive human trait; it is a small room with a low ceiling and not much of a view. A telling consequence of this has been to redirect human aspirations away from the confines of morality and toward the apparently limitless horizons afforded by the laboratory and the market.

Conditioned as we are by modernity's conception of the individual, the question of replacing avarice as the thematic motivation in the lives of persons is likely to leave us at a loss. What else could possibly serve? The purpose of this book is to propose the eudaimonistic answer, and that answer is love in the meaning of Eros. Thus understood, love is not exclusively or primarily interpersonal; it is first of all the right relationship of each person with himself or herself. The self to which love is in the first instance directed is the ideal self that is aspired to and by which random change is transformed into the directed development we term growth. When the ideal of the individual is rightly chosen, it realizes objective values that subsisted within the individual as innate potentialities, thereby achieving in the individual the self-identity that is termed "integrity" and that constitutes the foundation of other virtues.

Thus understood, self-love by no means precludes, but is rather the precondition of love of other persons. To love another person requires in oneself a number of developed capacities, beginning with knowledge of the values that are the other's responsibility to actualize, and courage to temporarily suspend one's own identity in order to achieve an internal understanding and appreciation of theirs. The motivation for the development of these capacities that interpersonal love requires is self-love. But Eros does not stop with interpersonal love; as Socrates, Plato, and Aristotle taught, it grows beyond to become love of all values together with the persons and institutions that embody them—yet without leaving behind interpersonal love, and all the while preserving self-love in the specificity of the individual's commitment to particular values. Eros is therefore aptly termed by Robert Nozick "the allure of value."[86] We propose it as the sole thematic motivation that is capable of elevating individuals in their development through progressively higher stages of moral life.

Modern morality is minimalist because it centers in rules that are regarded as governing the conduct of all persons identically and must therefore be compelling to persons of minimal development of moral character, and because "moral situations" comprise but a limited sector of human experience. By contrast the love that classical ethics relies upon is love of ideals, and it is characteristic of ideals that they are capable of enlisting and guiding higher human aspirations. Modern moral philosophers have typically been uncomfortable with ideals. They are believed to be inappropriate *res gestae* of moral obligations because they make extravagant demands that the average person is unable or unready to accept. In the words of P. F. Strawson, for example, ideals are the province of "the imaginatively restless and materially cosy."[87] It is true that by their nature as perfections, ideals can never be fully realized, hence the very best human conduct falls short of its ideal. But the criticism nevertheless involves a misconception, for under the guidance of an ideal what counts *now* for a person is the next step, and for persons next steps are always possible, which is to say that moral growth is always possible. Again, some moral philosophers discredit ideal morality because of a supposed resemblance of the moral idealist and the fanatic. And it is true, as Hare observes,[88] that a moral idealist may cleave to her ideal at the expense of her present interests; but to understand this as "fanaticism" is to condemn an important way by which "interests" are moralized. (The ex-alcoholic's personal ideal of sobriety must for a considerable time override his immediate desire to have a drink.) With respect to the moral idealist's stance toward others, it may be true that some seek to impose their own ideals,[89] but the fact that many do not ("Now I bid you lose me and find yourselves" is the parting message alike of Nietzsche's Zarathustra and the Buddha) attests to the contingency of such impositions. Eudaimonism's insistence on the autonomy of moral agents is the requirement for consent by whomever an ideal affects, and it condemns the imposition of the ideals of one person, or community, or party, upon resistant or unwitting others.

The place of the universalizability-principle in a morality of ideals can be illustrated by contrasting what I earlier termed the "Hobbesian truism" with what I will call the "Socratic truism." The Hobbesian truism is that for life to be bearable, (almost) everyone must conform to basic moral rules. What I propose as the Socratic truism is the proposition that any person may in the course of his or her life encounter one or more ultimate tests in which to pursue his or her chosen course of life, or to continue to become the kind of person he or she has chosen to become, is to risk his or her life or well-being. (Socrates, *Apology:* "This is the truth of the matter, gentlemen of the jury: wherever a man has taken a position that he believes to be best, or has been placed by his commander, there he must I think remain and face danger, without a thought for death or anything else, rather than disgrace.")

My leave to call this a truism rests in well-recognized cases, for example, when citizens are called upon to risk their lives in defense of their country; or when a parent must risk herself to save her child. Moreover it is not only supreme tests that are to be considered here, but all tests that are in any measure beyond the minimal moral requirements upon everyone, and all tests that surpass the individual's previous moral demands of himself.

The Hobbesian truism tells us that minimally acceptable conduct is required of everyone; the Socratic truism tells us that exceptional moral conduct may be required of anyone. The demands implicit in the Socratic truism are universalizable because moral growth is possible for everyone.

The prevailing modern way of handling exceptional moral conduct is by categorizing it as supererogatory, where this is understood to represent conduct that is morally good to do, but not morally bad not to do. But this means that exceptional moral conduct is not required of anyone, which is to say that moral development is not a moral requirement. Clearly this conception of supererogatory conduct reinforces moral minimalism.

The eudaimonistic handling of supererogation is discernable in the testimony of heroes and saints that their heroic or saintly conduct was perceived by them as their duty; yet at the same time (as Urmson observes)[90] they typically do not universalize their heroic or saintly duties. As a moral philosopher in the modern mode, Urmson judges the perception by saints and heroes of their heightened duties to be subjective, and employs the category of the supererogatory as capturing the truth of the matter; thus the "higher flights" of moral conduct are obligatory upon no one, notwithstanding the perceptions to the contrary of those who demand such "higher flights" of themselves. Against Urmson, eudaimonism supports the moral sense of those who expect more of themselves than minimal moral conduct. We can think of their situation on the analogy of the skilled swimmer who can accomplish a deep water rescue that is beyond the capabilities of a novice and a nonswimmer. As moral development increases, so do moral responsibilities, and in recognition of this the hero or saint demands more of himself than he asks of other persons, and more of himself than he asked of himself at prior levels of development.

In sum, eudaimonism's thesis is that some of what is obligatory at later stages of moral development is supererogatory (in the definition given above) with respect to earlier stages, while moral development itself is a universal demand upon humankind.

This is captured by the term *noblesse oblige* in its moral meaning. Thus understood, it was central to classical Greek and Roman ethics. Eradication of this principle has reduced modern moral life to a flatland, devoid of the peaks—the exemplars—that elevate our vision and elicit next steps.

But to identify the thematic motivation of moral development in a landscape where it is little in evidence and scarcely recognized, as we have done in this chapter, is to confront a practical problem that political philosophy, as an engagement in practical reasoning, cannot neglect. Beginning with the next chapter we shall be engaged with the question of how Eros can be summoned to life from its current condition of dormancy. It is a political question rather than an exclusively ethical one, on the eudaimonistic recognition of Socrates, Plato, and Aristotle, that moral aspiration in individuals requires a conducive social context. In Nozick's phrasing of the "allure of value" motif, value is what "would inspire and motivate us under valuable conditions."[91] Some of the valuable conditions are sociopolitical, and we must endeavor to map them. We will begin by examining the prescriptions of two theorists who sought to enlist the self-fulfilling initiatives of individuals—John Stuart Mill and John Dewey.

CHAPTER TWO

Individuality Reconceived and Redirected:
The Doctrine of Developmental Democracy

What will here be termed "developmental democracy"[1] is a nineteenth- and twentieth-century attempt to revitalize and morally enrich individualism by altering classical liberalism's conception of the individual, of the good life, and of good government. The tenets of developmental democracy are that the purpose of politics and government is enhancement of the quality of life of human beings; that the central agency of such enhancement is the initiative to self-development in individuals; and the paramount function of government is to provide the necessary but non-self-suppliable conditions for optimizing opportunities of individual self-discovery and self-development.

In this framework the concern for individual liberty is expanded to concern for an autonomy that includes considerations of enablement. It follows that while good government will certainly not be maximal government, neither will it be minimal government. And the conception of individuals as egoistic utilities maximizers, by nature and unalterably, is replaced by a developmental conception in which egoism is to be surpassed in the aspiration to worthy living, and material well-being is instrumental to that end.

It has sometimes been held that developmental democracy is a natural outgrowth of classical liberalism, the coming to fruition of ends that were implicit in classical liberalism from its beginnings. My own belief is that it is an incommensurably different conceptual framework, an alternative interpretation of the facts of human experience based on alternative premises and directed to alternative outcomes. We recall from chapter 1 that the realpolitik initiative that paved the way for classical liberalism was forcefully directed to the uprooting of Aristotelian-scholastic philosophy, conceiving of itself as a "new beginning." The clear indication is that Machiavelli, Bacon, and Hobbes perceived the new thinking as displacing the old, not modifying it. I think they were correct in this, from which it follows that if developmental democracy is a return to the ancient understandings of human nature and worthy living (as the present chapter is intended to show) this can only be by displacement, not modification, of the classical liberal understandings. To be sure, the vocabularies of developmental democratists retain key classical liberal terms—such as "individual," "liberty," "rights"—but the meanings of the terms undergo significant alteration.

In this chapter we treat with some care the developmental-democratic theories of two leading advocates, John Stuart Mill and John Dewey. We will look to them for the help they can offer toward finding firm footing for our own subsequent theorizing, and we will test the strength of key arguments directed against them. In particular we must attend to the counter-case mustered by political science in mid-twentieth century from empirical evidence of voter behavior, the effect of which has been widely thought to have sounded the death-knell for developmental democratic theory.

At the outset it will be well to consider an argument that, if valid, prevents developmental democracy from getting off the ground. It is the contention that the idea of individual self-development is contradicted by the idea of government. This is so, it is held, because government is coercive power (perhaps "the monopoly of legitimate coercive power") over individuals, whereas self-development implies the voluntary initiative of individuals and therefore cannot be coerced.

But this argument mistakenly supposes that whatever characterizes self-development must likewise characterize its conditions. To say that self-development is voluntary is to say that it is optional. If it has necessary conditions, then self-development is an option only when these conditions prevail. And this is to say that for the option of self-development to exist, supply of its necessary conditions is mandatory. To be sure, supply of the necessary conditions that are to be self-supplied by individuals falls within the option of self-development and is not mandatory. But conditions that must be furnished to individuals by external agencies do not partake of the voluntary character of self-development. Recognition that their presence is mandatory commensurates the provision of them with the coercive nature of government, while respecting the voluntary nature of individual self-development: individuals remain free to avail themselves, or not, of the provided conditions. It is mandatory, of course, that individuals contribute (notably through taxes) to the government that provides the necessary conditions that individuals cannot self-supply, but this is a different issue, namely the balancing of liberty with autonomy, where "liberty" is understood "negatively," as freedom from interference, but "autonomy," as "self-direction," entails positive conditions of enablement.

I contended earlier that developmental democracy employs an incommensurably different conception of the individual from that employed by classical liberalism. That Dewey recognizes this is abundantly clear throughout his writings and is his explicit theme in *Individualism Old and New*.[2] On the other hand Mill gives no express indication of a similar awareness, and his equivocation on the point is, I think, one of two deep-seated sources of occasional confusion and contradiction in his writings. The other is his attempt to infuse utilitarianism with eudaimonistic moral development. When Bentham said that quantity of pleasure being equal, pushpin is as good as poetry, he identified the conception of individuality at the heart of utilitarianism as centrally nondevelopmental. While it is true that an individual must grow out of egoistic hedonism to utilitarian consideration of others' happiness through recognition of what Bentham held to be the harmony between the interest of each and the general interest, no one has reason to question his own interests or modify them. By contrast, Mill's famous qualitative distinction among pleasures establishes a developmental framework consisting of stages, identified by the sources of one's pleasure, that are to be lived through and successively surmounted.

Mill's political theory of developmental democracy is built upon his conception of the moral development of the individual and is to be found primarily in his *Considerations on Representative Government*. But it relies upon his theory of individual moral development which is to be found in the just-mentioned qualitative distinction among pleasures, in the third chapter of *Utilitarianism* on the cultivation of the "sympathetic feelings," and in chapter 3 of *On Liberty,* entitled "Of Individuality as One of the Elements of Well-Being." But notice must first be taken of Mill's identification of two forms of self-government at the outset of *On Liberty*.

The two forms of self-government identified by Mill are collective self-government and the government of each individual by himself, and he unhesitatingly affirms the latter to be "the chief ingredient of individual and social progress." This is because "in proportion to the development of his individuality, each person becomes more valuable to himself, and is, therefore, capable of being more valuable to others." Indeed, Mill warns against the claim to priority of collective self-government, where "such phrases as 'self-government' and 'the power of the people over themselves,' do not express the true state of the case. The 'people' who exercise power are not always the same people with those over whom it is exercised; and the 'self-government' spoken of is not the government of each by himself, but of each by all the rest."[3]

In accordance with this, the purpose for which Mill argues in *On Liberty* for a private sector of life into which neither external government nor public opinion may intrude is in order that individuals shall have sufficient space in which to apply themselves to the work of becoming worthy human beings. The terms of this personal enterprise are set forth by Mill in *On Liberty*, chapter 3. There he presents a conception of the individual that is innatist, developmental, and individualist. He says, "Human nature is not a machine to be built after a model, and set to do exactly the work prescribed for it, but a tree, which requires to grow and develop itself on all sides, according to the tendency of the inward forces which make it a living thing."[4] He insists on the moral uniqueness of individuals according to the "ideal conception(s) embodied in them,"[5] he emphasizes that realization of these innate differences introduces distinctive values into the world, and he stresses that such realization can occur only on the initiative of each person in his or her own case. Thus, "He who lets the world, or his own portion of it, choose his plan of life for him has no need of any other faculty than the ape-like one of imitation. He who chooses his plan of life for himself employs all his faculties."[6]

It is this conception of individuality—innatist, self-directed, self-fulfilling, realizing distinctive objective values in the world—that Mill carries into *Considerations on Representative Government*. There he enunciates his foundational political principle: "The first element of good government . . . being the virtue and intelligence of the human beings composing the community, the most important point of excellence which any form of government can possess is to promote the virtue and intelligence of the people themselves."[7] In his subsequent explication and refinement of the principle, Mill discusses "virtue and intelligence" in terms of three types of excellences—intellectual, practical, and moral—and identifies each of the three as an aspect of the self-development of the individual. Thus "all intellectual superiority is the fruit of active effort. Enterprise, the desire to keep moving, to be trying and accomplishing new things for our benefit or that of others, is the parent even of speculative, and much more of practical, talent."[8] Regarding moral virtues he points out that while religion and conventional morality exhibit a preference for passive and submissive character in persons, in fact it is the character "actively engaged in the attempt to improve its own or some other lot" that cultivates in itself the excellences in question.[9] By the "practical excellences" Mill means the developed skills and capacities that enable a person to "improve his [and others'] circumstances," and these quite evidently are outcomes of the exercise of individual initiative.

In *On Liberty,* Mill supposes that the paramount conditions for the generalization of individual self-development are "freedom, and variety of situations." But in *Considerations* he advances a case for political apprenticeship, as uniquely afforded by representative government. We recall that for Mill democracy is not without qualification the best form of government: that distinction belongs to "the government of each by himself." But we can now see that democracy is the best form of collective government because it is uniquely qualified as the staging-ground in which the latent, merely potential capacities of individuals for self-government can be developed. This is because democracy is participatory collective government and thereby encourages the active character-type against the passive, and moreover because the kind of activity that is most particularly encouraged is the activity of government.

Representative democracy nurtures the active character by enlisting citizens in the processes of government. Such activity represents moral self-development in individuals because it serves the public interest rather than the exclusive self-interest of participants, and on this account Mill terms political participation the "school of public spirit."[10]

To underscore its effectiveness, Mill offers the following portrait of prepolitical life:

It is not sufficiently considered how little there is in most men's ordinary life to give any largeness either to their conceptions or to their sentiments. Their work is routine; not a labour of love, but of self-interest in the most elementary form, the satisfaction of daily wants; neither the thing done nor the process of doing it introduces the mind to thoughts or feelings extending beyond individuals; if instructive books are within their reach, there is no stimulus to read them; and in most cases the individual has no access to any person of cultivation much superior to his own.[11]

To this condition, political participation offers "salutary moral instruction." The participant must weigh interests not his own, as if they were his own, and he is mentored by experienced, high-minded public servants with whom he associates.[12]

Today we will not be likely to miss the air of unreality in Mill's presentation. His problem is partly that the role he assigns to political participation in the moral self-development of individuals requires a level of political participation that is too great to be generalized. Mill keeps the requirement of generalization clearly in view when he gets down to identifying the kinds of political participation he has in mind. He specifies voting, jury duty, and service on parish councils.[13] It is not unrealistic to regard this minimal participation as available to everyone; but it borders on giddy optimism to anticipate that from it the large strides in the moral self-development of individuals that Mill describes.

Additionally, today many will doubt that practical politics is the "school of public spirit" that Mill holds it to be. Part of the reason is the almost daily exposure of degraded motives of public officials, from Watergate through Iran-Contra to the Savings and Loan industry and the Department of Housing and Urban Development; but there is also the logic of the case. It is unquestionably true that political activity cultivates recognition in its participants of collective interests, desires, fears, and so forth, but it need not produce identification with them. What is to prevent it from producing contempt for the constituency, and use of the knowledge to manipulate the constituency for the politician's personal gain?

Mill of course recognized this possibility and sought to meet it by placing conditions on the politics that is to be the school of public spirit. It must (and, Mill believed, normally will) be the case that all sectors of politics will contain some practitioners possessed of moral and technical excellence who serve as examples to others. At the same time, those who are to learn from such exemplars must exhibit "deference" to them. But are these conditions realistic?

What Mill means by deference is an important virtue: it is the ability to recognize and the readiness to learn from persons whose moral development surpasses our own. But today the term connotes servile bootlicking and is seldom acknowledged as a virtue. From Plato to Nietzsche to Ortega y Gasset, the most penetrating critics of democracy have noted its egalitarian tendency to foster the conceit that no person is better than another, no judgment is better than any other, and all superiority is pretense. Mill acknowledges this propensity, as for example when he says, "But also democracy, in its very essence, insists so much more forcibly on the things in which all are entitled to be considered equally than on those things in which one person is entitled to more consideration than another, that respect for even personal superiority is likely to be below the mark."[14] Yet he relies upon the deference that the propensity he confirms serves to extinguish.

Mill likewise recognized the precariousness of his condition that some experienced political practitioners must be proximate and visible examples of technical and moral excellence. He acknowledged ever-present inducements to corruption, exploitation of office, and time-serving. To blunt them he proposed two devices, namely "plural voting" and a voting system designed by his contemporary, Thomas Hare (termed the system of the transferable vote).[15] Neither proposal is likely to be looked upon with hope or favor today.

Plural voting as Mill framed it gives persons of higher occupational status extra votes, on the supposition that they are above average in moral self-development and can better recognize, and will prefer, excellence in office seekers. Hare's system is complex and need not be reviewed here.[16] It afforded opportunities for national as well as local constituencies, and Mill saw in it a means to elect to office preeminent individuals of the nation, thereby (Mill thought) increasing pressure for better quality in local candidates.

That the suppositions underlying Mill's favor for plural voting are highly questionable need not detain us. (In the 1980s it is corruption in higher occupational status that has produced the public outcry for "more integrity.") The telling point is that if both plural voting and Hare's system can be shown to have the effect of electing persons of excellence to public office, their *adoption* depends upon the public desire to achieve this end, which is to say it depends upon prevalence of the "deference" that cannot be supposed to exist.

The mode of political theorizing we have termed "developmental democracy" was dealt a fatal blow by a series of empirical studies of voter behavior conducted in the United States and several other countries in the 1950s.[17] Although other avenues of political participation—such as jury duty, service on town and county councils—have not been subjected to comparable close examination, the voter studies have served as a paradigm supporting inferences in these other areas. The effect has been to brand developmental democratic theory as pie-in-the-sky unrealism.

Empirical studies by Bernard Berelson, Paul Lazarsfield, Robert

Dahl, Talcott Parsons, and others, disclosed minimal investment by voters in this form of political participation, and minimal expectations of it. In fact, according to Berelson, the evidence showed that less than a third of the electorate has any interest in politics; even fewer trouble to inform themselves about the issues; and even well-informed voters largely use the information they acquire to support their predispositions rather than to make rational choices.[18]

It is clear that the quality of participation as thus described undermines Mill's expectation of the self-development of citizens through political participation. Indeed, the effect of the studies and their analysis has been the root-and-branch displacement of the developmental democratic model of political theorizing by a new model, sometimes termed "equilibrium democracy," whose architects include Robert Dahl and Joseph Schumpeter. The new model abandons the traditional notion of maximizing citizen participation in collective self-government and expressly relies upon apathy in citizens as an important factor in stable government. In the words of one of its advocates, "an exceptionally high voting frequency may indicate an intensification of political controversy which may involve a danger to the democratic system."[19] Somewhat in the manner that classical liberalism "transvalued" avarice from a vice to a virtue (see chapter 1), so equilibrium democracy makes a virtue out of citizen apathy, and equilibrium democracy is in certain respects a return to the "protective democracy" of classical liberalism. C. B. Macpherson observes that equilibrium democracy "deliberately empties out the moral content which [developmental democracy] had put into the idea of democracy." Democracy becomes straightforwardly a market mechanism by which voters choose among bills of goods presented to them by political parties.[20]

This is not the place for a detailed criticism of "equilibrium democracy,"[21] but something must be said about the "realism" on which it prides itself as against the "utopianism" of developmental democracy. Unquestionably developmental democracy is not "realistic" in the sense that equilibrium democracy professes to be. This is patently so in virtue of the difference in kind of the two doctrines. Developmental democracy is by design normative political theory, while equilibrium democracy is by design descriptive. To compare the two while ignoring this difference is to make a category mistake. "Realism" in description consists in correspondence to existing facts; "realism" in normative theory consists in accurate identification of ends to be aimed at as values, and in practicability of proposed means for attaining proposed ends.

But as descriptivism, equilibrium democracy has normative effect—the effect of endorsing the status quo. This is because it considers no other possibilities than those that happen to be facts. The *unrealism* in this is that it fails to recognize human beings as essentially ends-seeking, aspiring beings, who are not long content with the status quo, both because of their imaginative capacity to envisage a better condition, and because of their ability to discern defects in the status quo. (It may be objected to this that many persons are at many times content for long periods, and even their lifetimes, with the *political* status quo. But the segment of a populace for which this is true is predominantly persons for whom the prevailing political conditions afford opportunity to continuously improve their personal situations. This leaves standing the contention for aspiration as a definitive human characteristic.) And defects there certainly are. Notice that the voter apathy that is accepted by equilibrium democracy is not an atomic, insular fact, but a fact embedded in the nexus of its conditions. Conditions that contribute to voter apathy are, for example, poverty and illiteracy. It is not possible logically to endorse voter apathy without endorsing the conditions that contribute to it. Accordingly endorsement of voter apathy is implicit endorsement, or at least fosters complacency, about poverty, illiteracy, and other conditions that contribute to feelings of helplessness and indifference in a populace.

In respect to realism, the proper comparison is between the worth of what exists and the worth of what normative theory proposes to attain, *in the measure of attainment that seems reasonable to expect.* The italicized words here, of course, return us to the matter of the means by which proposed ends are to be achieved. On this score, the findings of the voter studies serve to reinforce what we earlier recognized as the unworkability of Mill's proposals. The studies do nothing to overturn developmental democracy as viable political theory in itself, but they decree that developmental democratists must discern and propose more plausible means. Enter John Dewey.

We can properly place the strategy proposed by Dewey by first noting more explicitly a feature in the strategy of Mill. Mill sought to enlist the "active character" that is latent in every person through political participation. Now politics is a distinctive family of practices with distinctive qualities, yet as we have seen, Mill affirms the diversity of individual inclinations and propensities, perceiving them as guides to individual self-development. But if the "active character" of each person is best engaged through the individuated dispositions and inclinations of each, it is mistaken to look to one family of practices for the engagement of all persons—a point of inconsistency in Mill. It is important to notice that Dewey is not inconsistent in this way. What Dewey recommends as the backbone of a program by which to generalize the opportunity of individual self-development is not a particular kind of activity, but a method that is applicable to all activities. He terms it the "method of intelligence."

It is common to regard Dewey as a corporatist who opposed individualism, but this is to commit an error that Dewey himself identified—that of mistaking the "old" (classical liberal) individualism for the only individualism, and critics of the old individualism for opponents of individualism per se:

> Because of the bankruptcy of the older individualism, those who are aware of the breakdown often speak and argue as if individualism were itself done and overwith. . . . But in speaking as if the only individualism were the local episode of the last two centuries, they play into the hands of those who would keep it alive in order to serve their own ends, and they slur over the chief problems— that of remaking society to serve the growth of a new type of individual.[22]

The root defects that Dewey identifies in classical liberal individualism have each received consideration in our chapter 1. One of them is the failure to distinguish between "purely formal or legal liberty" and "effective liberty"[23] (between "liberty" and "autonomy" in our treatment). Another is the fixation of individual initiative upon economic interest, by which "instead of the development of individualities which it (classical liberalism) prophetically set forth, there is a perversion of the whole ideal of individualism to conform to the practices of a pecuniary culture." But even deeper damage was done by the older supposition that individuality is given, as unalterable matter of fact, when in Dewey's view it must be recognized as a developmental outcome:

> Only in the physical sense of physical bodies that to the senses are separate is individuality an original datum. Individuality in a social and moral sense is something to be wrought out. It means initiative, inventiveness, varied resourcefulness, assumption of responsibility in choice of belief and conduct. These are not gifts, but achievements.[24]

For present purposes we can focus upon one implication of the supposition that individuality is a datum, namely that individuality is inherently asocial, being associated only contingently in relations that remain external to individual natures. As Dewey expresses it, "Individuals, it is implied, have a full-blown psychological and moral nature, having its own set of laws, independently of their association with one another."[25] By contrast what Dewey terms the "new individualism" conceives individuality as inherently social. In the first place, persons begin life as dependent infants and children, who are "modified in mind and character" by their associations with family, teachers, and others of the adult communities in which they are reared. Secondly, the resources that individuals acquire in the process of their growth—tools, skills, intelligence—are social resources in the profound sense that they represent the funded contributions of many persons who are associated in the collectivities we term practices and traditions. Finally, human beings are social in the sense that the well-lived life is of worth to others, and intended to be such. As Dewey expresses it in one place, "Any individual has missed his calling, farmer, physician, teacher, student, who does not find that the accomplishments of results of value to others is an accompaniment of a process of experience inherently worth while."[26]

The recognition that individuality is in the beginning of the life of each person merely potential, in a condition of dependence upon external agencies, is the imperative to discern the requirements of developing individuality and devise the means and agencies by which to meet these requirements. Accordingly: "The problem of democracy becomes the problem of that form of social organization, extending to all areas and ways of living, in which the powers of individuals shall not be merely released from mechanical external constraint but shall be fed, sustained, and directed."[27]

Here is the recognition that spawned and fueled Dewey's lifelong preoccupation with the processes and aims of education. But we can follow him sufficient to our purposes by the single, concrete observation that the growth that education must support is from the dependence of childhood to the autonomy and relative self-sufficiency of adulthood. Basically, we care for children in order that they may subsequently achieve a level of development in which they are able to care for themselves. This furnishes Dewey with the paramount aim of education, which is "continued capacity for growth."[28]

The capacity for self-education is the ability to learn from experience (including, of course, the experience of others as transmitted, e.g., in books) and requires method, specifically what Dewey terms the "method of intelligence." It is significant that the method of intelligence is a problem-solving method, for in giving centrality to problems Dewey is affirming the problematic nature of human being. To be a human being is to be perpetually engaged at problems—how to drive a car; how to use a library; whether to marry, and whom; how to understand the Pythagorean theorem; and at bottom, how to solve the problem that one as a human being is to oneself, namely of deciding what to become and endeavoring to become it. Dewey's thesis is that the method of intelligence is the universal problem-solving method, applicable alike to all types of problems, though with differing degrees of refinement. It affords to individuals control over their circumstances and their lives, and is therefore the indispensable means of self-direction and self-development. The central goal of Dewey's philosophy of education is to equip all persons with working competence in the method of intelligence by which to choose their ends and move successfully toward attainment of them.

The method of intelligence is empirical-experimental method, which is to say it is "scientific method." In the first place, because its operation is a directed activity, and not random casting about, it requires an aim. But chosen aims require recognition of alternatives:

Where only a single outcome has been thought of, the mind has nothing else to think of; the meaning attaching to the act is limited. One only steams ahead toward the mark. Sometimes such a narrow course may be effective. But if unexpected difficulties offer themselves, one has not as many resources at command as if he had chosen the same line of action after a broader survey of the possibilities of the field. He cannot make needed adjustments readily.[29]

Dewey is neither first nor foremost among philosophers at explicating scientific method, but he is first and foremost at explicating it in ways that make it applicable by nonscientists to the conduct of daily life. In his endeavor to thus equip persons for the effective conduct of their affairs, he encounters at least three entrenched obstacles. One of them is that despite the success of the sciences, some realms of experience have sought to close themselves off from its methods of inquiry (religion and morality are notable examples); but because (on Dewey's account) these are the methods by which knowledge is acquired, the resistant realms are recognizably engaged at protecting dogmas. A second entrenched obstacle is the esotericizing of scientific method through the compartmentalizing of "pure science." A third obstacle is the propensity of the educational institution to divorce knowledge from practice, teaching "knowledge for its own sake" and disdaining problems of daily existence.

Regarding the second of these obstacles, what we commonly mean by "science" is inquiry at a high level of refinement: its problems are hypothetical, not concrete, and they are expressed symbolically in order to lend themselves to purely symbolic manipulations. These considerations serve to set "science" at so great a distance from the conduct of daily life as to afford no opportunity of commensuration. This distance is signified by the divorce of "pure science" from "applied science," the former being conceived as wholly disencumbered of practical considerations. Dewey opposes this divorce, holding that science is purposeful, systematic inquiry to acquire knowledge, not for its own sake, but for the improvement of practice. It is tied to practice at both its ends, so to speak, arising from problems initially encountered in practice, and returning with knowledge that successful practice requires. For holding this view Dewey has been accused of promoting the abolition of what we understand as "pure science," but no such consequence follows. Some pure science unquestionably receives the pragmatic justification that by the proportional release of some research from practical imperatives, practical requirements are in the long run better served.

We may say that Dewey is "reminding science of its origins." The important point in his so-doing is that science is commensurated with daily living, it is de-esotericized. To accomplish this is to avail ourselves of the recognition that learning and problem-solving in daily living are accomplished by the use of empirical-experimental method. It is not a case of altogether different methods, but of one method operating at very different levels of refinement. And as Dewey decisively demonstrates, effective use of empirical-experimental method at the level of refinement called for by the practical problems of ordinary living can be taught and learned. With respect to the self-directed, self-responsible living that it is our purpose in this book to foster and support, the central place for the application of the "method of intelligence" is to the life-shaping choices, and we will attend to such application in the next chapter.

The result of the esotericizing of science is not that science employs one problem-solving method, and a different method is employed by persons in the ordinary conduct of life. It is that persons are devoid of method for the conduct of daily life, which remains a catch-all of habit, custom, guess, hearsay, and dogma.

The divorce of classroom learning from problems of living is the effective divorce of living and learning, when the two must be conjoined. The result of the divorce is the impoverishment of both classroom and extracurricular life. Because classroom problems are remote from students' interests they require of students a manufactured interest (at bottom, their grade in the course becomes their compelling interest by default), and the intellectual capacities that are cultivated in classrooms are for the most part confined to the classrooms. To overcome this gulf, Dewey urged that classroom learning incorporate "the type of the situation which causes reflection out of school in ordinary life."[30] As positive measures he urged that schools incorporate laboratories, shops, gardens, dramatizations, and games.[31]

Such measures are no longer novel in our setting because in this respect Dewey's philosophy of education had great impact from the late 1930s through the 1950s. "Learning while doing" became a catchword of public schooling; laboratories, shops, and—yes—gardens were incorporated within the orbit of schools, and likewise dramatizations and games. Then in the late 1950s reaction set in at the disproportionate amount of attention to "nonacademic" subjects in the school day, as epitomized by "Driver Education," and the "back to basics" movement took hold. The justification for the reaction lay in the discrepancy between Dewey's philosophy of education and the wave of "Deweyism" that had adopted the trappings without the philosophy. What was left behind in practical classes was the "intellectual quality" that Dewey insisted should be paramount.[32] As with any other subjects, Driver Education or Gardening can be taught by inculcation of settled practices, in which case students learn to drive a car and to garden, but they learn next to nothing toward the self-directed learning, the "continued capacity for growth," that Dewey perceived as the central aim of education. Dewey correctly insisted that learning to garden, or to drive a car (for example) *can* call upon all of the elements of empirical-experimental method, elements that have general application to every problematic situation. But to make these elements visible, intelligible, and generalizable, they must be understood and emphasized by teachers. This was not done; teachers were by and large unprepared to do it; what they knew of driving or gardening—for example—they had themselves learned by rote learning of orthodox procedures, and this is how they taught—by rote. Left untouched in this case is the *originality* of both teachers and students. Dewey says, "We sometimes talk as if 'original research' were a peculiar prerogative of scientists or at least of advanced students. But all thinking is research, and all research is native, original, with him who carries it on, even if everybody else in the world already is sure of what he is still looking for."[33]

Nor was the distortion restricted to "nonacademic" subjects of study. Typically history is taught as dated outcomes, science is taught as results, and literature is taught as appreciation of masterpieces. The effects are not to be despised, but they do nothing toward the clarification of experience that is afforded when history and science are taught as processes, and literature is employed for the alternative perspectives upon the world and the self that it affords.

In sum, the validity of Dewey's enterprise to equip all persons to learn effectively from their own experience as well as from human experience in general is not contested by the reaction against Deweyism in American education, for that phenomenon left Dewey's enterprise behind.

Dewey provides a clear and concise picture of the employment of the method of intelligence in the discovery of values.[34] The first step is isolation of the relevant facts, and these consist in satisfactions that have been had. These, however (contra utilitarianism) are to be regarded not as values but as possibilities of value. The next step is to transform possibilities of value into conceptually realized values, and it is here that empirical-experimental method comes into full play. Each possibility of value is a hypothesis, to be confirmed or disconfirmed through experimental discovery of conditions and consequences. Knowledge of consequences must aim to be as complete as possible; further, such knowledge serves to disconfirm as values those immediate satisfactions that bring overriding dissatisfactions in their train. Knowledge of conditions has twofold importance. In the first place it introduces the recognition that all values are conditional, in the sense that they are values only in some circumstances. (This does not imply that there are no enduring values, for the conditions under which some values are values may endure, or endlessly recur.) For example, G. E. Moore has identified as intrinsic values aesthetic satisfaction and the pleasures of good interpersonal relations, such as good conversation. But we do not want to be awakened at two o'clock in the morning for good conversation; and aesthetic satisfaction appears to presuppose satisfaction of prior needs. To be overcome with hunger is for most people to be incapable of appreciating a still life of a bowl of delectable fruit *aesthetically*. As another type of consideration, a burning residence in a night sky has aesthetic appeal, but its appreciation in these terms is a distraction from the work to be done—rescue—and thus a situational disvalue.

Second, knowledge of the conditions under which a value is a value is essential to the enterprise of realizing the value in experience. For example, every good hostess or host is attentive to the conditions of good conversation; the mix of personalities, the topics, the timing, the amount of liquor and food served, the lighting, seating, and so forth.

This knowledge has been acquired by empirical-experimental method in its "common sense" form.

Determinations of value are central to the self-discovery and self-actualization that by our thesis are the backbone of self-directed, self-responsible living by individuals. This is because (as we shall seek to show in chapter 4) the integrity and moral necessity in such living result from the identification of oneself with certain values, where "identification" entails actualization, conservation, and defense.

It is evident that Dewey's strategy for the discernment of value, as just described, commits the "naturalistic fallacy" (if it is a fallacy) of deriving values from facts. What results from the application of the method of intelligence to satisfactions, regarded as possibilities of value, is not knowledge of values (it will be said) but only better-known facts. The straightforward line of response is taken by philosophers who today are challenging "Hume's law" ("no 'ought' from an 'is' "),[35] but I shall not follow the argument here. The thesis we are advancing is that significant gains in the quality of life can be realized by generalizing the opportunity of self-directed, self-responsible living, and we have contended that this aim translates into the enterprise of improving the "life-shaping" choices of individuals—among them choice of vocation; of whether to marry or not, and when, and whom; of whether to have children, and how many, and when; of avocations, friends to cultivate, locale of permanent residence (or vagabondage), religious and civic commitments. If this much is granted, then I take it to be beyond doubt that Dewey's program to afford to all persons sound capabilities in the "method of intelligence" is a most effective step, and a high priority.

Equally high priority must be given to a factor to which Dewey gives insufficient attention, at least explicitly; namely self-knowledge. Earlier we saw Mill's innatism together with his normative individualism in citations from chapter 3 of *On Liberty*. Dewey makes his own innatist normative individualism clear when he says, for example, "Callings have their roots in innate impulses of human nature but their pursuit does not merely 'express' these impulses, leaving them unaltered; their pursuit determines intellectual horizons, precipitates knowledge and ideas, shapes desire and interest."[36] In our terms, innate individuality finds expression by the identification of persons as individuals with certain values and not others. While each must learn to recognize and appreciate values other than her own, her responsibility to her own values—to actualize, conserve, and defend them—precludes her equal responsibility to other values, and facilitates her recognition of the corresponding responsibilities of other persons for the values with which they as individuals identify.

Dewey's three-stage strategy for the identification and realization of values, reviewed earlier in this chapter, is directed to values impartially considered, and is therefore unable as it stands to answer the question that poses itself to each individual qua individual: "Which distinctive values shall I identify with?" Our purpose in the next chapter will be to supplement Dewey by showing how the method of intelligence can be directed to this question. Our focus will be upon vocational choice, and therefore the values in question will be vocational values. The case will serve to illustrate how the method of intelligence can be employed with respect to every life-shaping choice. In chapter 4 we will attend to the virtue of integrity, understood as the integration of the several life-shaping choices.

We have noted that much of the Deweyism that had a shaping influence on American education into the 1950s left the heart of Dewey's philosophy of education behind: it was but the trappings, the vessel emptied of its contents. What had been by degrees overtaking Dewey and Deweyism, and eventually triumphed, was a combination of Thorndikean behaviorism, combined with the "scientific" management principles whose intrusion into public education we have noted earlier. These principles mandated total control of classrooms by teachers and corresponding control of teachers by administrators. Curricula were designed in board rooms, administrative offices, and learning-theory laboratories, which is to say, at a great remove from children in the classroom. This put an end to the interest-centered learning that Dewey sponsored. In so doing, it eliminated the elicitory form of teaching that moral development requires and supported teaching as inculcation. This coincided in our politics with the abandonment of the developmental model of democracy in favor of nondevelopmental "equilibrium" democracy, as discussed earlier.

CHAPTER THREE

Implementation of Developmental Democracy:
Focus Upon Adolescence

Political theory bears directly upon conduct and is therefore a species of practical reasoning. Where the theory is normative and revisionist, as ours is, it is answerable to two eminently practical questions—"What differences would acting upon the theory make?" and "How can such enactment begin?" In this chapter we will address ourselves to the second of these questions. Much of the remainder of the book addresses the first.

Where to begin is a particularly slippery question when what is proposed is not piecemeal alteration in prevailing thought and practice but an exchange of wholistic perspectives, for in this case everything changes, and each change is implicated in every other. This can appear to render any particular change—as a starting change necessarily is—impossible. But existing systems are less coherent than theoretical models and contain loose ends. The two loose ends in our social system that afford starting points are meaningful work and adolescence.

By "meaningful work" I mean work that is intrinsically rewarding to the worker, and too little of the work that is done today in our society qualifies as such. This is unsurprising, because by the modes of thought that have shaped our culture, earning a living is disconnected from self-fulfillment. The one is a hard necessity of life, whereas the other is typically considered to be a luxury if not a narcissistic self-indulgence. The need to rethink these matters is imperative. By the eudaimonistic conceptions of self and society that we are endeavoring to elucidate in this book, getting a living is an important strand in the true work that is the moral responsibility of every person, the work of living worthily by discovering and actualizing innate potential excellence. This work will be experienced as intrinsically rewarding and self-fulfilling; the individual will identify with it, invest himself or herself in it, and realize objective values in it. Earning a living should participate in this moral work. How can this be achieved for or by (or for and by) people in numbers sufficient to be said to characterize our society?

The central problem of adolescence is that its intrinsic developmental requirements go unrecognized. Our propensity is to regard it as a temporary aberration in an otherwise sensible life. To minimize the disruption we squeeze adolescence between prolonged expectations of childhood dependence and premature expectations of adult commitment. Inherently it is a stage for exploration among alternatives in the interest of making better life-shaping choices—choices of vocation; of whether or not to marry, and whom; and the rest as noted in chapter 2. In our investigation in this chapter we will focus largely upon vocational choice, but with the understanding that the type of exploration that is necessary to improve vocational choice is required also in preparation for every other life-shaping choice.

According to eudaimonism, a life-shaping choice is well made when it is founded in self-knowledge and serves to progressively actualize the ideal self that subsists in the individual initially *in potentia*. Accordingly the exploration that is the inherent requirement of adolescence is to the purposes both of experiencing alternatives afforded by the world and one's society, and of self-discovery. Self-discovery occurs, not by sheer introspection, but by exploration together with introspection upon the experience that exploration gathers. The reason that introspection by itself is ineffective is that pure unactualized potentialities are invisible to it. Introspection is retrospection whose material is actual subjective content. At the beginning of adolescence (prior to exploration) the only actual subjective content available to introspection is implicated in the conferred self of childhood. What transforms latent potentialities into material for introspection is some measure of enactment in the world. One is looking for courses of conduct that afford intrinsic rewards. Intrinsic rewards of activity are eudaimonic, constituting evidence that the activity is actualizing an individual's innate potentiality.

The relationship of introspection to the self's possibilities and potentialities might be encapsulated by saying: "You can't know if you will like playing the French horn until you begin to play the French horn." The reason that self-discovery does not require *excellence* at (in this example) playing the French horn is that unlike pleasure, which is reserved to the attainment of the goal of desire, eudaimonia is experienced with one's first footsteps on the right path.

In the interest of the exploration that is required for self-discovery and subsequent commitment, adolescence needs "freedom, and variety of situations."[1] And adolescence is admirably suited to its work by its temperament.

Adolescence is characteristically impulsive, rash, insecure, fickle, insolent, proud, clannish, extremist, and self-preoccupied. It is recognizable in the West by this portrait since the time of Homer, notably in the youthful Achilles. It is the portrait drawn by Aristotle,[2] by Shakespeare,[3] by Robert Louis Stevenson,[4] and by many others. As thus characterized, adolescence is not to be found in tribal societies, but neither is the degree of individuation and autonomy that we expect of adults. And the logic of development is such that if we expect a significant measure of individuation and autonomy in adults, then between adulthood and the dependence of childhood must occur an adolescence that is roughly characterizable as we are in the process of characterizing it.

Each of the traits with which adolescence was identified at the beginning of the previous paragraph is typically regarded by us as a defect calling for rectification. These traits appear so from the standpoint of adulthood because they are unsuited to the requirements of a well-lived life in adulthood. My thesis is, however, that the requirements of a well-lived life in adolescence are very different from those of adulthood, and are served—not disserved—by the listed traits. The problem is that we do not recognize adolescence as a distinctive developmental stage, different from both childhood and adulthood, with important developmental work of its own to do. In the words of James C. Coleman, chairman of the Panel on Youth of the President's Science Advisory Committee during the Carter presidency, "A capitalistic economy or market economy has no natural place for an intermediate status between full dependency, which a person is in when he is in school, and the full productivity that he is in when he is in the labor force."[5]

Coleman saw this structural defect as the deepest factor contributing to the alarming rise in youth vandalism and violent crime, drug and alcohol abuse, unemployment, teenage pregnancy, school drop-out, and suicide. He judged most proposed correctives to be superficial and argued for the basic need to establish a new status for youth as a compelling national interest.

But it is not only the visibly dislocated among our youth about whom we must be concerned. Margaret Mead spoke of well-behaved, "well-adjusted" young people when she says, "At present a very large number go from dependency on their parents into careers that have been chosen for them, or use marriage as a device to reach pseudo-adult status."[6] It is important to understand what Mead means by "pseudo-adult status," and we can do so by reverting to what I am terming the logic of development.

In concert with both common sense and developmental theory we will identify the definitive characteristic of childhood as dependence. Then adolescence begins in "separation" and leads to self-identification. Adulthood begins in commitment to a particular course of life comprising the life-shaping choices that we have referred to previously. Effective adult living requires the virtue of integrity, understood as integration of these life-shaping choices into an identity. The work of adulthood is realization of objective worth in the world through self-actualization. Each successive stage as here identified is dependent upon satisfactory (not perfect) fulfillment of the intrinsic requirements of the previous stage. If the life-shaping choices that inaugurate adulthood are to be what adult living requires, they must be genuine choices and they must be committed choices.

By a committed choice I mean a choice that keeps faith with its own unrecognized as well as its recognized entailments. For unless this is the case the choice is in jeopardy whenever trouble arises, whereas commitment sees its troubles through, seeking the best possible resolution, and learning from its failures. The crux here is that the individual identifies with his or her choice, such that it is constitutive of his or her being, a being that will be diminished by failure to stand up to the problems and troubles that lie in its course. The compensatory feature in problems and troubles that are faced is that identification produces growth in terms of resourcefulness and strength of character, when the choices that the individual makes are such as actualize that individual's identity. No aspiring life is without its measure of failure, but the failure of one's best efforts, in an enterprise with which one is unequivocally identified, carries eudaimonic compensation.

By a genuine choice I here mean one that fulfills the logical and developmental conditions of growth. The logical condition that counts most for present purposes is knowledge of alternatives, and the developmental condition is self-knowledge.

Then the pseudo-adulthood that Mead refers to is a life based on pseudo-choice. And pseudo-choice is certain to be more prevalent than true choice in a society that fails to recognize adolescence as the stage of development that is inherently responsible for acquiring the necessary preconditions of genuine choice.

In this light it is counterproductive to tie together adolescence and childhood in a pattern of education amounting to sixteen years at one sitting. Yet in the wake of the 1983 National Commission on Excellence in Education report, *A Nation at Risk,* together with the 1986 "Bennett Report," *First Lessons,*[7] state after state is lining up to support more schooling—longer school hours, more homework, shorter summer breaks. What a little foresight will tell us is that this will multiply the number of teenagers who are overdosed on classroom learning geared primarily to test-taking. The Bennett recommendations, if followed, are certain to widen still further the dismal disparity between childhood's exuberant curiosity and the leaden-eyed classroom presence of countless adolescents.

Compare the words of the Carnegie Council study, *Giving Youth a Better Chance:* "Young people received too heavy a dose of schooling for too long a period, unmixed with knowledge of the world of work or experience in work or community service. Work that takes the form of community service is particularly desirable, giving young people a feeling of involvement in community problems and of contributing to their solution."[8]

As sensitive teachers and parents recognize, youths who are leaden-eyed in class are intensely curious about the world "out there"; indeed, their attraction to "the real world" contributes to their resentment of the classroom that precludes the "real world" to them. Nor is it possible for classroom studies of the outside world to alleviate their hunger. Classroom study of "variety of situations" is not *experience* (even vicarious) of variety of situations. The reason for this is that the classroom is itself so imposing a situation as to homogenize whatever enters it. It is a narrow regimen of sitting, listening, and reading. As such it has its own strong flavor. Meanwhile every course of life in the world likewise has its own flavor, but these flavors are masked in classroom study of courses of life. It is the difference between reading about Alaska and being there, between preparatory study for a vocation and practice of the vocation; and too many persons, upon taking up the vocation for which they have prepared themselves, find that its flavor is altogether different than they expected.

It is a mistake to hoard the "real world" for twenty years from people whom we expect eventually to manage the world and manage themselves in it, and who for at least the last years of those years have hungered for experience of it.

Senator Sam Nunn of Georgia is but the latest in a long line of thoughtful and concerned national leaders who have proposed a National Youth Service. I believe there are strong reasons for supporting such a proposal on the developmental grounds we have sketched in this chapter. These same grounds call for the establishment of multiple opportunities to return to formal education in later life, thereby breaking up what former Secretary of Labor Willard Wirtz called the "time traps of youth for education, adulthood for work, old age for nothing."[9] Finally, I propose that a concern for good growth calls for opening elementary and secondary schooling to the community through apprenticeship and community service, and at the college level for reviving the "work-study" concept pioneered at Antioch and Beloit Colleges and Northeastern University, wherein semesters of formal study and semesters of work or community service are alternated.

I will lay out each of these proposals in more detail and respond to selected objections.

The idea of a National Youth Service (lately named a Citizens Corps) by no means originates with Senator Nunn and the Democratic Leadership Council for which he speaks. It has been strongly advocated in the past decade by such national leaders as Senators Bill Bradley, Paul E. Tsongas, Alan Cranston, and Mark Hatfield. It was advocated by Secretary of Defense Robert S. McNamara and Secretary of Labor Willard Wirtz, by Vice-President Hubert Humphrey, and by Presidents Roosevelt, Kennedy, and Johnson. At the outset of his administration President Johnson gave it top priority in the following words:

We must move toward a standard that no man [the choice of term should not be read to exclude women, whom he expressly included] has truly lived who has served only himself. . . . To move in this direction, I am asking every member of my Administration to explore new ways by which our young people can serve their fellow men. I am asking a group of Governors and Mayors to meet and study ways in which City, State, and Federal governments can cooperate in developing a manpower service that could work at every level of our society. . . . To the Youth of America, I want to say: If you seek to be uncommon, if you seek to make a difference, if you seek to serve, then look around you. Your country needs you. Your nation needs your services.[10]

Johnson's proposal was extinguished almost at birth by dramatic escalation in the fighting in Viet Nam.

The original proposer of something akin to a National Youth Service is generally acknowledged to be William James in his essay (originally delivered as an address at Stanford University in 1906) "The Moral Equivalent of War." James approached the problem of war by looking to it for certain values that could account for an attraction to it on the part of humankind. Noting, for example, the intense concentration, social cohesiveness, purposiveness, and invigoration that war typically achieves, James sought to afford them to young people by providing opportunities of important and adventurous work. Instead of cheering young people off to war, he proposed sending them to "coal and iron mines, to freight trains, to fishing fleets in December, to dishwashing, clothes washing, and window washing, to road building and tunnel making, to foundaries and stoke-holes, and to the frames of skyscrapers." He sought in this the cultivation of a self-confidence that would develop the nation's youth to become "better fathers ["parents" we will want to say today] and teachers of the following generation."[11]

For James, the basic purpose of a National Youth Service is developmental, namely to cultivate resourcefulness, maturity, and a judicious self-confidence in our youth, as preparation for effective adult living. In the time since James wrote, other rationales have been offered. One of them supports a National Youth Service as a means to stem disturbing social trends among our young people of the sort noted earlier in this chapter. Another stresses the mounting national and community needs that can be met by such a service. Both of these rationales have validity.

Regarding rising youth crime, drug use, teenage pregnancy, and the rest of the distressing litany, surveys by the Department of Labor indicate that mixing work and service is highly effective as a treatment. The fact that these surveys were done in 1973 will not trouble us if we recognize that they uncover a basic truth: the surest immunization against anti-social and/or self-destructive conduct is having something to do that one regards as important.

On the matter of national and community needs, President Johnson in 1966 said to young people, "Look at yourselves, and then look at our need at this very hour for more than a million medical and health workers in this Nation. Look at our need for more than a million teachers and school administrators. Look at our need for more than 700,000 welfare and home care workers; look at our need for more than two million people to help improve our cities. Almost half a million to serve in public protection of our homes and our families and our children." Johnson concluded, "The sign of your time is need,"[12] and today we cannot doubt that need remains the sign of our time by virtue of the steady erosion of social services since Johnson spoke. And since then we have been apprised of pervasive decay portending collapse in our system of public utilities—including bridges, roads, dams, reservoirs, sewerage systems, transit systems, waterways, ports, jails, prisons. The going estimate is that $3 trillion will be needed simply to halt the erosion process.[13]

So massive a national problem may seem to dwarf the potential resources of a National Youth Service—until we recall the effects of the Civilian Conservation Corps in the 1930s. In its nine-year existence the CCC planted over 2 billion trees covering 2 million acres; built 126,000 miles of tertiary roads and 46,000 vehicle bridges; constructed 62,000 buildings (not including CCC camps), restored 4,000 historical structures; put in nearly a million miles of fence, 89,000 miles of telephone lines, and 69,000 miles of fire breaks. It developed 800 new state parks, logged over 2 million person-days providing disaster relief, and 12 million person-days preventing and fighting forest fires.[14] (In 1935 the Forest Service adopted the epoch-making policy of fighting all forest fires in every part of the country, rather than letting many of them burn.[15] Such a policy could have been nothing but words on paper without the CCC.)

Curbing youth crime and meeting national service needs are appropriate objectives of a National Youth Service, but the deepest and most enduring benefits stand to be realized if the leading objective is the developmental one of equipping our young people for better living as adults. This is the dominant rationale in William James's proposal, and likewise in those of Margaret Mead, Erik Erikson, Theodore Hesburgh, Morris Janowitz, and—just now—Senators Nunn of Georgia and Barbara Mikulski of Maryland.

Senator Nunn believes that a Citizens Corps can inspire "a new spirit of citizenship and civic obligation in America."[16] So do I.

Young people who have helped families put their homes together in the aftermath of a flood are enduringly changed by the experience. The same can be true in a quieter way of the teenager who provides comfort and companionship to an elderly person. In the words of Senator Mikulski, "You know you've changed when maybe for the first time in your life you think about somebody other than yourself."[17]

Perhaps I can best show what I think our primary purpose should be by a personal example.

At the age of sixteen, I got a job fighting forest fires and was quartered in a tent camp near Priest River, Idaho. The fire call in question came through in the early afternoon, and we were trucked to the Ranger Station at Sandpoint for instructions. It was a big fire well north of us, on the Canadian border. Two thousand firefighters were already at work there, but the fire was not under control and was threatening a town, and we were to provide reinforcement. We rode north in our convoy of trucks the rest of the day and into the night. From midnight on, the fire was awesomely visible to us, reddening the night sky for nearly a quarter of the horizon. At 1 A.M. we rolled through the threatened town on its main street, which had been cleared of parked cars for our passage. To our astonishment the street was thronged with people; it seemed to us that every living soul in the town was there (I know I saw children); they cheered and clapped as we went by.

We got to the fire twenty minutes later. The immediate effect of the startling demonstration of the town was to give every one of us the strength of ten at battling the flames. The town was saved.

But what I want to speak of is the long-term effect upon me personally. It indelibly imprinted in me the feeling that "I can do it," and it did so at a highly impressionable age. At some subterranean level that feeling has been with me ever since, and I have had countless occasions to be grateful for it.

I recognize my good fortune in having been provided with the growth-experience just described. For many years I have surveyed my college students on their best work experiences. In the majority of cases their opportunity to venture forth from familiar territory has been curtailed by their obligation to help pay college expenses, together with a scarcity of available work. Typically they take summer employment at fast-food restaurants, do camp counseling, sell souvenirs at the beach, and the like. What I try to do is, first, show them (or remind them in some cases) that they have significant growth experiences nonetheless. Second, I try to show that more engaging or vivid circumstances may be available to them upon the exercise of a little more initiative. Two or three brief examples must here suffice.

The first is a growth experience that is not job-connected (as they certainly often are not; my survey of work experience is simply a place to start). A young woman described to me the circumstances of her grandfather's death, which occurred when she was at the age of twelve. He had been hospitalized for a week, and she had made ten-minute visits on alternate days with one of her parents, the other parent spending longer at the bedside. During this period she expected her grandfather to recover (though she could not remember whether she was told this or simply assumed it). On the morning of the day in question, her father informed her that her grandfather was dying, and requested that with him (her father) and her mother, she attend her grandfather to the end. She did so, and she reported to me that after some initial apprehension she felt comfortable in the situation with the three adults.

As with my fire experience, it was the lasting effects upon the young woman that she dwelled upon. And as in my case, the notable effect was a subterranean confidence that "I can do it," with special reference to attending dying or critically ill relatives or friends. She and I then reflected on the numbers of adults we both know who will avoid such occasions with words on the order of "I can't do it . . . I wouldn't know what to say."

One type of work experience that I keep track of for its growth potential is experience involving male-female role reversals. A compelling and amusing instance was a young woman who worked for a summer in downtown Washington, D.C., filling potholes in streets as a member of an asphalt paving crew. This had never been done before by a woman. She said there were about twenty such crews working different parts of the city. News spread rapidly, and other crews would drift by on their lunchtime to see this curiosity for themselves. "How did your own crew behave?", I asked her. She said for the first day they kept their language squeaky clean—just an occasional "damn" or "hell," accompanied by a quick glance in her direction. Laughing to me, she said she could see this put them under a severe strain; so on the second day she undertook to ease the situation by herself using stronger language. The effect of this, she said, was to raise hopes of her loose moral character in some of the men. Once she got them straightened out on that score, she told me, they were underway toward accepting her as an ordinary fellow-worker. Then *they* did the straightening-out of other crews that drifted by at lunchtime. A final note was that her boyfriend during that summer was working at an architectural firm. He dressed impeccably in three-piece suits while she was black to the knees each day after work, and reeked of asphalt continuously.

Another important category consists of jobs that afford to students a preview of their chosen careers. Last spring I interviewed a young man who had the previous summer worked in a law office and who learned from it that becoming a lawyer would be, for him, a mistake. A general lesson here is that the practice of a profession, and the course of study in preparation for it, are often very different in what I will term their "existential tonality."

Most employment reported by my students has at the objective level nothing out of the ordinary about it, and this lulls them to sleep. My job is to show them, where I can, that in their ordinary, even humdrum, experience is likely to lie hidden gold. I compare it to the case of persons who try panning gold for the first time. Pan in hand they step into the waters of a mountain stream, say in California or Oregon or Washington. They dip up into their pans some of the sand and gravel of the stream bed, together with a little water. They swirl this in their pan as someone has told them to do, but ineptly, all the while peering intently for the appearance of "colors." Typically they see nothing and will move to dump the contents of the pan into the stream. This is where the intervention of an experienced companion is required, for he or she can often swirl the pan expertly, and then point a finger: "There's your gold—and there—and there."

Our youthful prospectors of their own experience likewise are in need of the assistance of a trained eye.

And some of them can profit from the assurance that more interesting summer work of a number of kinds can often be tracked down with a modicum of persistence. To get a job fighting forest fires, for example, one need only write to three or four U. S. Forest Service Ranger Stations, the addresses of which are available in the reference rooms at most libraries. To get a job working on a salmon-fishing boat in Ketchikan, Alaska, is harder, but can be done. If one wants to teach children to swim at a summer camp, why not pick a summer camp in a state whose character is quite different from the state in which one spends the rest of the year? One of my students wanted to see the world but had no money; he hitchhiked to New Orleans and hired on as an apprentice seaman in a freighter bound for Rio de Janeiro.

The idea of a year of Citizens Corps service between high school and college arouses the anxiety that many young people will not return to formal education or will lose their study skills. But it is a matter of wide agreement that the best wave of students to pass through our colleges and universities was the returning G.I.s from World War II—men and women whose military service separated them from formal studies for from two to four years. Their academic rustiness was but a trifling challenge to their enhanced maturity and self-responsibility.

And with rapidly escalating costs of a college education, a Citizens Corps would afford college opportunity to the increasing numbers of young people for whom the costs are becoming prohibitive. The Nunn plan, for example, includes a $10,000 education voucher for each year of service.

A commonly voiced objection to a National Youth Service or Citizens Corps is its cost to the nation and thereby to taxpayers. And certainly to establish such a program would require substantial investments of money, as well as time and knowledge, by our society-at-large. But if we bear in mind that such programs as the CCC and NYA, VISTA, the Job Corps, and the Young Adult Conservation Corps have proved cost-effective, and that present mishandling of the growth requirements of adolescence is itself costly, a National Youth Service becomes recognizable as a "best buy."

By "cost-effective" is meant that in the programs just mentioned the dollar value of the work performed has been at least equal to total program costs. That it has sometimes far surpassed costs is evident in the following example from the CCC concerning reforestation in the Capital Forest area near Olympia, Washington:

During the 1920s and into the 1930s the Capital Forest area . . . was completely devastated by intensive private logging operations. The land was abandoned as being of no further use to its owners and was taken over by the state. During 1934–1939, 90,000 acres of this land was reforested by the CCC at an approximate cost of $270,000. In 1960 commercial thinning began and the first returns on this investment began to be realized. Today [1981] the acreage is being harvested with the timber value placed conservatively at $7000 per acre or $630,000,000 total.[18]

The "best buy" case has been presented in most detail in *National Service: Social, Economic, and Military Impacts* by Michael W. Sherraden and Donald Eberley. The book was published in 1981, but in proportional terms the figures remain indicative. Based on a National Service bill introduced into the House of Representatives by Paul N. McCloskey in 1979 (HR 2206), the Congressional Budget Office estimated the net cost per National Service participant at $6,660 per year. To compare with this, Sherraden and Eberley assembled the following per annum per person costs to the nation of certain alternatives: military service, $21,000; juvenile incarceration, $18,000; college education (public subsidy of various kinds), $8,900; minimum wage employment $6,968.[19] But the "best buy" case only scratches the surface in these figures. On developmental grounds we can expect, by the "freedom, and variety of situations" that National Service affords to youth, that the life-shaping choices of adulthood will be better made, more likely to afford intrinsic rewards, more likely to represent commitments in which adults invest the best of themselves, and more productive of objective values. In Margaret Mead's words,

Universal national service would provide opportunities for service abroad in a variety of capacities, service in different parts of the country, service in different climes and conditions. It should broaden all young people in the way in which those who have taken full advantage of service overseas and of the Peace Corps have been broadened and prepared for responsible citizenship and wider understanding of national and world problems.[20]

And from the experience in our colleges of increasing numbers of older returning students, we know that every increment of added maturity has a high probability of enhancing college performance. My experience at teaching in a large state university for twenty-three years convinces me that most undergraduate students at my institution and comparable institutions do not truly want to be there. They are there because they are told—by parents, teachers, community, and nation— that they must be there in order to "get a good job" and be a "success" in later life. Living on this secondhand initiative they are not committed students; they are only half-present in their classroom seats, being in their other half transported in imagination to where they truly want to be. Our healthiest response is to help them get to where they really want to be. When they return to us they will be twice the students they were before.

Overdosed on book-learning and classroom-learning, our students are victims of a myth that we have woven for them and also manage to catch ourselves in. I will call it the myth of over-preparation, by which the requirements for formal education are exaggerated.

Civil engineers, for example, do not need a Master of Science degree, or even four years of college to begin to practice in their profession. The design of small structures with which the practice of civil engineering typically begins is entirely feasible on the basis of high school mathematics and the guidance of an experienced engineer.

Similarly the formal requirement of a master's degree for a start in forestry today is inflated, and what is required in the first few years can be better gained by a lesser amount of formal study combined with practical experience.

What has been noted here of two professions is a pervasive condition. In his insightful study for the National Manpower Institute, *The Bound-*

less Resource: A Prospectus for an Education-Work Policy, Willard Wirtz paraphrased what he found to be the "prevalent employer view" as, "If the schools will just send us young people who can read and write and add and think, we will hire them—and do the job training ourselves."[21]

Recognition of problems created by "over-qualification" in terms of formal education has been growing. One of them is that the over-qualified job candidate is likely to expect more pay than the actual work he or she will be doing is worth. Another is that high-level abstract studies produce in some young persons a disdain for the menial-appearing work they are expected to do. Another (mentioned previously) is that the insularity of much classroom preparation nurtures misconceptions about actual job-practice, such that too many persons find, on entering upon practice of their chosen vocation, that they are disaffected by it.

Meanwhile some persons who have a native affinity for the work are barred from it by disaffinity for the inflated educational demands. The reader will know of examples, but for mine I offer the following.

From my youthful work in forestry I vividly recall my immediate superior of one season, a man named Dennis Fury, who had more woods-sense than any other person I have encountered. Fury had taught himself timber, land, and wildlife management and had a deep love of all aspects of the work. At fighting forest fires he was a one-man gang, and he had an instinctive sense of what a fire would do next. On a large fire in the Kootenai National Forest, northern Montana, it was Fury (not the half-dozen Rangers who were there) who each night coordinated the next day's attack on multiple fronts. Yet he was but a straw-boss, destined ever to remain such, for not only did he lack college education, but he was temperamentally disqualified for such by a metabolism that precluded the prolonged sitting that college requires.

Training at the upper levels may one day be called upon in any of the professions, but the typical case is that when that time arrives, the individual's classroom study lies so far behind as to be irretrievable, and he or she must take a refresher course. Or progress in the subject has been such as to render the individual's prior studies obsolete.

Together with a National Youth Service, the developmental imperatives of young people will be served by the breakup of the last year of high school and the first two years of college into periods of study alternating with periods of work in the world that are then studied upon return to the classroom. This is the "work-study" pattern pioneered at Antioch and Beloit Colleges and Northeastern University. It was originally developed at the University of Cincinati for use in higher education, but first employed in the high schools of Dayton, Ohio, beginning in 1913. Secondary school participation in work-study dramatically increased with the passage of the Vocational Education Act in 1963. But as with National Youth Service, so here also the rationale is crucial to what can be accomplished. Work-study can be conducted as vocational training on a "find a need and fill it" rationale, but in this case its deepest potential benefits will not be realized or even suspected. On a developmental rationale, by contrast, it is a means of affording some of the kinds of exploratory opportuities that contribute to self-discovery. Self-discovery then provides the basis for life-shaping choices whose enactments are self-fulfilling. That this is the native soil from which the moral virtues grow will be proposed in the next chapter. An individual who experiences his or her chosen course of life as self-fulfilling will identify with each of its several interrelated strands and will recognize dereliction with respect to their requirements as self-betrayal.

To be sure, under even optimum developmental conditions mistakes will sometimes be made by individuals in the matter of their life-shaping choices. Because this is so, our societal pattern should incorporate as far as possible what John W. Gardner terms the "principle of multiple chances." But re-choosing, after having lived a given life-shaping choice for an extended period, is invariably costly—to others, who had reason to rely on the individual to persist in the chosen course, and to the individual, in whom such re-choosing is necessarily at cost to his or her identity. Yes, the opportunity of a "fresh start" is in some circumstances invigorating, but these are usually circumstances that reflect long-term debilitation ("a dead end," etc.). And a new start typically entails considerable backtracking, including abandonment of skills and traits of character that were arduously acquired but are no longer useful. In this sense re-choosing is akin to some rites of ancient magic that, to be undone, had to be performed backward.

Such costs must sometimes be borne, because even under the best circumstances it cannot be expected that human beings will be infallible at choosing their courses of life. But it is clearly desirable to reduce these costs. The most effective way to do this is by securing, as far as possible, for as many persons as possible, the necessary preconditions of sound original choice.

On the problem of arriving at self-fulfilling courses of conduct, John Rawls offers what he terms an "Aristotelian principle." It says that "other things being equal, human beings enjoy the exercise of their realized capacities (their innate or trained abilities), and this enjoyment increases the more the capacity is realized, or the greater its complexity." He continues,

The intuitive idea here is that human beings take more pleasure in doing something as they become more proficient at it, and of two activities they do equally well, they prefer the one calling on a larger repertoire of more intricate and subtle discriminations. For example, chess is a more complicated and subtle game than checkers, and algebra is more intricate than elementary arithmetic. Thus the principle says that someone who can do both generally prefers playing chess to playing checkers, and that he would rather study algebra than arithmetic.[22]

But this leaves out the crucial Aristotelian-eudaimonistic point that we have been stressing in this chapter. A person who can play both chess and checkers but regards all board-game playing as a waste of time will disenjoy chess because it wastes more time. Similarly most readers will be able to cite realized capacities in themselves that they disenjoy exercising. For example in my early career as an engineer I was a skilled draftsman, but did not enjoy drafting, and I eventually learned to hide my skill to avoid inheriting all the drafting that was to be done in the various departments in which I was employed.

If increased complexity and subtlety of the work heightened the satisfaction of doing it, our "job enrichment" specialists would be on the right track in seeking to make work more meaningful by making it more demanding. But on the contrary, workers since the Industrial Revolution have been amenable to a pervasive de-skilling of jobs. When an American auto worker uttered the memorable and widely quoted line, "If I have to bust my ass to be meaningful, forget it; I'd rather be monotonous," he was reacting to the increased complexity of auto assembly at a SAAB plant to which he had been sent for an exploratory month by the United Automobile Workers.[23]

The dimension that is missing in Rawls's so-called "Aristotelian principle" is fully present in Aristotle. It is the innate individuation of persons. All that Rawls proposes is true of the individual who is engaged at enterprises he or she finds self-fulfilling, but is untrue otherwise. To find the enterprises one experiences as self-fulfilling is the self-discovery for which we are urging social support. Rawls misses this because it is embedded in eudaimonistic thinking that has long since been displaced by the modern thinking we sought to describe in chapter 1, to which Rawls is heir.

John W. Gardner offers the "principle of multiple chances" as central to the American democratic ideal.[24] An inspiring current example of it is the rising numbers of older returning students on our college campuses. Among the types of programs that are attracting them a notable example is the Master of Arts in Liberal Studies programs that are in place on about 150 campuses and are loosely confederated by the national Association of Graduate Liberal Studies Programs. They are designed for mature, vocationally established persons who want to supplement their earlier formal education. The guiding supposition is that persons in later life often recognize gaps in their formal education, as well as new educational interests, and should be accommodated by second (or third, or fourth) chances at higher education.

The uniform experience on campuses is that these mature returnees are superb students. They are excellent role-models for our ordinary students, and they inspire their teachers to heighten their teaching efforts, not only for MALS teaching, but also with ordinary students.

Demographers advise that "for the next decade, the only growth area in education will be in adult and continuing education," and that "by 1992, half of all college students will be over 25 and 20 percent will be over 35."[25]

Recently a parent expressed concern to me about the chosen course of study of her college-bound son. She was a person of cultivation and broad learning, and she was apprehensive that her son's narrow vocational track would prove limiting to him in the long run. I was able to picture for her the prospect of change in the pattern of formal education in our country, by which her son was likely to have second and third opportunities in later life.

The books-and-classroom overdosing that deadens the native curiosity of children begins in elementary school with the disregard of children's interests in favor of preparation for standardized test-taking. Sensitive teachers and parents know that elementary school children have an intense curiosity about the world "out there," and educational aims are best served by ministering to such curiosity. At one private elementary/secondary school in my area, the Newark Center for Creative Learning, resource people from the community—musicians, astronomers, potters, geologists, mountain-climbers—are continuously brought into the school, and children who want to follow up on the activities to which they are thus introduced are encouraged to do so.

And NCCL has an apprenticeship program for children ages twelve to fourteen. For a half-day each week Nathan and Matthew muck out llama pens at a nearby zoo. Kathryn works at a Newark travel agency.

Cory stocks shelves and waxes skis at a local ski shop. Chris helps with bicycle repair at a local bike dealership.

Cooperating businesses and service organizations report that their NCCL apprentices are very conscientious and responsible. "Too sick to go to school" is part of every twelve year-old's repertoire, but "Too sick to go to work" is a lot sicker. Employers say that apprentices try hard, usually successfully, to do their work well. "He's very determined" was the way one apprentice was described. At school, apprentices share their experiences and teachers seek to maximize the learning they afford.

According to parents and teachers, what is most conspicuous in the apprentices is new-found pride. They like having responsibilities and being accountable. Their growth is served by confirmation of their merits from sources more objective than parents and less child-oriented than teachers. What many of them recognize has been put best by Robert Frost: "Home is the place where, when you have to go there, they have to take you in" ("The Death of the Hired Man"). At age twelve a child knows that in the rest of the world one must earn one's way. He or she needs confirmation from sources outside the walls of home and school.

Interest-centered learning is the central principle at NCCL, and a parent gave me an example of it. Her son taught himself German beginning at the age of eight. How did this happen? "He liked to build models, and we bought him a model that was made in Germany. When he opened it, he found that the instructions weren't translated. He announced that, well, then, he would learn German. We bought him a couple of books, and one of his teachers coached him. Now he reads German very well, and is learning to speak it."

Just now in our country the importance of interest-centered learning is regaining wider recognition, specifically in respect to the beginnings of education, from kindergarten to third grade.[26] Educators call this "developmentally appropriate practice" and are recognizing the need to serve children's native curiosity from the beginning, when children's attitudes toward school and learning first start to take shape. But as we have sought to show, it is imperative to re-think the whole of formal and experiential learning in terms of the logic of development.

We concluded the preceding chapter by noting that Thorndike succeeding Dewey as the dominant influence in American education represented the abandonment of methods of elicitation in favor of methods of inculcation. The self-knowledge that is the foundation of moral development cannot be inculcated; and it depends for support upon pedagogy that emphasizes elicitation. Many of the basic terms of such a pedagogy are set forth for elementary education in *Caring: A Feminine Approach to Ethics and Moral Education*, by Nel Noddings.[27] Together with many advocates of a return to interest-centered learning today, Noddings references her thinking to John Dewey.

The several educational proposals in this chapter coalesce around the problem of acquiring self-knowledge, which for Greek eudaimonists was the starting point of worthy living. The next chapter argues that living in accordance with self-knowledge generates the cardinal moral virtues, foremost of which is integrity. If this can be established, it will cast our current flurry of piecemeal proposals to secure "more integrity"—in public office, in business, in the professions, in community and family life— in a cold light. They merely paper over the neglect for the past 400 years of the self-knowledge that is the foundation of the virtues. Our efforts to promote integrity and other moral virtues will be unsuccessful until we dig far deeper, down to the intrinsic developmental requirements of childhood and adolescence that support worthy living in adulthood and old age.

CHAPTER FOUR

Meaningful Work to Meaningful Living:
The Virtues and Politics

Political theorizing in the classical mode differs from political theorizing in the modern mode in ways roughly analogous to the differences in the two modes of moral theorizing. As noted in the preface, MacIntyre terms the modern mode of ethical theorizing "Nietzschean" and the classical mode "Aristotelian"; Richard Taylor contrasts "ethics of duty" and "ethics of aspiration," and I have elsewhere sought to distinguish "ethics of rules" from "ethics of character." To mark the comparable distinction in modes of political thought, Stephen G. Salkever employs the terms "politics of obligation and legitimacy" (modern), and "politics of virtue" (classical).[1]

Why "politics of virtue"? In modernity no direct connection between politics and virtue is recognized, therefore we must identify the connection here.

We may remind ourselves of the tenets of developmental democracy that were presented in the introduction and summarized to begin chapter 2. They are that the purpose of politics and government is enhancement of the quality of life of human beings; that the central agency of such enhancement is the initiative to self-development in individuals; and that the paramount function of government is to provide the necessary but non-self-suppliable conditions for optimizing opportunities for individual self-discovery and self-development.

In the conception of personhood and the good life that we are employing, "enhancement of the quality of life of human beings" means the acquisition by human beings of moral virtues, where moral virtues are understood as dispositions of character that are (1) personal utilities; (2) intrinsic goods; and (3) social utilities. (We will return to a careful consideration of these aspects.) Therefore politics and government whose purpose is the enhancement of the quality of life of human beings must be concerned to generalize opportunities of individuals to acquire moral virtues. In the phrases "meaningful living" and "enhancement of the quality of life" we are employing a values sanction: a meaningful life is a valuable life, and enhancement of the quality of life is enhancement of its value. The value is objective, which is to say it is valuable to whoever meets the conditions for appreciation and utilization of value of the particular kind in question. This includes the values-actualizer—her life is intrinsically valuable to her—but extends to such others as fulfill the conditions. To appreciate the music of Brahms one must first of all know of it—the condition of acquaintance—but one must also possess cultivated sensitivities to harmony, orchestration, rhythm, and melody.

In this context, an important distinction is to be made between "cardinal" virtues" and "distributed virtues." What we will mean by the former is virtues that are indispensable to worthy living of every kind, examples of which are Plato's famous four, namely wisdom, courage, temperance, and justice. What we will mean by "distributed virtues" are virtues that are indispensable to worthy lives of some, but not all, kinds.

And following Aristotle, it is important to distinguish between "a virtuous act" and "an act done virtuously."[2] "A virtuous act" is an act done as virtue requires, but not necessarily from virtue. Thus an honest answer may be given by a dishonest person; or a person may do a generous act but without generous motivation—perhaps because he or she has been trained to perform such acts, or because he or she wishes to be regarded as generous.

This distinction enables us to recognize that possession of the virtues is to the credit of persons who possess them; it is the result of their own initiative. Where politics and government have their part to play is in the engagement of that initiative. It is, to be sure, the initiative of individuals in their own self-development, but it is subject to external conditions both of obstruction and of facilitation. Extreme poverty, for example, is an obstructive condition, exaggerating the requirements of survival at the expense of the considerations of living well and becoming a better person. Likewise such political crises as war and threat of impending war are in one important aspect obstructions, for they usurp the total attention of most persons.

The reason that facilitating conditions require attention is that the initiative to self-directed self-development remains merely latent in persons in the early stages of their lives, where it is overlaid by external demands. This pattern of responsiveness to external requirements is reinforced by repetition to acquire the strength of habit and the comfort of familiarity, such that persons are in need of conducive conditions if they are to discover and be responsive to their inner initiative of self-direction. On the side of facilitation, the problem, then, is the engagement of latent initiatives.

Our thesis is that these initiatives are engaged when persons make contact with themselves. This accounts for the emphasis upon self-knowledge in the eudaimonistic tradition, beginning with the great Greek imperative, *gnothi seauton*—"Know thyself." In the last chapter we argued that by the logic of individual development, the opportune place for this is the stage of life we term adolescence and youth, and we held that the facilitating conditions are, in Mill's words, "freedom, and variety of situations." To afford an illustration of how these conditions serve the purpose of self-discovery we focused upon vocational choice, contending that discovery by individuals of the kind (or interrelated kinds) of work that each experiences as intrinsically rewarding to do is an important increment of self-discovery.

In this chapter we contend that the initiative that is engaged by self-discovery—whether the self-discovery occurs in the context of preparations for vocational choice, or of preparation for any of the other life-shaping choices—exhibits an inherent propensity to spread from the realm in which it is first engaged to other realms. This is to say that self-knowledge and the initiative to self-actualization inherently seek to overcome the compartmentalization of modern life into unrelated and often contradictory "roles." To be sure, this is no more than a tendency; it can be overwhelmed by countervailing conditions of which there are many. But it deserves to be fortified against such conditions, for it is the movement toward the moral virtue of integrity, which—so I will argue—is the foundation of the other moral virtues. In this sense I will be defending the classical thesis of the "unity of the virtues."

As we here use the term, "moral integrity" has three-dimensional meaning. In the first place it means integration of separable aspects of the self—notably faculties, desires, interests, roles, life-shaping choices—into a self-consistent whole. Second, it implies "wholeness as completeness" by which it is distinguishable, for example, from fanaticism and monomania. The third dimension of meaning may be preliminarily described as a deeper kind of honesty, and it is this dimension that has prominence in popular usage, as for example when newspaper editorials demand "integrity" of politicians and business managers.

An example will help us at this point. It is for his unsurpassed exemplification of moral integrity that Socrates has a permanent place among the moral heroes of the world. In the *Apology,* Socrates is offered many inducements to save his life on condition that he change his conduct. He refuses in every case because, he says, he acts on an authority higher than that of his judges. He insists that if allowed to go free on payment of a fine he must resume his life in Athens in the same terms as before. Similarly in exile he must do just as he has done, and very likely to the same discomfiture of authorities and the same outcome. He refuses to envisage an afterlife except as a further opportunity to ply his vocation, this time among the immortal souls of the departed. To the entreaties of friends (*Crito*) that they be allowed to arrange his escape from prison and the hemlock, he replies that far from doing them a favor, he would be doing them the disservice of betraying in himself everything that made him worthy of their friendship. Most telling of all, throughout the trial, Socrates so conducts himself as to vividly demonstrate the very conduct for which he is condemned.

The "higher authority" to which Socrates maintains steadfast allegiance is variously translated as "my commander," or "my god," or "the god." The Greek word here being translated is *daimon*. It is Socrates's higher or true self, by which his course of life has been guided. He describes it (and thus himself) in three aspects, namely as philosopher, as gadfly, and as midwife. He is a philosopher, he says, in that he had sought wisdom lifelong, which is to say he has been engaged at the conduct of inquiries. Because many people pretend to knowledge and wisdom that they do not possess, and thereby obstruct inquiry, he has been obliged to become a "gadfly," administering the sting of exposure and refutation to such pretense. His "midwifery" is his distinctive method of teaching. Based on his theory of innate knowledge, an implicit knowledge that requires to be made explicit, Socrates teaches not by inculcation but by elicitation, or coaxing forth.

In the life of Socrates as thus presented to us are generalizable and nongeneralizable aspects. What is generalizable is the virtues he manifests, beginning with integrity. Indeed, the broader eudaimonistic thesis is that all virtues subsist *in potentia* in every person; thus to be a human being is to be capable of manifesting virtues, and the problem of moral development is the problem of discovering the conditions of their manifestation. What is distinctive to Socrates is the particular course of life on which his virtues were manifested. For each person there is such a course of life, but the course represented by the conjunction of philosopher-gadfly-midwife is Socrates's uniquely.

Using the model of Socrates, we can understand the origin of integrity as the identification of the individual with certain values. Objectively considered, "identification" here signifies a person's commitment to actualize, conserve, and defend those values. It will be evident that on this meaning, no person can identify with all values, because of what Leibniz termed "the imperfection of finitude." Perhaps our finitude does not discredit the aspiration to recognize and appreciate all values (though achievement will certainly fall short of the aspiration), but it precludes identification (as just defined), because just as in a single lifetime one cannot do all things, so one cannot do for all values what identification requires. The question for each individual, then, is with which values shall I identify? Some philosophers (the Sartre of *Being and Nothingness* is a leading example) have held that the choice is arbitrary; what matters is not in the least which values are chosen, but only that choice occurs, that it is choice with commitment, and that it is acknowledged as choice. But I think that introspective evidence speaks to the contrary. Among the values a person recognizes are sure to be some with which he or she is disinclined to identify, and a select few with which he or she is inclined or even (in personal feeling) compelled to identify. Moreover many persons will have had the experience of trying to identify with certain values, but against innate inclination, with troublesome results. Indeed, a not unfamiliar source of self-deception is the unreadiness of the individual to acknowledge unsuccessful identification: the priest who is equivocally a priest, the nurse who is equivocally a nurse, the spouse or parent who is equivocally spouse or parent, and so on. In the cases that are to our present purpose, it is not that the person comes to question the worth of the priesthood (or marriage, or parenting, etc.), or to discredit the relevant values. It is, rather, the perception (unacknowledged in cases of self-deception) that the particular values are "not my values."

This leads us from values-identification (I am using the term here to mean, not identification *of* values, but the individual's identification of himself or herself *with* certain values), objectively described, to an inner criterion. Values-identification is not arbitrary or noncriteriological in respect to the particular values with which given individuals identify—it is qualifiable by right and wrong, better and worse. The right values-identification by an individual is his or her explicit identification (in terms of actualization, conservation, and defense) with the values with which he or she is implicitly—that is, innately—identified. These are the values in the service of which the individual will experience the intrinsic rewards of personal fulfillment. This is to say that values-identification is the actualization of an implicit identity. But if the identity antecedently exists, in the form of the unique potentialities within the individual, what is the point of actualization? Its point is the value-enhancement of actual human existence. Metaphysically considered, a potentiality is a possibility, and the meaning of possibility is "possible existent." Where the possible existent is a value it inherently lays claim to existence. But as possibilities, values are powerless to bring themselves into existence; they can only be actualized by existing entities, and the existing entities upon whose agency they depend are those in whom the possible values subsist as potentialities. In sum, to be a human being is to be responsible for certain values.

The fact that human beings are differentiated with respect to values-potentialities entails a division of labor in the work of values-actualization. The interdependence of values-actualizers confirms the inherently social nature of human beings. This social nature has earlier been noted in the dependence of infants and children, in virtue of which every person is, in the beginning of his or her life, a "social product." The just-noted division of labor in the primary work of values-actualization confirms the inherent social nature of developed individuals. This sociality in the outcome will be explored under the name of community in chapter 6. One of the questions to be probed there, for example, concerns the nature of the autonomy that can be attributed to and discerned in individuals who are interdependent in the fundamental moral enterprise of values-actualization. Meanwhile we may observe that the division of labor in values-actualization entails, in particular, two cardinal virtues that have not previously been commented upon. One of them is the developed capacity in individuals to recognize and appreciate values other than those with which they as individuals are personally identified. We shall name this virtue "liberality." The other is the readiness to respect others' responsibilities for the values with which they are identified, as against the impulse to arrogate those responsibilities for ourselves. The folk-maxim says, "If you want the job done well you must do it yourself," but we are here introducing the crucial proviso—unless it is a job that is someone else's to do, where this means that for the other not to do it is a failure in self-responsibility. To respect another is to recognize and affirm the fundamental moral responsibilities of that other; to appropriate for oneself the responsibility of another is an especially deep form of disrespect. The virtue of respecting others' fundamental responsibilities for self-actualization we shall term "deference."

Aristotle says that persons who have experienced the satisfactions of self-fulfilling activities will not exchange them for gratification of any other kind. The Greek term for the feeling that constitutes the intrinsic reward of self-fulfilling activity is *eudaimonia*. It refers both to the feeling and to the condition of which the feeling is the subjective indicator, namely the condition of "living in harmony with oneself." Its contraries are, in the Greek, *athlios, akrasia, kakodaimonia,* or (rarely) *dysdaimonia,* meaning "living in opposition to oneself," or "living at odds with oneself," or simply "inner faction (or division)."

Here we come to the meaning of moral integrity as a deeper kind of honesty. Eudaimonism identifies it as lying well beneath "truth telling" in truthful living, that is, living in truth to oneself, where the self consists of the innate potential values that one is responsible for discovering, actualizing, conserving, and defending. Thus Aristotle speaks of "pursuing the truth in words and deeds," which he says occurs when "each man [person] speaks and acts and lives in accordance with his [or her] character."[3]

The feeling of eudaimonia is the intrinsic reward. of the virtue of integrity, understood as "living in truth to oneself." Supposing for the sake of discussion that Aristotle is correct in saying that a person who experiences it will not trade it for gratifications of any other kind, it must be added that such a person will naturally seek to experience it, not just in one dimension of his or her life, but in other dimensions as well. This recognition does two things. It connects "integrity" in the meaning of "living in truth to oneself" to integrity understood as integration of the separable aspects (faculties, roles, desires, interests, life-shaping choices) of the self. And it affords an account of what we earlier contended was the inherent tendency of self-actualization to spread, from the dimension of life in which self-discovery first occurs (the situation of preparation for vocational choice was our focus in chapter 3) to other dimensions. An implication of the "unity of the virtues" thesis is that the occurrence of self-discovery in a dimension of an individual's life is the beginning of a progression to other dimensions.

The feeling of eudaimonia is a benefit to the person who possesses the virtue of integrity. In this sense, "integrity is its own reward." But integrity also benefits the person who possesses it as a personal utility. We can recognize this by reverting to the eudaimonistic account of human being as problematic being: to be a human being is to be obliged to decide what to become and endeavor to become it. Significant success at endeavoring to become what one has chosen to become requires integration of faculties, desires, interests, roles, and life-shaping choices, such that aspects in each of these categories complement others, and all aspects alike contribute toward the chosen end. This integration must be achieved out of an initial disorder that was enduringly depicted by Plato in his image of the human soul as chariot, charioteer, and two fractious horses, one struggling to rise aloft while the other seeks to plunge below (*Phaedrus*). In this condition the chariot cannot move and is at risk of being torn asunder. It symbolizes the disordered and internally contradictory condition of the self in which integration has not in significant measure been achieved. Such a self will be ineffective at achieving its ends and equivocal or contradictory in its identification of them. We are familiar enough with this condition: to begin with, it is entirely typical of young children, whose transitory desires pull them in many directions at once. But it is also familiar in the adult whose desire—say for a new car—is not extinguished by the knowledge that she cannot afford one. It is exemplified by the adult who marries, but with the covert intention of preserving to himself the prerogatives of bachelorhood. It is illustrated by the adult whose pursuit of his career is at cost to his marriage. That such cases are common is evidence not, I think, that the fragmenting conditions of contemporary life are irresistible, but that the problem of achieving integrity is neglected.

We are speaking of the benefits of the virtue of integrity to persons who possess this virtue and will shortly argue for the personal benefits of every virtue to its bearers. But is this appropriate? Are we not engaged at the reduction of moral virtue to prudence that, as F. H. Bradley said, "degrade(s) and prostitute(s) virtue"?[4]

In answer, it should first be noticed that the propensity to regard prudence and virtue as mutually exclusive is shared by some versions of Christian theology and some modern moral philosophies (Kant is a leading example), but not by classical moral philosophy, according to which prudence is itself a moral virtue. The basis of the judgment that the two are antithetical is the supposition that self-interest is either nonmoral or immoral, and is to be counteracted by morality. But if, as the Greeks supposed, the true interest of persons is to lead worthy lives, then prudence is a virtue because the self-interest that it serves is a moral interest. This is what underlies the consistent effort by Socrates, Plato, and Aristotle (and many lesser classical moral theorists) to show that persons stand to gain by being moral. Presently there are some signs of a revival of this understanding, as for example when Robert Nozick concludes: "Plato's vision is right; we are better off being moral, it is a better way to be," adding: "It is a mistake, however, to squeeze this into the view that being moral serves what a person feels to be his self-interest, serves his felt motivations."[5]

If we do not suppose in persons a self-interest in being moral, the question, "Why be moral?" becomes unanswerable. Such answers as "to achieve salvation in an afterlife" or "to be accepted within the moral community" play to the self-interest that has been adjudged nonmoral or immoral, whereas answers that posit an obligation to be moral are circular, resting on premises that are acceptable only to those who have accepted the conclusions drawn from them. This cul-de-sac gives us good reason to entertain once again the classical premise that a life that is better for others and a life that is better for itself are not mutually exclusive.

Nozick correctly notes that the Platonic vision requires that persons' true interests be distinguished from their perceived interests. As we had occasion to consider in the introduction, persons may misperceive their interests through ignorance and through evil. Ignorance misperceives for a personal good something that is not such. The evil will actively seeks destruction of the good, but is a reactive phenomenon—in Nietzsche's term a phenomenon of *ressentiment*—representing the perversion of the native desire to live a worthy life, in response to obstruction of that desire by obstacles in the world or in the self. We indicated in the introduction that a social enterprise to generalize the opportunities of self-actualization must guard itself against misperceived self-interests of both sorts, and we there proposed the constraints of (1) the law, (2) universalizability, and (3) forecasted objective worth. But preoccupation with curtailing the effects of self-misdirection must not be allowed to leave unattended the constructive work of providing social conditions that optimize the opportunities of individuals to enlist their self-actualizing initiatives. This has been our principal concern beginning with chapter 3 and will continue as such for the remainder of this book. Just now we are endeavoring to show how the moral virtues are generated out of the recognition of the potential worth of the self, which is the recognition of important work that requires to be done by each individual.

It is the recognition of something of importance that one has to do that generates a perspective on virtues and vices that is expressed, for example, by John Cowper Powys: "Conceit seals up the exploring antennae of your free sensibility. Malice and hate distract you and waste your life-energy. Possessions make you a fussy super-cargo."[6] Vices squander the resources that are available to do the worthy work that is ours to do; virtues both are (in themselves) such resources, and also serve to organize and focus personal resources—physical, mental, emotional—that are not themselves virtues in the moral sense. It is the perspective that led Thoreau to give a large place to "economy" in moral life.

Identification with certain values generates moral integrity, understood on one hand as integration of personal resources toward the end of actualizing, conserving, and defending those values, and on the other hand as "living in truth to oneself," where the self is conceived as incomplete, to be finished or fulfilled by actualization, conservation, and defense of those values. Knowledge of these values is, therefore, self-knowledge, and self-knowledge is a measure of wisdom. Wisdom is classically defined as "knowledge of the good," and self-knowledge, understood as knowledge of the values whose actualization, conservation, and defense will complete or fulfill the self, is knowledge of the good of the self. To be sure it is not complete wisdom, which is complete knowledge of the good, but it is partial wisdom, and as such it is the starting point of the moral self-development of every person.

Our thesis is that self-knowledge and integrity conduce toward the manifestation of the other cardinal virtues by the individual. This is to speak, not of a necessity, but of a tendency. It can be illustrated in the example of courage. Courage is not a "portable attribute," like the six-guns of the movie gunslinger that are available for hire to the highest bidder. It is not a mere *addition* to one's character, whatever that may happen to be. Neither is it a disposition granted by the "natural lottery of birth" to the few, leaving the rest empty-handed. As Lester H. Hunt has shown, courageous acts involve a "limiting principle." They are "ones which are done from the principle that one's own safety . . . has no more than a certain measure of importance."[7] It is not misleading to speak of an "instinct of self-preservation" that has primacy in human beings *until* they discover the values they will identify themselves with. But to discover these values is in the case of each individual to discover "what is worth living for," which is also what is worth placing oneself at risk for. What sets a limit to the importance of one's own safety is something that one cares about more. There are of course countless things that a person may prize more than his or her own safety. Mothers are disposed to place themselves at risk for their children; romantic lovers are often ready to risk themselves for the beloved (whose reciprocal love serves to control this self-sacrificing propensity); I know a man who risked his life to prevent his parked sports car from rolling off a cliff. How are we to distinguish true courage from such of its pseudomorphs as foolhardiness, rashness, and so forth? The answer, I think, is by the intrinsic value that this virtue, with other virtues, possesses. The intrinsic value in each virtue derives from the end that it serves as means—the end is *in* the means—and thus presupposes the value of the end. Where that end is not a value, the apparent virtue is not a virtue. Courage, as defined by Hunt, is a relation between values, namely between the value sought and the value risked. There are many situations in which the value sought is higher than the value risked, and the basic one is the situation of self-actualization, where the objective worth of the actualized self, or the outcome, is greater than that of the present self.

But do we not attribute courage to the bank robber and the international jewel thief? Indeed so, but mistakenly, and the mistake is not far to seek. The fact is that many of us are fascinated by such figures, who exhibit an adventurousness and irresponsibility that we sometimes envy. It is our glamorization of them that results in our attribution to them of courage. This Walter Mittyism becomes culpable, however, when it induces us to contrive a moral philosophy that vindicates it. If we shift from bank robbers and jewel thieves (whom, conveniently, most of us are not likely to be victimized by) and try to attribute courage to sadistic rapists, wanton torturers, and brutal murderers, I believe we will choke on our words. Yet it is unquestionably the case that these latter sorts often exhibit as much or more daring as the former. The difference is that we cannot amuse ourselves by admiring what they do.

The eudaimonistic thesis is that courage is likely to be manifested by any person who discovers and identifies with the values that are the right values for him or her. Such manifestation represents the moral growth that is the natural tendency of human beings. To be a human being is to be *in potentia* a bearer of moral virtues, and the problem of moral development is that of discovering the conditions for their actualization.

The social utility of the virtues is apparent in their direct contribution to the well-being of others. The person of integrity can be relied upon to do what he or she accepts responsibility for; the courageous person better serves the collective interests to which she lends herself by her unwavering resolve when trouble arises. But the virtues also afford social utility by rendering individual enterprises congenial to one another (justice, temperance, tact, liberality, discretion, and civility are conspicuous in this respect). Legal and other institutional means are also required for this purpose, but they must not undermine, or usurp the role of, the virtues.

It is lately a commonplace of moral philosophy to categorize virtues as predominantly "self-regarding" or predominantly "other-regarding." We may take it that the personal utility of the predominantly "self-regarding" virtues is sufficiently recognized. Our thesis that all virtues are personal utilities (as well as intrinsic values and social utilities) meets its test in the virtues that are typically adjudged to be predominantly other-regarding. Accordingly we will here take up two of these—generosity and honesty—while reserving to chapter 5 the additional two of justice and temperance.

By general agreement generosity is the virtue that is expressed in acts whose characterizing intention is to benefit someone other than the agent. It is doing something for the sake of one or more others. Paradigmatically a generous act is an act in which something is given by a donor to a recipient for the purpose of benefiting the recipient. A condition of generous gift-giving is that the donor has reason to believe that her gift will have value for the recipient. That this belief proves to have been mistaken does not in itself deny the generosity of the giving. For example, John may (generously) give to Robert a copy of a book that, as it happens, Robert purchased for himself a day previously. But if John had no reason to think what he gave to Robert would be of value to Robert, John's act would not be generous in our meaning of the word. Most obviously this will be the case if the gift is utterly valueless—say an article of used clothing with no wear left in it. (I will shortly show that this is not in fact disputed by Schopenhauer's and Emerson's esteem of the giving of "useless" gifts.)

Generosity will also not be present, however, if the gift has no value for Robert because John has not troubled to acquire sufficient knowledge of Robert to know what will be valuable to him. To see this requires, first, that we overturn the present propensity to study virtues in "atomic" acts, that is, acts that are considered independently of the agent's general conduct of life. Philippa Foot refers to the propensity when she says, "The reason why it seems to some people so impossibly difficult to show that justice is more profitable than injustice is that they consider in isolation particular just acts."[8] We hold that what she says applies identically to generosity (and to every virtue)—it is embedded inextricably in the texture of the life of the generous person and must be studied in that context. This is part of what Aristotle is saying in his identification of virtues as *dispositions* of character.

Generous gift-giving begins to acquire its context in the recognition that it is necessarily situated in prior giving, namely the giving of the attention of the prospective gift-giver to the person of the prospective recipient in order to perceive what kind of person he is and what will benefit him. This does not preclude the possibility of giving generously to persons with whom one is not personally acquainted. It can be enough, for example, to know that persons in another part of the world are starving to give food generously. To be given generously some gifts require only such knowledge as is to be inferred from the fact that the recipients are human beings, whereas other gifts require knowledge of the distinctive needs and interests of the recipient. Our contention, therefore, is the general one that generosity requires "proportional" knowledge, where the requisite amounts and kinds of knowledge vary with the circumstances.

When Schopenhauer and Emerson contend that generosity is often best expressed in the giving of "useless" gifts,[9] they are in spite of appearances not contradicting the aforementioned condition of generosity, that the gift be such as the giver has reason to believe will benefit the recipient. They are advising that when a gift is devoid of material utility, this will serve to make more apparent other values it possesses. They are not offering the (fatuous) advice that recipients who most of all need material values should be given gifts that are devoid of such values. They are advising that most of us who are not in serious material need are nevertheless so preoccupied with material values as to be unable to recognize the higher values that true gifts confer.

What is particularly interesting in Schopenhauer's and Emerson's advisement is the tact and discretion it embodies, specifically in regard to the ever-present possibility of confusion between generosity and charity, and the effect of this confusion upon such a relationship as friendship. Through the ages, friendship has been recognized by those who have attended carefully to it (from Socrates, Plato, and Aristotle to Montaigne, Schopenhauer, Emerson, Thoreau, Buber, and C. S. Lewis) as a "horizontal" relationship, that is, relationship among equals. It makes no difference if one member of the pair of friends is president of the United States and the other is wholly without power or prestige—in the friendship such disparities do not appear. (Though, to be sure, such a disparity as has just been cited renders friendship in that case unlikely to arise. Similarly, for example, friendship between husband and wife is unlikely in social circumstances characterized by male dominance.)

That generosity is a horizontal relationship is attested by the fact that it is compatible with friendship, whereas charity is not. Charity is a "vertical" relationship from sufficiency to deficiency. Indeed, such is our sensitivity to this verticality that charity is only a virtue on condition that it includes the tact that deemphasizes its downward direction—deemphasizes, but cannot eliminate. An important attribute of the "useless" gift is that it cannot be mistaken for charity.

But the "useless" gift makes a profounder point. By eliminating the distraction of material utility it facilitates recognition that what the generous giver gives in her gift is herself. Her gift signifies her appreciation of the worth, whether actual or merely potential, of the recipient. This presupposes two capacities in the giver—knowledge of the distinctive worth of the recipient and actualized worth in the giver that is conferred in the giving of the gift. In other words, she gives herself in her gift, having beforehand taken the trouble to see to it that the self she gives is a worthy self.

Nevertheless the "useless" gift of Schopenhauer and Emerson is a significant symbol; it is not an ideal toward which generosity is aimed. Generosity *can* be distinguished from charity in normal gift-giving. And that it is at bottom himself that the generous gift-giver gives is sufficiently clear to the alert witness in countless cases where the gift is, not a material thing, but the judgment, sympathy, encouragement, and so forth of the giver. Likewise it is fully evident here that the giver is responsible for first having taken the trouble to make his judgment sound, his encouragement worth having, and so forth. This will be evident in our personal histories as recipients. In our youth we were so eager to receive approval of any sort, thanks to our radical uncertainty of our own worth, that we did not dream of questioning its source. But our subsequent development led us to become more selective in the matter of whose judgments about us were to be taken seriously. We learned to value most the goods of this sort that were tendered by persons whose own development in the relevant respects surpassed our own.

Because the generously given gift must possess value, and as it is at bottom himself that the generous giver gives, it is recognizably the case that generosity is connected to self-interest, understood as each person's interest in living in such a way as to manifest his or her potential worth.

In the early stages of development a person may wish to be generous but not know how. Becoming capable of being generous is part of the process of self-development; it is dependent upon progressively acquired powers of discernment, discrimination, understanding, patience, evaluation, and sympathy (understood as the capacity of imaginative participation in the lives of others). The central motivational power in this process of self-development is the self-love that Socrates, Plato, and Aristotle recognized as the precondition of love of others.

As a developmental outcome, generosity may be said to have its seasons. One of the richest rewards of a mature person's achievement of secure *place* is the liberty it affords for relating generously to others. (A tenured university professor, say, who does not use his secure place to help younger colleagues of promise is depriving himself of one of the deep intrinsic rewards of tenure.) At the lowest end of development, children can be said to be generous only in an appropriately diminished meaning of the term. This is because, as dependents, children give what they have received from others. This remains true even if we suppose that in giving they give themselves, for the selves of children are social products. And though adolescents can be generous, the virtue is not well lodged in this season, because adolescence is the stage in which a person recognizes the self as his or her own first problem, and is intensely self-preoccupied. To be sure, adolescents sometimes exhibit extravagant generosity, but the very extravagance is our clue that the adolescent, in accordance with the exploratory, experimental temper of the stage, is experimenting with generosity (as an adolescent will test himself for courage by, for example, climbing the town water tower and emblazoning upon it his or his girlfriend's initials).

If Carol Gilligan is correct that women in their development from girlhood typically move from an egocentric stage to a stage centered in caring for others, and only thereafter (and with great difficulty, thanks both to inner conflicts and to social expectations) to recognition of the responsibility to care for oneself,[10] then I think the stage of caring for others contains an anomaly that can be expressed as giving oneself before one has a self to give.

And what of the personal utility of generosity? It lies first of all in the intrinsic reward of giving oneself when one has a worthy self to give. But generosity also exhibits the "reflex-arc" that characterizes personal development. This is expressed in Thoreau's words: "Genius is only as rich as it is generous; if it hoards it impoverishes itself."[11] Self-development is the necessary foundation of generosity, and generosity contributes to self-development by confirming the objective worth that self-development aims to manifest. As objective, the worth of the self in the degree to which it is actualized is meant to be recognized, appreciated, and utilized by persons other than the self (though by no means to the exclusion of the self), and it is incomplete without such recognition, appreciation, and utilization in appropriate measure. To be sure, this is not the whole of self-actualization. Unfortunately history attests that worthy lives have been lived with little or no contemporaneous recognition, appreciation, or utilization of their worth by others (Nietzsche and Thoreau received small appreciation in their lifetimes; El Greco and Van Gogh received almost none). It may be regarded as the consummating increment.

It should be clear that the personal utility we have discerned in generosity does not compromise the virtue. This is so because the self that is served is not alien to the virtue but is instead the foundation of it as well as of other virtues. That there is personal utility in the aim of worthy living does not alter the aim; indeed, that aim remains the moral aim it is even if personal utility should be a conscious secondary aim, for the utility in question serves the moral aim. Were personal gain to be the primary intent, the virtue would be hopelessly compromised. But "personal utility" logically implies priority of the end that the utility serves, and where the end is worthy living, the virtue of generosity is not compromised.

As was set forth in the introduction: in eudaimonistic perspective, each person's true work is his or her life, to which the person's "job" in the work-a-day sense should be contributory. The contribution of the job to the life is a mark of integrity (whose measure, of course, includes corresponding contributions by marriage and family, avocations, friends, religious and civic commitments, and all other distinguishable strands in the life of the individual). We have defined "meaningful work" in the primary sense as meaningful living, understood as valuable living, and more specifically as actualization of particular values that realize the implicit identity of the individual. It now requires explicit statement that on our thesis, meaningful work is the foundational case of generosity. We can recognize this in the phenomenon of "objectivization," by which the person of the friend is in the friendship, the person of the painter is in her paintings, the person of the engineer is in the finished bridge that he designs, the craftsperson is in her crafted products. Identification with the work produces objectivization, by which, in Emerson's words, "the inmost in due time becomes the outmost."[12] He refers to the objectivization of what is initially subjective in the self, by which what is at first private becomes public and available to others (as a poem, say, starts in one's head and is subsequently written down and perhaps printed). For human beings the process of living is inherently a process of objectivization—it is *ex*-isting, understood as living from oneself outward, into the world. It is *ex*-pressing oneself into objective situations by which one's self becomes available to others. This constitutes generosity in the cases of persons who have striven to make the self and its expressions as worthy as possible.

Consistent with his thesis of the inherent criteriology of all virtues, Aristotle says that the generous person "will give to the right people, and the right amount, and at the right time, and fulfill all the other conditions of right living."[13] This has sometimes been held to prescribe a degree of calculation that is inconsistent with the virtue, but I think it can be shown instead to express the dependence of generosity, with every other virtue, upon wisdom, understood as practical knowledge of the good and how it can be attained. We shall look more closely at the inherent critiera of generosity, beginning with "the right amount."

Is it possible to be "excessively generous," such that the excess undermines the generosity? Certainly a person can give away more money (say), or time, or food (etc.), than he or she can afford to be without. At first sight, however, this appears to be a failure, not of generosity, but of prudence. Or if the excess is said to be "more than the recipient deserves," the case appears to involve failure in respect to justice rather than to generosity.[14]

We can agree that some intended criticisms of "excessive generosity" are mistargeted while denying that this is so for all, and thereby preserve Aristotle's case for an inherent criteriology.

A form of excessive generosity that is not chargeable to imprudence or injustice (in the modern sense) is giving more of something to someone than is good for him or her. That too much can be as debilitating as too little is a neglected implication of the Greek counsel of *sophrosune*, or "proportion." But do we need to be reminded that excessive power, or wealth, or adulation, can seriously disorient their recipients? Moreover "help" of any kind becomes oppressive when it usurps responsibilities that are properly those of the persons "helped," responsibilities that must be exercised by them in the interest of their own self-development. To recognize others as ends in themselves, and self-responsible, is implicitly to affirm that generosity has intrinsic upper limits. There are cases in which conduct that recognizes others as ends in themselves exemplifies generosity. Suppose that shortly after your marriage you exhibit a budding interest in photography, in which, as it happens, your bride has in her past acquired expertise. If, because she sees your pleasure in your growing skill (though her own skill greatly surpasses it), she leaves the family photography to you, she behaves generously. For the most part, however, the more appropriate term for conduct in recognition of others as ends in themselves is "respect."

And what of the inherent criterion of giving "to the right people"? If it meant giving to deserving people what they are entitled to, it would be a matter not of generosity but of justice, but this is not Aristotle's meaning. The "right people" criterion reflects the fact that persons are qualitatively individuated such that for what a particular person has to give, only some persons are appropriate recipients. One does not generously give a bottle of whiskey to a teetotaler, or a Union Jack to the Irish patriot Parnell, or one's attentions to someone who finds them an unwanted intrusion. This may seem to be a question, not of giving to the right person, but of giving the right gift, but the relevance of the "right person" criterion will be evident if we call into play our previous recognition that it is at bottom herself that the generous giver gives. Each person is distinctive, manifesting distinctive values, which only some others are prepared to recognize, appreciate, and utilize. Emerson is calling attention to his when he says, ". . . cleave to your companions; I will seek my own."[15] Our appropriate "companions" are persons who can recognize, appreciate, and utilize our distinctive worth, as we do theirs. In a certain sense what one has to give selects its recipients, namely those persons by whom the particular values in the gift can be recognized and utilized.

Here generosity points to its foundation in personal integrity: one must give in truth to oneself; it is not one's part to give what anyone or another may happen to need, or what anyone or another may importune one to give, but what one has to give by virtue of what one is. The foundation of generosity in integrity prevents the dissipation of the self of the giver that is attendant upon "being all things to all people."

In our society as in many others, women are conditioned (whether in accordance with woman's "nature" or not is here irrelevant) to be "caring." But until limits are set to the scope of each woman's caring, dissipation of her self is the result. The particular form of this dissipation is the woman's inevitable and continuous feeling of guilt, arising from the fact that while she is caring for one thing (oftenest a person, though candidates include pets, houseplants, wildlife, the natural environment; the first person to make a practice of speaking tenderly to houseplants was quite certainly a woman), she is not caring for many others. The conclusion to be drawn is that responsibility for caring must be limited (as must any conception of responsibility, in recognition of persons' finitude). But how shall it be limited? Traditionally the circle of the family has been employed, but ineffectively, because it is immediately evident that the need for care extends beyond it, and care is inherently responsive to need. In accordance with what has been said above, the appropriate limitation of responsibility will be set by self-knowledge and the responsibility to care for oneself in recognition that this is a necessary condition of caring for others. To care for oneself entails knowing oneself and being oneself, which qualify the kinds of care one can give in truth to oneself. Carol Gilligan marks the recognition by women that their caring must include self-care as the threshhold of the crucial consummating stage in the moral self-development of women.[16]

From the task of disclosing the personal utility in the "other regarding" virtue of generosity, we turn to the corresponding task with respect to the virtue of honesty, but here we shall be brief, for the line of thought is the same.

No argument is needed to show that what we ought to mean by honesty is more than truth-telling, for human beings express themselves in forms of conduct other than speech, and may deceive no less by these other forms. To recognize aspiration as a definitive human characteristic is to be aware that human beings are always aiming at an intended future. It follows from this that all human conduct is promissory and is read as such by fellow human beings. (Our perennial underlying question in all social intercourse is what we are to expect of the other: what we are to expect next, what we are to expect after that, what we are to expect ultimately.) Accordingly the deceiver is one who contrives his conduct to misrepresent his intended future (as, in a simple case, if you had fallen, and I extended my hand to you, and then withdrew it as you reached to take it), and the honest person is one whose conduct accurately expresses his intended future. But this drives the question of honesty beneath the matter of truth-telling to truthful living. The problem is that we understand by "truth" a relationship (some sort of "agreement") between something and something else. In the simple case of descriptive sentences, it is a relationship between the sentence and what the sentence describes. But we have just seen that verbal conduct alone is insufficient to the meaning of honesty. We gain the requisite breadth if we conceive of truth as the relationship between "appearance" and "reality." When we apply this to the prima facie puzzling notion of truthful living, we find that we can conceptualize the notion in the idea of "living in truth to oneself," where "living" is appearance (i.e., expression in the world), and the "self" is the reality. In eudaimonistic thought, as we know, the self that is the reality is the person's distinctive innate potential worth, which his or her actual self—the self that exists in the world and is available to others—may express or misrepresent. "Living truthfully," then, is actualizing one's innate potential worth in the world, and "living untruthfully" is failing to do so (that this may be either deliberate or inadvertent need not detain us here).

Earlier we offered a three-part definition of moral integrity as: (1) integration of separable aspects of the self: faculties, desires, interests, roles, courses of conduct determined by life-shaping choices; (2) wholeness as completeness (by which is meant "completeness *as an individual*," not as a Marxian "species being" in whom all human potentialities are to be realized); and (3) a deeper kind of honesty. We have now identified the "deeper kind of honesty" as "living in truth to oneself," that is, as self-actualization. Therefore the case for the personal utility of honesty is the same as the case for the personal utility of moral integrity, which has been set forth previously. It consists, first, in the intrinsic reward in the virtue, which is the feeling of eudaimonia. We translate it as "happiness," but it is a distinctive quality of satisfaction that can be described as inner harmony as against inner dissonance. And second, it is the effectiveness at goal attainment that is exhibited by inner organization as against inner disorder and division. To be sure, there are also the benefits of being trusted by others because one is trustworthy, but this is one of the reflexive effects of the social utility of the virtue of moral integrity, and the social utilities of the virtues are not our present focus.

Thanks to the modern divorce of morality and politics and its effect upon our thinking, it will be well to reiterate here our unconventional thesis of their inherent connection, which we have termed "politics of virtue." It consists of the following three steps. First, the primary responsibility of government is to enhance by such means as are available to it the quality of the lives of the governed. Secondly, enhancement of lives in its profoundest sense means moral development to the end of worthy living. And third, because all persons are (*ex hypothesi*) invested innately with both potential worth and incentive to moral growth, the crucial first step in the enhancement of quality of lives, considered as a social endeavor, is to secure conditions under which most persons are likely to "make contact with themselves," that is, to recognize their own innate potential worth, thereby engaging their incentive to live so as to actualize that worth. In sum: because good politics is concerned with good living, it must be concerned with cultivation of the moral virtues.

A "unity of the virtues" thesis underlies this chapter and must be spelled out. We hold that self-knowledge, understood as knowledge of one's potential worth, is inspirational: it enlists the incentive to growth, it generates the identification of the individual with certain values which marks the beginning of moral integrity, it generates courage by providing the values with respect to which (in Lester Hunt's keen observation) the individual perceives her or his own safety as having "no more than a certain measure of importance," it generates generosity and honesty. A part of our "unity" thesis is our contention that the discovery by a person of her potential personal worth in one aspect of her life actualizes a tendency to seek the self in other aspects of life, and to wish to actualize the potential worth of the self in all domains of the individual life. Here is the larger utility in our proposed programs of chapter 3, which were aimed at facilitating self-discovery in the realm of work in the work-a-day sense. Our purpose would be served by self-discovery in any other dimension of life, hence for vocational choice might have been substituted an investigation of the conditions of any of the other life-shaping choices. What is needed is a starting point of self-knowledge in individuals.

A correlative aspect of our "unity" thesis, announced at the outset of this chapter, is the tendency in the individual for the acquisition of one virtue to lead to the acquisition of other virtues. An account of this tendency must necessarily involve subjective factors, but it also entails, in logic, the mutual interdependence of the cardinal virtues. In this chapter we have sought to exhibit this interdependence in the case of wisdom, integrity, courage, generosity, and honesty. In the next chapter we shall endeavor to do the same for justice and temperance.

This is a "unity-of-the-virtues" thesis, and theses so-named are famously associated with Socrates, Plato, Aristotle, and Aquinas. They are just as famously attacked, and this propensity has been especially notable of late, even in moral philosophers and classical scholars otherwise disposed favorably to the theorizing of the principals. What I shall be most concerned to call attention to, by way of conclusion to this chapter, is that attacks on "unity of the virtues" as advanced against Socrates, Plato, Aristotle, and Aquinas are in many cases mistaken about the kind of unity that those philosophers held to obtain. In short they are wide of the mark, exposing errors that Socrates, Plato, Aristotle, and Aquinas did not commit, while leaving the mistaken impression that "unity of the virtues" is indefensible.

For example, some critics[17] suppose that by "unity of the virtues" Socrates meant that "wisdom," "courage," "justice," "temperance," and "piety" are one and the same virtue, or even that their names are synonyms. Then Socrates is refuted by the simple measure of showing that courage is different from wisdom, justice is different from temperance, etc. Remarking on the prevalence of this interpretation, Gregory Vlastos says, "This is how Socrates is being understood today,"[18] and Vlastos proceeds with great care to demonstrate the misunderstanding. We shall here follow him briefly and merely in outline. Our aim is to arrive at a defensible understanding of the Socratic-Platonic-Aristotelian thesis that in some sense to possess one of the cardinal virtues is to possess them all.

Vlastos demonstrates that Socrates cannot reasonably be supposed to have held that the virtues are identical. What Socrates says of piety in the *Euthyphro*—that it is a single idea (Form) that recurs self-identically in every pious act and can be used as a standard by which to determine whether a given act is or is not pious:

He would say, *mutatis mutandis,* of every one of the other virtues. How then could he possibly tolerate, let alone uphold, the notion that each is identical with each? Could one think of him, for instance, conceding that if Euthyphro were to give him the definiens of Courage, he could use *that* as a "standard" by which to judge whether Euthyphro's prosecution of his father was, or was not, pious? As for claiming that the names of the five virtues were all synonyms, that would imply that any of those five words can be freely interchanged in any sentence (in a transparent context) without changing its sense or truth. Try substituting "Courage" for "Piety" in (1) "Piety" is that *eidos* in virtue of which all pious actions are pious" (*Euthyphro* 6D), or "Justice" for (2) "Piety" in "Piety is that part of Justice which has to do with service to the gods" (*Euthyphro* 12E). The substitutions would falsify (1) and make nonsenee of (2).[19]

The strategy chosen by Vlastos is to start with what he terms Socrates's "biconditionality thesis" and then apply what is arrived at to the "similarity" thesis (above) and the "unity of the virtues." The biconditionality thesis is the thesis that a person who possesses any one of the virtues will (*in some sense*) possess them all. The key to it lies in Socrates's contentions that "courage is wisdom," "justice is wisdom," "temperance is wisdom," "wisdom is courage," and so on. We are to understand by this, Vlastos says, that all five virtues are interpredicable—not however, in the sense of the subject of each predication as the abstract entity named by its term, but in the sense of the subject as instantiation of that abstract entity. In other words, "justice is temperance" means, not that the concept "justice" is the concept "temperance," but that the just person is also temperate, the temperate person is also wise, and so on. And the key to understanding this is what I will term the "interpenetration" of the meanings of the virtues (not their identity).

To illustrate this, we earlier held that integrity results from the identification of the self with certain values, and this means that integrity participates in wisdom, for knowledge of those values is knowledge of (certain) goods, and knowledge of the good is wisdom. (Knowledge of certain values is, as we said, not the whole of wisdom, which would be knowledge of all values, but is a part of it.) Then we argued (drawing upon Lester Hunt) that courage implies placing a limit upon the importance of one's own safety, and that the placing of this limit occurs in the identification of the self with certain values—to actualize, conserve, and defend them—which is to say that courage participates in wisdom. Likewise wisdom participates in courage, in that courage is implicit in the recognition of the values one will actualize, conserve, and defend. It awaits the occasions that require it (which is to say with Aristotle, it is a disposition). This demonstration can be carried out to arrive at the interpenetration of all of the cardinal virtues. For example, "temperance" is desiring no more than what one is due, and what one is due derives from the values one identifies with, knowledge of which is wisdom. And justice seeks for all persons what is due them on account of the values that are theirs to identify with: therefore it requires a more extensive measure of wisdom, which includes knowledge of the goods of others as well as of the self. It is not possible here to undertake the lengthy task of demonstrating the interpenetration of each cardinal virtue with every other, and I must trust that what has been offered is indicative of the terms and direction of such demonstration.

Now we must consider an immediate objection to the "biconditionality thesis," which is that, quite evidently, many persons manifest some of the cardinal virtues but not all. What I wish to show is that to grant this (as I do) need not be damaging to the biconditionality thesis. The supposition that it overturns the biconditionality thesis leads (in one direction) to regarding the virtues as independent of one another. It is evident in Protagoras' rejoinder to Socrates: ". . . you will find many men who are unjust, most impious, most intemperate, and most ignorant, but exceptionally brave."[20] It results in regarding virtues as "portable attributes" that may be learned independently of one another and applied to otherwise unvirtuous courses of conduct,

an approach resisted strenuously by Socrates. Our leaning in this direction today is exhibited, for example, in "applied ethics," and specifically in the practice of *adding* "ethics" to each of the professions by
requiring a college course—such as "business ethics," "medical ethics,"
"engineering ethics"—in the educational program of each profession.
This "quick fix" approach ignores the thesis that ethical conduct expresses traits of character—the moral virtues—whose cultivation will
transform the various professions. In short, the relationship of ethics
to practices that have arisen from other grounds and are directed to
other ends is not just additive but transformative.

Earlier we used the examples of the jewel thief and the bank robber
to note that each virtue (courage was the virtue there treated, but the
point is general) has its pseudomorphs. Some of the "Protagorean"
difficulty with the biconditionality thesis will be removed by learning to
distinguish pseudomorphs of the virtues from the virtues themselves.
Nevertheless it is sure to be the case that in the matter of the genuine
virtues, persons will be found who manifest some of them but not all.
The reason this is not inconsistent with the biconditionality thesis is
that virtues in their manifestation are developmental outcomes, and
persons do not develop in all aspects of themselves at the same rate. To
expect all of the virtues to become manifest in an individual at the same
time would be as illogical as to expect that every (or any) individual will
make all of his or her life-shaping choices at the same time. But by the
understanding of development as the actualization of potentials, it is
entirely consistent to recognize mutual implication among the virtues
without holding that all must be manifest at once, because the implication (say) of wisdom for courage may be of actualized wisdom for as-yet
unactualized, that is, merely potential, courage. Moreover this implication, though logically "of necessity," in Socrates's phrase, does not entail
existential necessity, for the actualization of a potentiality partakes of the
contingencies of existence. Therefore we do not interpret the
biconditionality thesis to hold that where (say) wisdom exists, manifest
courage must necessarily follow: we interpret biconditionality in the
weaker terms of the *tendency* for each virtue to elicit into manifestation
the other virtues.

Understood in this way, the thesis of the "unity of the virtues" is
consistent with the basic tenets of eudaimonistic philosophy. Unlike
Vlastos, I will not by detailed exegesis and interpretation endeavor to
demonstrate that this is what was meant as "unity of the virtues" by
Socrates (or by Plato or Aristotle). My task has been to show, against

modern criticism, that a defensible meaning of the thesis exists. It enables me to argue that a politics that is aimed at improvement of the quality of life must look to the establishment of institutions that afford to the maximum number of persons the best prospect of coming in touch with themselves—their own inner potential worth—at any point. I have granted that from this beginning the growth of self-knowledge, wisdom, identification with certain values, integrity, courage, generosity, temperance, and justice does not follow of necessity. My eudaimonistic thesis is in behalf of no more than the tendency of this development. The question then is: can we afford to ignore, obstruct, or—deliberately or inadvertently—extinguish this tendency?

CHAPTER FIVE

Responsibilities and Rights

A. I. Meldin says that to establish the existence of rights "we need nothing more than the concept of persons, whose features as the moral agents they are suffice for the possession by them of their fundamental moral rights."[1] The Robert Nozick of *Anarchy, State, and Utopia* held that rights obtain simply by virtue of persons' "separate existences."[2] As Ronald Dworkin has shown, John Rawls relies for the plausibility of his "original position" upon the shared presupposition by persons in that position that they are bearers of rights, beginning with the right to equality.[3] And Dworkin in his own general theory of rights says that the basic right to "equal concern and respect" is "axiomatic," that it is an "intuitive notion" that cannot be demonstrated but must be "assumed."[4]

Beneath important differences, the political theories of the four thinkers we have just cited are all "liberal" in that they are rights-based. According to the definition by Leo Strauss (for example), liberalism is "that political doctrine which regards as the fundamental political fact the rights, as distinguished from the duties, of man and which identifies the function of the state with the protection or the safeguarding of those rights."[5]

What the citations exhibit is that within the liberal tradition the existence of rights is not demonstrated, it is presupposed. The rights of individuals are "God given," or "intuitively self-evident," or included in what it is to be a human being by stipulative definition. Insofar as the question "Why rights?" is the request for the grounds of rights, it finds no answer in classical liberalism, for which rights are themselves the ground of the political theory. To ask for their grounds is to seek a prior starting point, which is to say that the request is illegitimate within the framework of liberalism. So well is this understood that H. L. A. Hart is exceptional among liberals for his caveat, ". . . if only we could find some sufficiently firm foundations for such rights."[6]

In this chapter we will endeavor to provide grounds for the rights of individuals, and from what has just been said it will be clear that in doing so we will be leaving the confines of liberalism in its classical definition. Our argument is that rights derive from responsibilities. This approach signifies the exchange of liberalism's "rights-primitive" conception of the individual for a "responsibilities-primitive" conception. By "primitive" I mean "logically primitive" as distinguished from "logically derivative." Liberalism's conception of the individual is rights-primitive in that it includes rights, but not responsibilities, in its irreducibly minimum conception of the individual human being. On the other hand eudaimonistic moral and political theory is responsibilities-primitive, including responsibilities, but not rights, in its irreducibly minimum conception of the individual human being. To be sure, having started with rights, liberalism must and does move to a theory of responsibilities (more typically termed "duties" in accordance with the etymology by which duties are "due to" someone); and having started with responsibilities, eudaimonism must and does move to a theory of rights. Nevertheless the exchange of a rights-primitive conception of the individual for a responsibilities-primitive conception is an alteration in the foundations of political theory affecting every aspect of the superstructure that subsequently arises. Our intent is to examine some of the more telling changes.

One of the changes is that in a responsibilities-primitive framework, rights are furnished with grounds. And today it is necessary to supply rights with grounds.

In the historical beginnings of liberalism (examined in chapter 1) it was distinctly advantageous and probably necessary that the existence of the rights of individuals be regarded as an unquestionable presupposition. This is so because the immediate task was to enfranchise individuals against the sovereignties of church and state, and this cause needed not an argument that provoked counterargument, but a manifesto. But today this "ipsedixitism" (as Bentham termed it)[7] has become a liability. In the words of J. M. E. McTaggart, "When a man asserts that he has an immediate certainty of a truth, he doubtless deprives other people of the right to argue with him. But he also—though this he sometimes forgets—deprives himself of the right to argue with other people."[8]

"Ipsedixitism" will not suffice today, first because political liberalism is now situated in a world that knows it well, and some sectors of the world judge it wanting, whereas other sectors have serious questions that cannot be blunted by stipulative definitions. Secondly liberalism is now a tradition, which is to say that its basic principles have an extended historical embodiment. This has served to explicate many implications of the principles, not all of which were initially recognized (indeed, we "learn from history" precisely because it is the case that theory never by itself recognizes all of the practical implications of its concepts and principles). The result is that internal to liberalism today are issues about the kinds of rights that persons have that are irresolvable by classical liberalism. They can be resolved by uncovering the grounds of rights, but to hold that rights have grounds is to depart from classical liberalism.

Our contention in this chapter is that the rights of individuals are not weakened but strengthened by deriving them from something prior to them. This is because today the question "Why rights?" must be answered, and the only effective way to answer it is by introducing the grounds of rights, from which they are derived. To be sure, every inquiry necessarily contains presuppositions that are not questioned in that inquiry. The basic presupposition of our present inquiry is that to be a human being is to innately possess potential worth, and (because potential worth inherently lays claim to actualization) to bear the moral responsibility to discover and progressively actualize this worth. Why is this presupposition sounder than that of liberalism? The answer is because today wider agreement can be achieved upon it. In the first place it affords a ground for rights in the proposition, "The rights of individuals must be respected because such respect is a necessary condition for maximizing the realization of potential human value." The rest of the answer consists not in an insupportable claim of "indubitable truth" for the presupposition, nor in deductive demonstration or empirical verification (both of which are inapplicable to rock-bottom presuppositions) but in "pragmatic vindication," which is to say in terms of the consequences of adopting the presupposition and acting upon it. Accordingly in what follows we will seek to show on eudaimonistic foundations: (1) that rights are not inherently adversarial, and therefore social relations are not in essence competitive; (2) that "negative" and "positive" basic rights can coexist without contradiction; (3) that while "welfare" rights exist, they are circumscribed by responsibilities such that they cannot endlessly proliferate, and they cannot endorse individuals in the disregard of their responsibilities.

But these and other changes are the issue of differing answers of liberalism and eudaimonism to the question of wherein the essential dignity of the human being lies. The liberal answer receives vigorous expression by Joel Feinberg:

> Having rights enables us to "stand up like men," to look others in the eye, and to feel in some fundamental way the equal of anyone. To think of oneself as the holder of rights is not to be unduly but properly proud, to have that minimal self-respect that is necessary to be worthy of the love and esteem of others. Indeed, respect for persons . . . may simply be respect for their rights, so that there cannot be the one without the other; and what is called "human dignity" may simply be the recognizable capacity to assert claims. To respect a person then, or to think of him as possessed of human dignity, simply *is* to think of him as a potential maker of claims. Not all of this can be packed into a definition of "rights"; but these are facts about the possession of rights that argue well their supreme moral importance.[9]

To test whether " 'human dignity' may simply be the recognizable capacity to assert claims" let us first look to the reflexive case: does an individual's sense of his or her own dignity rest in his or her capacity to assert claims? Now it will be illuminating to set this question in developmental perspective. It is typical of small children to issue unending claims—"I want this," "I need that," "You promised me this," "Johnny got that and I want one too." But I think that a child's sense of his or her own dignity comes not from these miscellaneous and disordered pronouncements, but from what is conveyed to the child by parental response. Parental response will be discriminate, honoring some of the child's claims but disregarding others. If the child's sense of dignity lay simply in the claims, parental response would be irrelevant to it. We can if we wish say that that the child's demands and entreaties are merely "claimed claims," some of which are identified as genuine claims by parental response. But such parental response to claims is only a small part of parental caring, and it is in parental respect for the child, conveyed by many forms and expressions of caring, that the child gains the sense of its own dignity. Caring is nurture of good growth, which requires a projection of the child's future. Is it their child's future as a rights-bearer that parents first of all aim at, or is it their child's future as a worthy person? Recognizably it is the latter, for as a future rights-bearer their child is identical to every other, but what parents attempt to read in their children is signs of individuation—not any child's future but Sarah's, or Timmy's—and worth admits of individuation as (classical liberal) rights-bearing does not.

But if the young child's sense of his or her own dignity comes from parental caring, it is a conferred sense. The same is true of an adult's sense of his or her own dignity that rests in claims understood as "legally recognized," for legal recognition is by the state. To find the inception of an original (in the meaning not of "first" but of "self-originated") sense of self-worth we must look to later childhood or adolescence, and there we find it associated, not with claims, but with responsibilities. It begins with the discovery that "Here is something I can do," and the fact that one is entrusted with the responsibility for doing it affords invaluable confirmation.

Feinberg says that it is as rights-bearers that we have "that minimal self-respect that is necessary to be worthy of the love and esteem of others." I think he is correct in connecting love and esteem to worthiness, which is to say to worth; but he is mistaken to identify worth with rights. To be a rights-bearer says nothing about one's worth—unless rights are so defined as to presuppose worth, and they are not thus defined by liberalism. For eudaimonism love is a response to worth, actual or potential, and rights are instrumentalities for the actualization by individuals of their innate potential worth.

Is dignity merely imputed, or is it recognized? An analogous question is whether honor is merely imputed, or directed to what is honorable. If, as eudaimonism holds, value is objective, then it exists to be recognized, honor is properly directed to what is honorable, trust is properly directed to what is trustworthy, and moral development has objective ends (to become trustworthy, to become honorable, to become just, to become courageous, temperate, patient, resolute, kind). But rights are not objective in this sense; we cannot identify a rights-bearer by what she does, but only by others' conduct toward her that signifies respect of her rights. She may make claims, take liberties, exercise powers, and presume immunities (to employ the categories of rights identified by Wesley Hohfeld),[10] but these are perceptible as rights only in the conduct of others in respect to them.

(It does not follow, of course, that whether or not an individual has moral rights is determined by whether or not others respect those rights. Others may fail in their responsibility to respect the rights that a given person has. Our point is simply that rights are not enacted into the world by their bearers; they must be imputed to their bearers and inferred from the conduct of such others as exhibit respect of someone's rights.)

By contrast individuals perceptibly enact responsibilities. It is true that in order to affirm the basic dignity of all persons we must impute responsibilities to persons unknown to us and also to persons who have not assumed their basic moral self-responsibility (children are the conspicuous case). We do this on the premise of innate potential worth in all persons, which is at the same time responsibility for actualizing this worth. It remains the case that a dignity based in responsibilities is objectively based. It is first recognized and thereafter generalized by imputation; and if it were not recognizable, imputation would be impotent against denial of the dignity it imputes. Because rights are imperceptible, a rights-based dignity is impotent against denial.

We will now outline a eudaimonistic theory of responsibilities and rights and then explore some of its implications especially as they speak to current issues in rights-theory.

The basic moral responsibility of every person is to discover and progressively actualize his or her innate potential worth. From this responsibility basic rights follow, by the logic that "ought" implies "can," as moral entitlements to what the individual needs in order to recognize and undertake his or her basic moral responsibility. Before turning to the form and substance of these rights we must consider the logical principle that "ought" implies "can" in its present application.

It is incoherent to hold persons responsible for doing what is strictly impossible for them to do—to fly, for example, by flapping their arms, or to live forever. But beyond cases of strict impossibility, "can" and "cannot" acquire complicating modalities; for example the distinction must be made between "can try to" and "can succeed"; and "cannot" has psychological and moral modes no less than physical.

For the "ought" of self-actualization to be attributable to individuals, it must be the case that they can discover and progressively actualize their potential worth. But "can" here divides into an unconditional and a conditional sense. The unconditional "can" pertains to the abstract possibility for a person, by the general nature of personhood, to discover his or her innate potentiality and to try to act upon it. It is the possibility in principle of these things. On the other hand the conditional "can" reflects the fact that persons exist in and are affected by situations. These situations are sets of circumstances which will be conducive to, obstructive of, or neutral with respect to the individual's exercise of his or her basic moral responsibility. The effect of the abstract "ought" upon these circumstances is to mandate the utilization of conducive circumstances and the removal or overcoming of obstructive circumstances. The effect of this bifurcation of the meaning of "can" and "cannot" is that individuals who are blocked by the circumstantial "cannot" are not relieved of the abstract moral obligation; they must strive against the obstacles. William James and Jose Ortega y Gasset are but two modern moral philosophers who echo the ancient eudaimonistic and Stoic wisdom that moral struggle cultivates the personal resourcefulness and strength of character that in many cases will prevail over initially daunting obstacles. But extreme circumstances can in some instances thwart self-actualization or prevent recognition of the responsibility for it from arising. The judgment to be made in such cases is not that the person is absolved of his or her basic moral responsibility, which is inalienable, but that he or she bears proportionally diminished liability for his or her failure in that responsibility. The next step is to determine the measure of culpability of the society, for some of the necessary conditions of self-actualization by individuals cannot be self-provided but can be socially provided. By the ubiquity of the abstract and unconditional "ought," noted above, it is the first responsibility of any society to provide such conditions for all persons. And by that ubiquity, individuals cannot use obstructive circumstances to deny their own basic moral responsibility ("I cannot, therefore I ought not").[11]

On this derivation, the basic rights of individuals divide into two classes according to what they are rights to, or substantively, and likewise into two classes formally, that is, according to their derivation. We have referred to the two substantive classes, which are distinguished according to whether what they entitle the individual to can or cannot be self-provided. Rights that can be self-provided are essentially *to things* and not *against other persons,* but in Hart's phrase they require a "protective perimeter" of negative rights, that is, rights to noninterference. Some rights that cannot be self-provided are "positive" rights, that is, rights to positive performances by others. Formally, some rights are possessed by the individual by virtue of unactualized potentiality—potentiality simply as such—while other rights obtain by virtue of actualized potentiality. Rights of the first kind are inalienable (in the strict sense of "indefeasible," i.e., "can't be lost or taken away") because potentiality is ineradicable. Rights of the second kind are self-alienable because actualized potentiality is subject to lapse.

On the eudaimonistic view as I am presenting it, what one has a right to is what one needs and can utilize in one's primary moral work of actualizing one's innate potential worth. As thus conceived, rights are in their essential character *to* things, and only secondarily *against* other persons. This was recognized in the ancient world, but gave way in modernity to the legalistic conception of rights as "claims against." When rights are defined as "claims against," it will appear that the ethics of Socrates, Plato, and Arisotle are devoid of the conception of rights, whereas in fact rights are included, but under a different definition. And if the concept of "individuality" is thought to be coincident with the concept of the rights of individuals, understood as "claims against," it will be concluded that individuality is a modern notion, whereas Greek eudaimonism defined individuality in terms of responsibilities.

A recent writer whose view corresponds to the ancient conception in this respect is H. J. McCloskey:

My right to life is not a right against anyone. It is my right and by virtue of it, it is normally permissible for me to sustain my life in the face of obstacles. It does give rise to rights against others *in the sense* that others have or may come to have duties to refrain from killing me, but it is essentially a right of mine, not an infinite list of claims, hypothetical and actual, against an infinite number of actual, potential, and as yet nonexistent human beings . . . Similarly, the right of the tennis club member to play on the club courts is a right to play, not a right against some vague group of potential or possible obstructors.[12]

But McCloskey is an exception to the modern propensity to model ethics upon law. Moral requirements are framed as rules, moral rules together with law serve the certain purpose of maintaining social order, moral judgments mirror judicial decisions in terms of impartiality and impersonality, and moral rights are conceived on the model of legal rights. The effect upon the conception of moral rights is apparent in Carl Wellman's contention that "the essential presupposition of the language of rights [is] the adversarial context in which its use alone makes sense."[13]

Wellman offers four reasons for modeling our conception of moral rights upon our conception of legal rights: paradigm cases of rights are more apparent in law than in morality; the content of legal rights is more precisely defined; the practical relevance of legal rights is more apparent; and the literature of jurisprudence lays out alternative theories of legal rights with more precision and detail than the literature of moral philosophy lays out alternative theories of moral rights.[14]

But if we are traversing a forest, a map of city streets is unhelpful whatever may be its precision and detail. In the modern setting Wellman's legal modeling of moral rights sits comfortably; but from a eudaimonistic standpoint it is a grand distortion to represent moral rights as inherently adversarial. In a theory that grounds social relations among individuals in respect for their rights, the effect of conceiving of rights as inherently adversarial is to render social relations inherently adversarial. To be sure, cooperation can be engendered on this foundation, but because it necessitates forfeiture, relinquishment, or waiving of (some) rights, and the operative conception of the individual is rights-primitive, it is the cost of cooperation that is emphasized.

By contrast, when rights are understood as deriving from responsibilities they are conceived as inherently nonadversarial because responsibilities are not inherently adversarial. Instead, responsibilities manifest a division of labor which expresses the interdependence of mature human beings thanks to their finitude as individuals. Each is responsible for the actualization of certain values, but each requires for satisfactory living values other than those he or she personally actualizes (as for example in this book I have been utilizing the ideas of a great many other philosophers), for which he or she is dependent upon the work of others. For this reason, as noted in our introduction, the operative conception of the "autonomy" of the individual cannot be total self-sufficiency, but must be compatible with interdependence. We hold "living autonomously" to mean: determining for oneself what one's contributions to others will be, and determining for oneself which values from the self-actualizing lives of others to utilize, and how.

It is the finitude of responsibilities that limits the scope of rights, precluding the ad hoc proliferation that constitutes the crucial problem for rights-theory today. The problem is epitomized in the contrast between Locke and the Universal Declaration of Human Rights, adopted by the General Assembly of the United Nations on December 10, 1948. According to Locke all human beings are invested by their nature with the inalienable rights to life, liberty, and property, each of which is to be understood negatively (see definition of a "negative right" hereafter). The U. N. Declaration reads in part:

Everyone has the right to a standard of living adequate for the health and well-being of himself and his family, including food, clothing, housing and medical care and necessary social services, and the right to security in the event of unemployment, sickness, disability, widowhood, old age or other lack of livelihood in circumstances beyond his control.[15]

Commenting on the proliferation of purported rights, Bertrand de Jouvenel says, "It is a major folly of modern times to fill the individual with ideas of what society owes him rather than of what he owes to society."[16] In similar vein H. B. Acton suggests that when fundamental needs (he cites health care, housing, and the education of children) are provided by the state, persons "will come to regard their basic requirements as somebody else's business and to regard amusement as the chief aim of their free choices."[17] Again, Iredell Jenkins says,

Under the impetus of a steadily expanding concept of the new human rights, we are mobilizing an immense political and social effort to satisfy the needs of men. But at the same time, under the influence of the traditional doctrine of individual rights, we reject any proposal that would require men to contribute to society to the measure of their ability. . . . We are placing the state under the legal duty to make good all of the basic needs of men, but we are placing men under no duties of discipline, responsibility, and service to support the effort made in their behalf.[18]

The thought of each of the philosophers just cited falls squarely within the classical liberal tradition, and in what each says we find resistance to both the proliferation and the changing character of rights, and also frustration at the inadequate handling of responsibilities (duties, obligations) within the classical liberal framework. Liberalism's bulwark against proliferation of rights has traditionally been its distinction between "negative" and "positive" rights, but it is ill-suited to this service, and it curtails obligations, preventing them from expanding to provide for expanding rights. This latter feature today leads liberals who have some sympathy for a limited inclusion of welfare rights (Martin Golding for example) to expand duties by terming them "mandatory rights." But first we will consider the traditional bulwark consisting in the distinction between negative and positive rights.

Traditionally defined, a right is "negative" when the correlative duty it imposes upon others is merely to abstain from interference with the right-holder in the exercise of the right; rights are "positive" when the correlative duties of others are positive performances. In orthodox classical liberal terms, all basic human rights—rights held by human beings simply by virtue of their humanity—are negative rights, and the idea of positive basic rights is precluded by the logic of the case. The paramount values according to liberalism are liberty and equality, and rights protect these values. Liberty is served by basic rights, and the requisite kind of equality is the possession by all individuals identically of basic rights. To serve liberty, these rights must be exclusively negative, for to respect negative rights requires no more of others than that they mind their own business. But positive rights intrude coercively upon the liberty of others by mandating particular courses of conduct of them; therefore the very notion of positive basic rights is self-contradictory and introduces a damaging contradition into politics. Nothing here precludes the existence of positive *special* rights, however. If George promises Arthur a job, Arthur acquires a right to the said positive performance by George. There is no contradiction because the right and the correlative duty are created voluntarily by both parties.

The first problem with this is that the "negative-positive" distinction is difficult to maintain. Advocates of welfare rights can and do define them as serving "the essentially negative goal of preventing or alleviating helplessness."[19] Going further, Henry Shue argues that so-called negative rights are actually rights to the establishment and maintenance by government of protective agencies. Such establishment and maintenance by government is positive performance which in turn can be maintained only by positive performances (notably taxpaying) by citizens.[20]

But the erosion of the bulwark against positive basic rights that marks the historical development of welfare liberalism out of classical liberalism received a powerful push from two other factors, one historical and the other lodged within the self-conception of individuals promulgated by classical liberalism.

Historically, modernity is identified with the growth in influence and power of centralized government. At the time at which Hobbes and Locke wrote it was unthinkable to look to government as the distributive agency for basic benefits, required by all persons, because government lacked the requisite resources. But between that time and ours, in countries such as our own, government has become the principal repository of wealth, the major landholder, the largest employer, and the dominant manager of the conditions of public life. In this situation it becomes reasonable to address welfare-claims to government—provided that what is understood as "welfare" is a distributable commodity.

This proviso was satisfied by the economistic self-conception that was promulgated by classical liberalism, as described in chapter 1. Liberalism's objective of enfranchising individuals against the sovereignties of church and state made sense only on the presupposition of independent initiatives in individuals. The initiative astutely seized upon by *realpolitik* and classical liberal thinkers as the most universal and reliable was the desire for material gain. To vindicate it they first sought to discredit higher, and thus rarer and less reliable, human initiatives as hypocritically disguised egoism; they released the desire for material gain from the strict limits placed upon it alike by the medieval church and ancient Greek and Roman moral philosophy; and they transvalued the resulting avarice by invisible hand arguments. The outcome is a conception of the self whose welfare is conceived in terms of material goods. Because material goods are distributable, "welfare" as thus conceived is distributable, and it becomes reasonable to look upon a wealthy and powerful state as a welfare distributor. This generates the impasse described by Jenkins in our earlier citation: "We are placing the state under the legal duty to make good all of the basic needs of men, but we are placing men under no duties of discipline, responsibility, and service to support the effort made in their behalf." The reason we are not exacting the counterbalancing duties and responsibilities is that to do so would be to overtly infringe the liberty that our politico-moral tradition defends. In this tradition all persons are rights-bearers, but bear only such duties as are correlative to the said rights (duties of noninterference), and such obligations as they voluntarily undertake.

An attempt at a corrective within the liberal framework is the concept of a "mandatory right" as distinguished from a "discretionary right," or in Martin Golding's terms, a "welfare-right" as distinguished from an "option-right." An option-right for Golding is "an area of autonomy within which a right-holder is free to decide."[21] But what Golding terms a "welfare-right" leaves no option: it must be exercised, and others have no duty not to interfere if it is not exercised. In Feinberg's terms, "If I have a mandatory right to do X then it follows logically that I have—not a right not to do X—but rather a *duty* to do X."[22]

Golding's principal example of a mandatory right is the right of all children to education, and Feinberg says that on this point "very likely there is no gainsaying Golding."[23] The problem is that in the notion of mandatory rights the concept that has been consecrated to creation and preservation of individual liberty is being used to curtail it.

To those who are disturbed by this paradoxicality, Feinberg proposes a way out: "That is to interpret the right as a claim that each citizen has to live in an educated society. On this construction, each person has a right that all the other persons be educated, and in virtue of the right that the others have that he be educated, he has himself a duty to attend school."[24] But surely this is a convoluted way to arrive at a duty. It is analogous to saying that if I want to become a lawyer, then because the lawyers I will eventually associate with have the right to expect that their colleagues have received training in the law, I have a duty to acquire training in the law. Why should not the duty derive directly from my aim to become a lawyer, by the principle that from one's chosen ends comes the responsibility for utilizing the appropriate means for their achievement? Feinberg's account has the virtue that it does not compromise the liberty-preserving function of rights, as Golding's does, but it avoids this by deriving the duty from a right, which forces it into the indicated convolution.

Compromise of the liberty-preserving function of rights, and gymnastic derivation of performative duties from others' rights, are avoided by preserving the distinction between rights and duties. In this interest we endorse the general definition of a right—encompassing all four kinds of rights distinguished by Hohfeld—as a "respected choice,"[25] with legal rights constituting "legally respected choices" and moral rights constituting "morally respected choices." Under this definition a right is bilateral, that is, to do or not to do, and a right also inherently includes the bearer's option to choose not to exercise it on those occasions on which it can be exercised.

It is entirely possible to speak of both a duty and a right to do something without conflating the meanings of "right" and "duty," and without regarding it as a mere case of the same thing seen from different viewpoints. The duty to vote, for example, is also the right to vote, because indispensable to performance of the duty is the "protective perimeter" (in Hart's words) that the right provides. But this understanding requires a source of duties that is other than the source of rights.

Recognizing this enables Henry Shue to avoid the compromises of Golding and Feinberg. "Probably," Shue says, "some rights actually ought to be exercised. . . . But any duty, if there is one, to take advantage of a right you have would not be a duty correlative to the right, but the quite different kind of duty that flows from a moral ideal of a rich or fulfilled life." I think this is correct. Shue then adds, "Such ideals and their associated duties may well be important, but they simply are not part of a theory of rights."[26] This would be accurate if it had been qualified by ". . . within our political tradition," but is inaccurate without such qualification, for eudaimonism is an alternative political and moral tradition in which ideals and their associated duties are the source of rights.

The sole source of duties that are not generated as correlatives of rights, in classical liberalism, is voluntary agreement. On this understanding an individual can with impunity avoid all duties and responsibilities except the duty to respect the rights of others. Such an individual perhaps does no harm, but also does no good, and a moral viewpoint that is obliged to endorse this as a commendable life is clearly minimalistic. Other persons would be just as well off if this individual had never existed.

In concert with Hart we have defined a right as a protected choice. Any equivocation with the centrality of choice to the concept of rights introduces the risk of compromising the liberty and autonomy of individuals which it is the function of rights both to secure and to preserve. Accordingly we must eliminate the equivocal notion of "mandatory rights" and recognize what they refer to as duties. All rights, then, are liberty-rights. "Claim-rights" protect the choice to lay claim to something or not; "power-rights" protect the choice to exercise a power or not; "immunity-rights" protect the choice to exercise an immunity or not. But the reason choice is to be protected is not to release the individual from all requirements, but to release him or her from external requirements for the purpose of supporting self-imposed requirements. In other words the freedom here supported is not *libero arbitrio,* but self-determination as against determination of the self by external agencies. It provides the condition under which to recognize the self as first of all a responsibility, namely the responsibility for discovering and progressively actualizing the potential worth that it innately possesses.

This fundamental moral responsibility is not just a responsibility *regarding* oneself, it is a responsibility in the first instance *to* oneself. Is this a coherent notion? Kant held that one has a duty to oneself to develop one's talents, and others have held that one has a duty to oneself not to injure oneself. One of the often-noted problems with the concept of a reflexive duty or responsibility is that it requires a duality in the self between that to which the duty or responsibility is owed and that by which it is to be fulfilled. But eudaimonism's conception of the person, we will recall, is as an initial multiplicty—of disordered and conflicting faculties, in Plato's presentation—into which order and integration must be introduced. The essential duality that accommodates the notion of a responsibility to the self is between the ideal self, or daimon, and the actual self. Self-responsibility is the responsibility of the actual self to the ideal self.

But beyond questions of the logical cogency of the notion of a responsibility to oneself, there is presently, I think, compelling practical reason to return to it. In the preface, in chapter 1, and again just above, we have sought to show that modern moral theory, whose mode we termed "rules morality," makes minimal demands upon individuals. What it demands is what others are entitled to expect of an individual, which by the terms of impartiality and universalizability is what they are entitled to expect of anyone in "relevantly similar circumstances." But the "anyone" here includes persons of little or no moral development, and by the modern understanding of universalizability, what can be expected of them is the limit of what can be expected of others. The effect of social conditioning in this moral minimalism is to produce persons who expect of themselves nothing beyond minimal moral performance.

Persons who aspire to higher moral thought and conduct in a morally minimalistic setting cannot be supposed to be responding to others' expectations of them, and I think we make sense of their conduct best by understanding it as their responses to self-originated expectations of themselves. And if the notion of expecting something of oneself is cogent and useful, I see no reason that the same cannot be true of "holding oneself responsible," and of having "duties to oneself." Harry Frankfurt's analysis of "second order" desires is relevant here.[27] What he terms a second-order desire is a desire to desire, as for example in the case of a person who does not have the desire to listen to classical music, but has the desire to have that desire. Thus understood, it will be evident that second-order desires play a central part in character development. The person one seeks to become is the bearer of qualities, including desires, that one presently lacks, and the desire to become that person is the desire to learn to act, think, feel, and desire as that envisaged person does. If this character development is a moral responsibility, then it makes sense to say that one recognizes a duty to oneself to learn to act, think, feel, and desire as does the person one aspires to become.

But because the self is inherently social it cannot be conceived as exclusive of other selves, or "atomically," and a duty to the self can be at the same time a duty to others. A good way to recognize what eudaimonism holds to be the basic moral responsibility of the individual as a duty to others is in terms of culture as tradition. In its aspect as tradition, culture is cumulative knowledge and practices bequeathed to each new generation by its predecessors. It means that every human being begins life as a recipient and is responsible in subsequent, productive stages of life for recognizing and repaying this debt. As a debt to prior generations it cannot be repaid to them, but is a responsibility to conserve and enrich the culture that the next generations will receive. However, the effect of recognizing this responsibility as also a responsibility of the individual to him- or herself is to ascribe to each individual the responsibility for determining in what coinage his or her debt is to be repaid. In a self-fulfilling life, it will be repaid by actualization of the particular values for which the individual is innately responsible.

Derivation of rights from responsibilities will generate both "positive" and "negative" rights. This is because, while "welfare" cannot be distributed, some of its necessary conditions can be, and among them are some that a good society will distribute because they cannot be self-supplied by individuals. In this latter category some conditions are negative, for example, protection of individuals against unwarranted intrusions by other persons, groups, or institutions, protection against fraud, protection of society against invasion. But some are positive, including guaranteed subsistence, provision of appropriate education for children, facilitation for adolescents of "freedom and variety of situations" as discussed in chapter 3, provision of a public information service as will be proposed in chapter 6, and some part in providing good organizational management as such management will be defined in chapter 7.

In eudaimonistic perspective, "positive" rights are not entitlements to "welfare" but to conditions for the exercise of responsibilities by individuals. This is because "welfare" is at bottom the well-being of persons, which consists in their own developed moral character, the principal agency of which is individuals themselves. In this light it is seriously misleading to use the term "welfare" to refer to public programs such as Social Security, Medicare, Aid to Dependent Children, and unemployment compensation.

While derivation of rights from responsibilities generates both positive and negative rights, it curbs the ad hoc proliferation of purported rights by the inherent limits of responsibilities. In accord with many rights-theorists today let us regard the declaration of a right as the laying of a claim, and the establishment of a right as the establishment of a "justified" or a "valid" claim. The point to be noticed is that the activity of claiming has no inherent limits; an individual may, without doing violence to the meaning of "claiming," lay claim to anything and everything at once. To refer claims to desires, as for example Hobbes does by inferring the right to self-preservation and felicity from the instinctive desire for these, does not alter this picture, for like claims, desires are without intrinsic limit. Accordingly a theory that is rights-primitive has but two recourses in order to restrict rights by distinguishing what are genuinely such from what are falsely declared to be such: it can try to do so by definition, as in the contention that basic rights are exclusively negative; or it can introduce criteria from another source. The first recourse is vulnerable (as we have seen) to the charge of stipulative definition, whereas the second cannot avoid an ad hoc appearance.

By contrast rights that derive from responsibilities are restricted by the inherent finitude of responsibilities. The exercise of a productive responsibility (as self-actualization is) is a concrete course of conduct by a particular individual which, during the time required, precludes to the individual alternative courses of conduct. To be sure, an individual can undertake alternative courses of conduct successively; but when the responsibility of the individual is to live a determinate life, it precludes to him or her the living of alternative lives. The principle once again is Spinoza's *omnis determinatio est negatio*. And if rights are entitlements by the individual to what he or she needs and can utilize in living the life that he or she is responsible for living, then what we may call the "constraint of finitude" is an inherent limitation upon his or her rights.

We intuitively recognize the constraint of finitude in respect to responsibilities, for although a person may desire all things for himself, no one is ready to accept more than a very limited number of productive responsibilities. (There is no corresponding limit on responsibilities of abstention, for to do any one thing is at the same time to abstain from doing an infinitude of other things. Likewise we can simultaneously fulfill our duties of noninterference to a limitless number of other persons simply by minding our own business.)

Moreover the individual who possesses self-knowledge and lives by it manifests justice, first by not laying claim to goods that he or she cannot utilize, and second by actively willing such goods into the hands of those who can utilize them toward self-actualization. What is expressed in both cases is not "selflessness," but the proportionality of a self-responsible self that is situated in relations of interdependence with other selves that are, or ought to be, self-responsible. An individual who possesses self-knowledge and lives by its direction recognizes goods to which he or she is not entitled as distractions from his or her proper course of life—"loud and noisy things," in Nietzsche's expression, "emphatic trifles" in Emerson's. And to will to others their true utilities is at the same time the concrete expression of respect for them as ends in themselves and recognition that we stand to gain from the worthy living of others. Eudaimonistic individualists from Socrates to Thoreau have sought to remind us that our needs of others—whether of parents, teachers, plumbers, carpenters, doctors, lovers, or friends—are best served when those others are self-identified with what they do and experience it as self-fulfilling.

By eudaimonism's responsibilities-primitive conception of persons, the fundamental moral responsibility of each individual is for moral self-development, and the derivative basic rights are to subsistence, protection, and enablement.

We will define subsistence as adequate food, shelter, clothing, and basic health care. The right to subsistence derives from the *potential* worth of every person and is inalienable by virtue of the inalienability of this innate potentiality. In earlier citations from Jouvenel, Acton, and Jenkins we can read the objection that a right to subsistence confirms a recipiency orientation within which persons can with impunity live on the basis of others' efforts. But in a responsibilities-based understanding, subsistence is the first condition of the exercise of responsibility and carries the expectation of such exercise. A fair expression of this difference is the recent transformation in some states of "welfare" to "workfare," but the latter must be sensitive to the distinction between bare productivity and self-fulfilling productivity. If it is the latter that constitutes the well-being of persons that society exists to promote, then workfare must include opportunity for exploration and choice among a wide range of types of work, and this mandates national administration.

To summarize: the right to subsistence is the license to live unproductively if the conceptual framework within which it is introduced is rights-primitive; however, the right to subsistence will serve to generalize productive living when the setting within which it appears is responsibilities-primitive.

Rights to protection are the "protective perimeter" that exercise of responsibilities requires. Central here are the Lockean rights to life, liberty, and property, but responsibilities-primitivism significantly alters their meaning.

The liberty in question becomes so-called "positive" freedom, that is, "freedom for . . ." and not merely the negative "freedom from . . ." As effective freedom and not merely formal freedom it includes considerations of enablement, starting with the subsistence that we have just addressed. The very idea of positive freedom has been famously held to be the seed of despotism by Isaiah Berlin in his "Two Concepts of

Liberty."[28] The charge is apt in reference to the Absolute Idealisms, such as of Hegel and Bradley, that Berlin has in mind and also in reference to a "closed teleology" type of eudaimonism such as was Aristotle's on the "dominant end" interpretation of his thought.[29] What Absolute Idealism and "closed" eudaimonism have in common is that each claims a priori knowledge of the good of all human beings, defines freedom as pursuit of this good, and takes measures to discourage other courses of conduct and other conceptions of the good. But the "open" eudaimonism that we are setting forth in this book is immune to Berlin's charge, for the ideal it promotes is the self-identification of individuals according to their chosen ends. Self-identification had conditions, such as the "freedom, and variety of situations" we considered in chapter 3, that only an open society can provide.

According to Locke, the right to property is an ownership right, but in eudaimonistic terms it is a use right. The primary difference is that the latter is inherently limited whereas the former is not. From the standpoint of ownership there is nothing to be said against such a distribution of wealth as exists in the United States today, where the top fifth of families owns almost eighty percent, while the bottom fifth owns two-tenths of a percent.[30] But so extreme a disparity will be condemned by a eudaimonistic use criterion.

In Lockean terms, ownership begins with the self and extends to material goods through the labor that the self "mixes" with them. The effect of this is that the identity of the self is "mixed" with its material possessions. But in the absence of a self-knowledge that is independent of its material possessions, this is an inducement to identify oneself *as* one's material possessions. In this case moral growth will be discounted in favor of the endless accumulation of material possessions.

Finally, in Lockean terms "ownership" is defined exclusively because it is the extension of a self that is conceived atomically, as "a private dominion exclusive of the rest of mankind."[31] This entails exclusivity in regard to the interests of each person, and the division of experience into "public" and "private" sectors. The private sector of experience serves to protect those interests of each person in which, by the atomic conception of personhood, other persons have no legitimate interest. But to preclude legitimate interests of others in the essential personhood of each is, as communitarian critics of classical liberalism charge, to preclude to persons the community that meaningful living requires. On the other hand communitarians typically argue for the legitimate interest of each person in the welfare of other persons by affirming the priority of shared interests over distinctive individual interests and calling for the sacrifice of the latter to the "common good."

For eudaimonism the common good is no more and no less than the particular goods of individuals *in complementary interrelationship*. The requirement for complementary interrelationship is implicit in the fact that the good that is to be actualized, conserved, and defended—the good that represents the individual's achieved identity—is an objective good, that is, it is of value to others no less than to the individual who actualizes it. Because this is so, no life can be said to be fulfilled whose worth is not recognized and utilized by (some) other persons in their own self-actualizing enterprises. Correspondingly every well-lived life must utilize values produced by (some) other well-lived lives. And this is to say that within a society, every person has a legitimate interest in the essential personhood of every other. (The move here from "some others" to "every other" is legitimated by the fact that those upon whom you or I rely have need of values produced by others, who have need of values produced by others.) This is the foundation of a form of community that in chapter 6 we will term "community of true individuals" and consider in more detail.

In this form of community individual self-determination, self-direction, and self-fulfillment are not sacrificed to the "common good" but nurtured as the foundation of the common good. Is the very notion of "privacy" abolished by the recognition that the inmost personhood of every individual is of legitimate interest to other persons? Not when the essence of personhood is understood as the responsibility for self-actualization by each individual, on his or her autonomous initiative. For this dictates that others' interest in each must begin with respect for the autonomy of each. In chapter 4 we termed the disposition to this respect the virtue of deference. Our expectations of others must defer to their self-expectations.

Eudaimonism endorses a right to privacy, but not on the grounds that experience itself contains a domain of privacy. The classical claim that experience inherently includes a private domain is advanced by Mill in the first chapter of *On Liberty*. The effect of this within classical liberalism is to render the individual's use of his or her privacy non-criteriological. By the definition of the domain the rights of others are not violated by the individual's private conduct; and because other obligations are voluntarily undertaken, an individual who chooses to accept none, has none, and freedom in the private domain becomes *libero arbitrio*. To be sure, on his eudaimonistic side (as expressed in chapter 3 of *On Liberty*, in his qualitative distinction among pleasures, and in his conception of the good state in *Considerations on Representative Government*), Mill sought to rectify this. But in so-doing he introduced contradictions into his thought, because the eudaimonistic and the classical liberal conceptions of individuality and moral obligation are not commensurable.

Robert Nozick refers to privacy as "moral space,"[32] but he does not mean space in which moral work is to be done. His concern is with the question of authority, which in his classical liberal view must begin with the self-authority of individuals, who may then transfer some of their self-authority to such institutions as protective agencies and the state. As a form of individualism, eudaimonism agrees that primacy of authority is borne by individuals and that the state must respect this self-authority. But eudaimonism differs significantly from classical liberalism in what kind of state best exhibits this respect (our theme in chapter 7). And by eudaimonism's responsibilities-primitivism, rights serve responsibilities, and the privacy that is protected by right is not the domain of *libero arbitrio*—it is the domain of freedom for self-determination as distinguished from the determination of the self by agencies external to it.

The right to privacy creates a domain of privacy, it does not validate a domain that is inherent in experience. To see this, consider what is the most promising candidate for such a domain. This candidate is subjectivity, understood as the content of the self—feelings, thoughts, perceptions, and so forth—to which the individual alone has immediate access, while the access of other persons depends upon the mediation that is afforded by various forms of expression. But subjectivity is not an inherent domain of privacy because it is not a "domain"; instead it is part of a process, namely the process of objectivization by which persons live their lives into the world. In Emerson's words, ". . . for always the inmost in due time becomes the outmost. . . ."[33] Because living must be into the world, subjectivity from the beginning contains implicitly within it its objective issue from which it cannot be divorced. The poem that begins with an image or a line in one's head is already aimed at expression.

In this light privacy is a right of individuals because it is a necessary condition of self-discovery and self-actualization. To hear one's own inner voice requires the opportunity of chosen occasions on which the vociferous world is stilled. And the reason that the autonomy of individuals must be protected is that in the beginning it is tentative and vulnerable, wholly unequal to the buffeting that awaits its expression in the world. This is a developmental consideration. It is true that individuals long disciplined in self-directed living will have acquired the strength of character by which to make their way undeterred. Nevertheless the right to privacy continues to serve, for self-actualization is perpetual origination; if it has built firm dispositions behind, yet at its forward extremity it is, in Abraham Maslow's good term, a tender "growth-tip."[34] In a word, the right to privacy serves the process of incubation. When Isaac Newton was asked how he arrived at his theory of the mechanical laws of the universe, he replied, "*Nocte dieque incubando*"— by incubating them night and day. To live originally, out of oneself, is to be perpetually aware that some of one's fresh thoughts, feelings, and experimental traits of character are not yet ready to see the light of day. The right to privacy enables individuals themselves to control the process by which "the inmost in due time becomes the outmost"; it shelters incubation.

The right to personal property is necessary to individual autonomy, both as protection and as enablement. It is the former function that receives emphasis in the words of the elder William Pitt: "The poorest man may in his cottage bid defiance to all the forces of the Crown. It may be frail; its roof may shake; the wind may blow through it; the storm may enter; the rain may enter; but the King of England may not enter; all his force dares not cross the threshold of the ruined tenement!"[35]

A just and temperate person seeks to possess what he or she is entitled to, neither less nor more. Eudaimonistically conceived, what each person essentially is is a work of self-actualization for which he or she is responsible. Accordingly each person holds natural entitlement to goods he or she needs and can utilize in the exercise of this responsibility. As noted earlier, some of these entitlements obtain merely by virtue of the individual's potential worth, and because potential worth is inalienable, so likewise these rights are inalienable. The right to subsistence is an inalienable right, and to correlate it with the growth-responsibility of individuals, the subsistence cannot be "bare," but must include a growth-increment. For another example, imprisoned criminals regardless of their crimes are entitled to be treated with respect in acknowledgment of their potential worth, and in almost all cases the operational meaning of "respect" must include opportunity for rehabilitation. The demand of rioting prisoners at Attica, Graterford, and other penitentiaries to be "treated like human beings, not like animals" is valid.

Earlier in this chapter we considered the case of persons whose socioeconomic conditions obstructed their recognition and fulfillment of the moral responsibility of self-actualization. Here we will briefly address the question of how eudaimonism's "rights from responsibilities" doctrine affects persons who are from birth or injury severely handicapped, either mentally or physically, or both.

In the great majority of such cases, the innate potentiality to manifest moral worth remains present, though it may be in varying measure restricted. For example in the case of feeble-mindedness, as was noted in the introduction there are many virtues—for example, lovingness, fidelity, compassion, honesty—that do not depend upon even average intelligence. Persons who possess the potentialities for such virtues are entitled to the conditions of their manifestation and to social supply of such of the conditions as they cannot self-supply. The judgment that only "superior" or "normal" persons can manifest virtues is parochial. A listing of historically recognized human virtues (cardinal and distributed) would exceed a hundred,[36] and persons in whom handicaps preclude manifestation of some of them will be capable of manifesting others. The first order of business here is the educational work of correcting the prevailing narrow recognition of but a few virtues—a parochialism that is one of the consequences of modern moral minimalism.

In eudaimonistic conception a being with no moral potentialities whatever is not human. Sadly this describes some entities that might have been human, for example infants born without a brain, and some entities that once were human, for example comatose accident victims in whom all or most brain-function has been destroyed. Such creatures have no rights; but morality is not limited to respect of rights. Are moral responsibilities toward them entailed in particular cases by worthy individuality? By the eudaimonistic definition of a good society? I find compelling an argument by Jane English for what she calls the "coherence of attitudes." She contends that

our psychological constitution makes it the case that for our ethical theory to work, it must prohibit certain treatment of non-persons which are significantly person-like. If our moral rules allowed people to treat some person-like non-persons in ways we do not want people to be treated, this would undermine the system of sympathies and attitudes that makes the ethical system work.[37]

Returning to ordinary cases: on a responsibilities base, no one is entitled to more of a good than he or she can utilize, and no one is entitled to incommensurate goods, that is, goods whose utilization serves a course of life alternative to that of the person in question.

Persons directly responsible for others who require to be cared for—their children, their infirm or aged relatives—have correspondingly increased entitlements. "Caring for one's children" is to be understood as preparing them for self-responsible, self-directed living and ceases to entail provision of material goods when this has been achieved. The desire of parents to secure their grown children against misfortune by means of inheritance must not be entirely thwarted, but a ceiling on inheritance is required as a measure toward rectification of the gross inequity in present distribution of wealth (see figures cited earlier). I know of no studies of the effect of large inheritance upon the recipients in terms of their character-development, but my guess is that in the aggregate, harm approaches benefit at $100,000 and outweighs it at $500,000. What must be considered is not just the effect upon the individual of inheriting substantial wealth at, say, the age of forty, but the effect upon him or her of knowing of the prospective inheritance from perhaps the age of twenty.

The admonition that "our possessions possess us" (Stoics, Nietzsche, Thoreau) is particularly apt in reference to incommensurate goods. To possess such goods is to live with a perpetual distraction from one's true course of life. If one succumbs to the distraction, one's actualization of one's own innate potential worth is compromised. If one does not succumb, one wastes the value of the potential good. How many of the people who own Porsche or Ferrari automobiles are capable of or situated to utilize the potentialities of these machines?

Or consider if you will—umbrellas. For years I carried, with perfect peace of mind, a twelve-dollar model purchased at a local department store. Then two years ago I was irresistibly attracted to one at Harrod's in London that was made from a Yorkshire walking stick and cost the equivalent of seventy-five dollars. From that point on I was deathly afraid of losing my umbrella; and when rain was accompanied by wind I carried it furled for fear it would be blown inside-out. Two months ago, to my blessed relief, I contrived to lose it for good.

For a last example: the Association of University Women holds an annual used book sale in my town. It is eagerly awaited and thronged equally by students from my university and the many townspeople for whom reading is an important activity. The first time I went to hunt treasures, I noticed a man who was pushing a train of shopping carts into which he was carelessly scooping whole shelves of books. When I encountered him again the next year, behaving as before, I inquired of one of the attending AUW women if she happened to know who he was and what he was doing. "Yes," she replied. "He is a building contractor who puts up residences for people. The houses contain what he is pleased to call 'the library,' and he takes pride in the fact that he saves floor space by slicing the spines from the books he buys and gluing the spines to the walls. He throws the pages of the books away." I clutched tightly the out-of-print two-volume *Letters of Joseph Conrad* I had found, and reflected on the persons who were denied their comparable joys by the bandsaw bandit.

It is important to notice that establishment of an individual's entitlement to a good does not address the question of how the entitlement is to be met. By the priority that eudaimonism ascribes to individual autonomy, individuals are themselves responsible for self-supplying such of their utilities as can be so supplied without serious compromise of their own self-actualization. The reason for the qualification is that for any person the bare "can" is much broader than the applicable "ought." Literally a musician, say, can (learn to) grow her own food, build her own house, repair her own car, and tailor her own clothes. But if she is responsible for every such "can," she will make little or no music. It may be the case that one or another of such "cans" is a useful complement, in her case, to her music-making, and is thereby included within her "ought"; but others will conflict and should be avoided in the interest of her integrity. It is normally to be expected that her music-making will provide her with monetary income by which to contract for the utilities she requires, and in this case we regard the said utilities as self-provided at a one-step remove. But no one in the early stages of life is capable of such self-provision, and in subsequent stages some conditions of worthy living by individuals are by their nature insusceptible of self-provision. Justice requires provision of non-self-suppliable necessary conditions by the appropriate social institution, that is, by family, community, workplace, or state.

By its provision of non-self-suppliable utilities to individuals, society expresses its legitimate interest in the deepest interests of individuals. There is no sphere of privacy from which legitimate social interest is locked out. But because the social value of individual lives is to be realized on the autonomous initiative of individuals, autonomy requires to be protected by a right of privacy as we have previously indicated, and this right creates a sphere of privacy.

Accordingly the property right we are here defending is better termed the right to personal property than the right to private property. This is because within the classical liberal tradition "private" bears the connotation of exclusivity that is associated with atomic individuality. In Locke's terms, private property is for the "benefit and sole advantage of the proprietor."[38] But the notion that true benefit to the individual can be his or her benefit exclusively is a deep-seated modern misconception, and virulently corrosive of social and personal life. Its prevalence reflects the modern moral minimalism that disregards (or judges "supererogatory") the intermediate and higher stages of moral development where, as Plato and Aristotle insisted, the goods sought and realized by individuals are objective, that is, good not for the self exclusively, but likewise for whoever is capable of recognizing and appreciating them as what they are.

And what of the ground-level material goods of survival? It is of course true that because one consumes the food one eats, it cannot be shared. Nevertheless it does not serve one's own good exclusively, for its status is that of a utility in the enterprise of attaining to an objectively worthy life. To recognize it as such requires that our rights-primitive conception of human beings be exchanged for eudaimonism's responsibilities-primitive conception.

CHAPTER SIX

Community as the Sociality of True Individuals

The thesis of this chapter is that the route to the just and good society lies in the cultivation and the perfection of individuality, not in its suppression or extinction. Our tasks are to understand how the contrary belief now bids to prevail, and why it is mistaken.

The making of a conceptual distinction introduces a tendency moving next to disjunction and thereafter to antagonism between the disjunctive elements. In the case at hand, evidence from cultural anthropology suggests that human beings in the beginning had purely social identities—each was the instantiation of tribe, clan, and phratry. The subsequent distinction of the individual from his or her social grouping—the beginning of individuality as we know it, that is, as qualitative rather than merely numerical—led to the disjunctive "oneself or society" and thereafter to the antagonisms of individual against society and conversely. The good of the individual and the common good became conceivable, and conceived, in mutually exclusive terms. This antagonism is conspicuous in current disputes between "individualists" on one side and "communitarians" and "traditionalists" on the other. Individualists condemn the conformity that they perceive to follow from deriving individual norms from a conception of the collective good, and communitarians and traditionalists hold individualism responsible for the dissolution of meaningful community and tradition.

Our contention is that the charges by anti-individualists are telling against some varieties of individualism but not against others, and that by often failing to distinguish among varieties of individualism, its attackers spread confusion. There are in fact many importantly different varieties of individualism,[1] but by the pattern established at the outset of this book we shall concentrate upon just two, namely classical liberal individualism and eudaimonistic individualism.

We shall argue that classical liberal individualism is correctly perceived as in key respects destructive of meaningful community and meaningful tradition, whereas eudaimonistic individualism, on the contrary, supports and strengthens both. A pivotal issue that will occupy us throughout this chapter centers in the difference between the community and the tradition that each person inherits with his or her birth, and the community and tradition that each person laters joins by choosing his or her course of life. We will term the first case one's "received" community and tradition, and the second case one's "chosen" community and tradition. It follows from classical liberalism's insistence upon freedom of choice that such community and tradition as it can consistently endorse must be chosen by the individual. Eudaimonism also insists upon chosen community and tradition, out of its recognition of individual autonomy as essential to individual moral development. But this resemblance between the two individualisms issues from a profound difference, namely that for classical liberalism there is nothing obligatory in an individual's choice of this or that community or tradition, whereas for eudaimonism there is in the case of each person the *right* community and tradition, which he or she is required to endeavor to find as part of the inherent moral obligation of self-discovery and self-actualization.

In short, community and tradition—and more specifically the right community and tradition—are necessary to individuality as conceived eudaimonistically, but are merely contingent within the understanding of classical liberalism. What is necessary to classical liberalism is the social contract that ends the "war of all against all" by establishing and preserving a social order consisting in protection of individuals' rights by consensual government and just resolution of conflict through impartial judicial decision. But this is not community, it is society-at-large—a very different thing. Society-at-large is necessarily impersonal association, whereas community is interpersonal association. What is referred to as the "legalism" and "formalism" of classical liberalism is its embrace of the impersonality of society-at-large as a governing ideal, and its attendant endeavor to perfect this impersonality by active depersonalization. We will argue that impersonality of large-scale social relations, and active depersonalization of them, are very different things. Impersonality of large-scale social relations is inevitable because the relations are of interutilization in which persons appear to one another merely as utilities. Although there are dangers in this, they can be ameliorated by the underlying knowledge that the utilities are in fact aspects of persons, in accordance with the Kantian imperative, "Never treat other persons as means merely, but always also as ends in themselves."[2]

But when social relations are deliberately depersonalized, then by the second part of the Marxian truth that human beings make history, and history makes human beings, individuals are induced to depersonalize themselves, finally in their very self-conceptions. When this has occurred, community is by definition impossible, for it consists in interpersonal relations. Our examination of classical liberalism's active depersonalization of relations in society-at-large, then, will be support for the case of communitarians against classical liberal individualism, namely that it fosters in individuals a self-conception that is incompatible with community. We also aim to show why community is necessary to self-actualizing individuality and will speak in exploratory fashion to the problem of strengthening community and reversing the depersonalizing effects of society-at-large.

Communitarians and traditionalists of course recognize the possibility of chosen community and tradition, but argue against it that choice is a weak bond, incapable of establishing and sustaining the strong allegiance that tradition and community require. In a characterization of American individualism, for example, Bellah et al. say: "No binding obligations and no wider social understanding justify a relationship. It exists only as the expression of the choices of the free selves who make it up. And should it no longer meet their needs, it must end."[3] These authors attribute our weakening ties of kinship, religious fellowship, and civic friendship to the liberal endeavor to found them upon choice, and commend relations that are "independent of the individual's will and can to a considerable extent be taken for granted."[4] In similar vein, Alasdair MacIntyre holds liberal voluntarism responsible for our "rootless cosmopolitanism" as it appears in individuals who "temporarily adopt the standpoint of a tradition and then exchange it for another, as one might wear first one costume and then another, or as one might act one part in one play and then a quite different part in a quite different play."[5]

But it will be evident that the attribution of dilettantism to chosen association is simplistic if we remind ourselves of some of history's many instances of chosen commitments that were lived out unwaveringly: the conversions of St. Paul and St. Augustine to Christianity, the conversion of Cardinal Newman to Roman Catholicism, the commitment of Socrates to philosophy, the commitments of Heloise and Abelard to one another, not to mention the commitments of countless immigrants to America. The simplistic explanation overlooks what few of us fail to recognize in our everyday experience, namely that there are choices, and choices. Some choices are made by persons who have no intention of being bound by unforeseen implications, which is to say they are not commitments. Some "choices" are made with almost no knowledge of the available alternatives, and therefore are not true choices. Some choices are made by persons who, as we say, "don't know their own minds."

I do not deny the prevalence of the dilettantism in respect to communities and traditions that is decried by MacIntyre, Bellah et al., and many others, but I think we cannot attribute it to individualistic voluntarism until we pose the question of the kind of individuals who are involved. And here we confront a disparity between classical liberal individualism and eudaimonistic individualism. For eudaimonistic individualism, individual self-actualization is inherently social. This is so because it manifests objective worth in the world which, as objective, is incomplete without recognition, appreciation, and utilization by appropriate others. Accordingly for every person there is a "natural community" comprising those others who recognize, appreciate, and can utilize his or her worth in their own self-actualizing enterprises. The obligation of the individual to relate to this community is identical with the inherent moral obligation of self-actualization; her choice of herself is her choice of this community; and the choice(s) must be true commitment(s) if it (they) is to fulfill her inherent moral obligation. The effect of this is to ground both choices in self-knowledge and to support the teaching of common sense that commitments by persons who "know their own minds" are trustworthy.

Eudaimonistically conceived, there is in the same way a "natural tradition" for every person and also a "natural meta-tradition." The self-directed life of any given person is necessarily a life of a particular kind. Such a person has predecessors in the general enterprise of self-directed living, and predecessors also in the particular chosen course of life. The former comprise his meta-tradition, and the latter his tradition. Therefore to "choose oneself" is inevitably to choose one's meta-tradition and one's tradition, and the moral imperatives to self-actualization and to identification with one's traditions are identical—they are the same thing viewed in different and complementary ways. Moreover the imperative to self-awarely recover and avail oneself of one's natural traditions are evident, for to grow and ultimately to excel in one's chosen course demands the acquisition of skills, tools, resources, and virtues that traditions gather, conserve, improve, and bequeath. This is equally the case with the tradition and the meta-tradition.

We have identified commitments to community and tradition with the commitment to self-actualization that is the basic moral imperative according to eudaimonism. But to be sure, self-knowledge is corrigible, and life-shaping choices are sometimes mistaken. The inalienability of the moral imperative entails that mistaken choices be rectified, and in the case of life-shaping choices such rectification inevitably involves some damage to self and others. Here as elsewhere, mistakes are costly. Our proposal is to minimize the damage by recognizing in the lives of individuals a period for experimentation in the interest of self-discovery. The appropriate period is adolescence, and it is in order to facilitate the developmental work just described that adolescence is termed a "moritorium" by Erik Erikson.[6] It is a period in which persons are not to be held to their promises. Here the experimental exchanges of perspectives, lifestyles, and traditions that MacIntyre disapproves are, in fact, appropriate and functional. But their function is to facilitate the growth of individuals toward committed living.

By contrast, classical liberalism endorses the freedom of individuals at the expense of committed living and is vulnerable to the charge of promoting dilettantism or "rootless cosmopolitanism." This case is made best by Michael Sandel in *Liberalism and the Limits of Justice*.[7] He argues that liberalism inculcates a conception of the self as independent of whatever interests, aims, and attachments it may have at any given time— "never identified by [its] aims but always capable of standing back to survey and assess and possibly to revise them."[8] What has happened is that freedom has been divorced from moral responsibility, stripping choice of any moral obligation save that of respecting others' rights. Choice is determined by individual preference, and preferences are private, subjective, and arbitrary. But matters stand differently according to eudaimonism, for which preferences are right and wrong according as they contribute to or impede the individual's moral work of actualizing his or her worth in the world. For liberalism, persons can change their allegiances with moral impunity. For eudaimonism, persons are morally obligated to discover and maintain the natural allegiances—the communities and traditions—that their self-actualization discloses.

Sandel contends that selves are political products, and it will be useful to look to both classical liberalism and eudaimonism on this important point. Speaking against liberalism's conception of the self as prior to the political association that it establishes by contract, Sandel says that "By putting the self beyond the reach of politics, it makes human agency an article of faith rather than an object of continuing attention and concern, a premise of politics rather than its precarious achievement."[9] Does liberalism "put the self beyond the reach of politics"? Clearly so in its depiction of an aboriginal and apolitical state of nature peopled by selves; but more importantly it does so also in its central principle of consensual government, for it bases express and tacit consent alike upon a rationality in persons that is presumed authoritative because it is presumed objective, which it cannot be if it is conditioned by politics. What shields the individual's rationality is the liberal conception of the self as, in Sandel's words, "antecedently given and finally fixed,"[10] and thus impervious to its contingent associations, including its political context.

The telling objection to this picture is the sociological recognition that selves are in the beginning social products. Thanks to the dependency of persons in the beginning of their lives, their rationality is the product of enculturation and is both social and political, embodying shared presuppositions and relations of power within the society.

The grievous consequence of treating the self as a datum, when in fact it is a developmental outcome, is that the conditions of its achievement are ignored. This is reflected in the neglect of the problems of the development of moral character by modern "rules morality." This same consequence attends liberalism's treatment of freedom as given, whereas for eudaimonism freedom is an achievement whose conditions must be, in Sandel's words, "an object of continuing attention and concern." In summary on this point: liberalism is a doctrine for fully formed and equipped individuals and has bordered on indifference to persons who are as yet less than such.

But it does not follow from the truth that selves in their beginning are sociopolitical products that this is what they must remain to the end. They will remain so if no other agency intervenes, but the novel agency that is available for intervention is the initiative and originality of the individual himself. In childhood it is unavailable because it is purely latent, but it becomes available with the birth of autonomy in adolescence. Whether to exercise this initiative or not is the choice of the individual; the force of habit and the comforts of familiarity work against it. At the same time the prospect of discovering new ground to stand upon and explore is a powerful attraction to the inherent adventurousness of adolescence. By exercise of the initiative one distances oneself one by one from the terms and associations of one's prior identity, holding them, so to speak, in suspension. The developmental purpose is to identify those merely contingent (because products of contingent enculturation) associations and identity-elements and learn to recognize the elements and associations that are essential to the life that is one's own to live.

Am I positing *something* apolitical in the individual? In a sense, yes; and to acknowledge that persons are in the beginning political products is not to agree that they are so wholly and without remainder. But the apolitical something that I am positing is nothing so rounded-out and finished as a self. It is in the beginning no more than certain potentialities that have remained until now latent and are unconditioned. Indeed, the adolescent only learns what they are experimentally, by trying out alternative aims and courses of conduct. Here is the beginning of self-discovery; but the self remains to be *made,* and the making is an interactive process between the individual and political society involving the agencies of both. We are, therefore, not committing the mistake of regarding the essential self as a *fait accompli* instead of a "precarious achievement"; but we are avoiding the mistake of supposing that the agency of the self's formation lies exclusively in political society.

To return to the beginning of this portion of our inquiry with what we have just arrived at: the life-shaping choices of individuals who are possessed of self-knowledge are reliable commitments—more reliable, indeed, than is thoughtless perpetuation of received tradition with its assigned commitments. The person in the latter condition is like the man who has married his childhood sweetheart without troubling to acquaint himself with other possibilities. At the next turn of a corner he may encounter a woman who shatters the thin shell of his equanimity and tumbles his world. But for the reasons identified by Sandel, self-knowledge has been neglected by liberalism, with the result that choices, being the expressions of preferences that are themselves arbitrary, have not been commitments. In this context it is unsurprising that community and tradition have been eroded.

The reader will notice that by our argument, strength of community and tradition are dependent upon strength of character in individuals as individuals. This runs directly counter to the contention by many communitarians that to manifest allegiance to community, individuals must diminish or extinguish their allegiance to themselves. But before proceeding with this issue and related ones it will be well to define "community."

To begin with, community in the meaning we employ is a form of association intermediate between the individual and society-at-large. The term "intermediate association" has qualitative as well as quantitative connotations for sociologists and social philosophers which can be expressed by saying that between the personal and the social lies the region of the interpersonal. In *I and Thou*,[11] for example, Martin Buber argued for the continuity of the personal and the interpersonal (the region of "I-Thou" relations), but the discontinuity between these two regions and "the social" by virtue of the impersonality of social ("I-It") relations. Social relations, understood as distinct from interpersonal relations, are relations of utilization in which persons appear to one another not as persons but as pragmatica (roles, offices, and the like). Buber recognized the necessity of "I-It" relations and did not propose (as some careless commentators have mistakenly supposed) that they be transformed into interpersonal relations.[12] (This latter is the explicit or implicit proposal of spokespersons for, for example, "political community" or the "global village.") Instead, he argued that neglect of intermediate association leaves individuals vulnerable to their own depersonalization under the powerful influence of impersonal society.

To identify community as interpersonal association is to say that within it persons interact with one another as whole persons. In society-at-large, by contrast, the bank teller is no more than a bank teller, the traffic policeman is but a blue uniform and hand signals. Interpersonal association does not mean, of course, that everything that is the person appears in each of his or her expressions, for that is clearly impossible. It means that everything that is the person is continuous with what appears in each expression and supportive of it. In Sartre's words a person "is a totality and not a collection."[13] This is the case when each of a person's expressions reflect one or another of her life-shaping choices, and her life-shaping choices are themselves complementary to one another and contributory in their distinctive ways to the individual's enterprise of self-actualization. Such integration, to be sure, is not a datum but a developmental outcome, and community is the matrix of its development. It contrasts with the fragmentation of persons into unrelated or conflicting personae by their life-shaping choices—everyday conduct condemned by professed religious and moral beliefs, vocation at cost to marriage and family, and so forth.

As a third characteristic, persons who compose a community are united by certain shared beliefs that are embodied in institutions and practices, and MacIntyre holds that this requires recognition of certain texts as canonical, though the list of such texts is open to addition and subtraction, and their interpretation is matter for ongoing debate.[14]

Fourth, the interpersonal relations of community are caring relations, where "caring" is understood as the most universalizable form of love (Aristotle's "civic friendship" is I think properly regarded as a form of it), and "love" is defined as willing the well-being of others for their sakes. From this it follows that community includes principles of mutual aid (Walzer)[15].

Fifth, Bellah et al. insist that within community, work has the sense of "calling,"[16] and I believe this is rightly included among definitive conditions of community because it is entailed by the definitive condition that community relations are relations among whole persons. For work-relations to be such, an individual's work in the work-a-day sense must be part of his or her larger work of self-actualization, and in this case it is intrinsically rewarding and self-fulfilling, which are the marks of "calling."

Finally, Walzer reminds his readers that community entails the distinction between members and nonmembers, together with recognizable marks of membership[17] (e.g., acceptance of the canonical texts as canonical).

With this working definition of community, we may now define a tradition as a community viewed longitudinally, extended over time, where the temporal extension is essential because present and anticipated future are continuous outgrowths of the past and cannot be understood without understanding the past, while at the same time the past is understood partly by the historically enacted future that it produced. Granted that all communities are traditions, and all traditions are communities, it remains useful to retain both terms for their difference in emphasis between relations viewed primarily longitudinally or primarily cross-sectionally.

Perhaps the most relentless criticism of individualism in the name of community comes from communitarians who place the "shared beliefs, shared values" condition of community uppermost. Supposing that it is possible for individuals to conduct their lives according to values that are not shared, then the creation or conservation of community will seem to require the rectification of this, whereas normative individualism endorses it, seemingly in defiance of community. The *locus classicus* of this conceived antagonism is Rousseau's political works, most notably his *Second Discourse* and *Social Contract*. Here Rousseau famously argues that to be good citizens, persons must be "denatured," by which he means that their original nature must be exchanged for a "second nature."[18] To effect this work is the function of the relentless civic education modeled by Rousseau on the quasi-military training of ancient Sparta. Civil association mandates the exchange of the natural freedom of individuals for what Rousseau holds to be its civil analogue in "a form of association . . . by which each one, being united with all, only obeys himself and remains as free as before."[19] To the question of how this is possible, Rousseau's famous answer is that it is accomplished through the reconstitution of individuals as identical instances of the General Will. The General Will is specified by Rousseau as "general in its objects as well as in its essence."[20] By general in its object Rousseau clearly means that it wills the good of all rather than the individual's good. But what of "general . . . in its essence"? This means that the will *in* each person is the will of all, and by implication that the good of all, as willed by each, is that good, not as each perceives it, but as all perceive it. In Durkheim's words the General Will "is a single, indivisible soul which moves all the parts in the same direction by depriving them, to the same degree, of all independent movement."[21] This draws Ortega y Gasset's observation, "There is no such collective soul, if by soul is meant—and here it can mean nothing else—something that is capable of being the responsible subject of its acts . . ."[22]

There are many reasons why Rousseau's "denaturing" program finds little support today in behalf of society-at-large, prominent among them being the unacceptability of Rousseau's rigorous indoctrination of children and youth as the pattern of education in a free society. But it has found a home among communitarians, most of whom hold that priority for the collective good calls for relinquishment by individuals of their pursuit of individual goods. And this conception of the collective good is unerringly recognized by normative individualists as their adversary.

When such individualists as Kierkegaard and Nietzsche castigate "the crowd," and "the herd" they are often mistakenly thought to be antagonistic to all forms of association. Likewise for Emerson, when he says "Society everywhere is in conspiracy against the manhood of every one of its members."[23] But that Emerson is not attacking association of every kind is clear when he subsequently says, "Cleave to your companions; I will seek my own."[24] For Emerson as for Nietzsche and Kierkegaard, our true companions are persons whose distinctive worth we recognize and appreciate, and who recognize and appreciate ours. These normative individualists attack forms of association that are built upon the suppression or extinction of individuality, but endorse forms of association that support and utilize the distinctivenesses of associates. Rousseau's prescribed form of association together with conceptions of community that are modeled upon it epitomize the first category.

To see that normative individuality does not preclude community by precluding shared values and beliefs, it is necessary to recognize that values and beliefs are formulated at different levels of abstraction. Shared beliefs and values of sufficient generality are entirely compatible with diverse lifestyles. To cite the eudaimonistic case, supposing that everyone in our community agrees to place very high value upon human "flourishing"—the agreement is not jeopardized if the course of life through which flourishing is achieved is different for every individual. To fail to distinguish levels of abstraction with respect to values and beliefs is to fall into what might be termed vertical category mistakes. A simpleminded example is the person who reads Thoreau's *Walden* as his recommendation to all persons to live for two years in a cabin in the woods. Thoreau is indeed recommending something to all persons, namely self-knowledge, and he descends a step toward increased concreteness by formulating universalizable elements of a strategy for the acquisition of self-knowledge; but how these are best implemented will vary widely among individuals.

Communitarians who on the Rousseauvian model call for the extinction of individuated values in the creation of a "second (communal) nature" are attempting by fiat to dispense with the never-ending work that is community's to do, namely the *harmonization* of diversity, including diversity of values-identifications by individuals. It is often held that as organized diversity, community is restricted to a merely instrumental place in the lives of individuals (serving their ends as individuals, where the ends and the individuality antedate community and are independent of it) and cannot occupy a constitutive place in their self-conceptions. But the organized diversity of community is recognizably part of the self-conception of individuals who understand individuality itself—their own and others'—as organized diversity. Personal integrity denotes this organized diversity in eudaimonism's conception of individuality.

Perhaps the charge against individualism that most clearly finds concensus among communitarians is that it promotes unmitigated competition, thereby fostering predatory feelings and precluding caring feelings. When primary goods are in short supply, and individuals are defined in terms of their preferences for these goods, then competitiveness has prominence in their self-conceptions. It is particularly noteworthy that individuality conceived in this way has no intrinsic limits or counterbalances to its competitiveness. Persons are MacPherson's "infinite utilities maximizers"[25]—and whatever constraints or counterbalances are to be brought to bear must be imposed upon individuals externally. A society of such individuals is described by Philip Slater as "a jungle of competing egos," and by Carol Gilligan as a "contest of selfishnesses," whereas Christopher Lasch refers to it as a thinly disguised Hobbesean "war of all against all."[26]

In chapter 1 we sought to show that an absence of internal constraints on material acquisitiveness is indeed characteristic of the self-conception promoted by classical liberalism. We must now see that the eudaimonistic self-conception, by contrast, is importantly self-constrained.

Under the tutelage of *sophrosune*, Aristotle identifies the primary goal of moral education as learning to desire the right things in the right amount. The right things are those that constitute utilities to the individual in his or her self-actualization. This marks a qualitative constraint on each individual's desires. The person who knows himself will not desire those things that are of kinds that his self-actualization cannot utilize; he does not desire them because he recognizes that his possession of them will be distracting to him, while at the same time they hold prospect of helping appropriate others. The "in the right amount" constraint embodies the recognition, noted in chapter 4, that in respect to most goods, too much can be as debilitating as too little. Both of these internal constraints derive from self-knowledge, whereas the omnivorous desires that pursue all goods in ever-increasing amounts attest to the absence of self-knowledge. For such a life we might employ the image of many cats with their tails tied together, their movement not a direction but a frenzy.

The one class of goods of which too much cannot be had is that of the virtues of character, but these are goods of unlimited supply; no amount of them possessed by any number of persons lessens the supply for others. Moreover they are good not just for their possessors but likewise for those with whom their possessor associates, thus the honesty or justice of a person benefits those who relate to her. (Notice that here persons are conceived as inclusive of one another, not exclusively as for example in the paradigmatic thesis of Locke. An exclusive self-conception can accommodate only instrumental community, whereas an inclusive self-conception can include community within itself as con-stitutive community.) For these reasons competition among persons in respect to acquisition of moral virtues is to the detriment of none and the benefit of all. Here the evils of the "war of all against all" are absent. The virtuous society is a collective good that knits together, rather than circumventing, the goods of individuals.

Yet another frequent charge against individualism is that it conduces to the privatization of interests at the expense of public interests (Tocque-ville, *Democracy in America*),[27] and to self-preoccupation amounting to narcissism (Christopher Lasch, *The Culture of Narcissism*).[28]

Tocqueville, whose genius at analyzing the democracy he observed in the United States is evident on every page, had the courage to perpetu-ally risk contradiction in his study of that complex phenomenon. An example of this is his insistent condemnation of *individualisme*, coupled with his resolute support of *independance individuelle*. His repeated prox-imity to contradiction in this matter he fully recognized, yet in the end managed to avoid. Though it is often hidden beneath his description and analysis of what he witnesses in the United States, Tocqueville's allegiance is to liberty, pluralism, and *independance individuelle*, against what he regards as the immanent dangers of centralization, despotism, and *individualisme*. What he perceives in the form of *individualisme* is a "calm and considered feeling which disposes each citizen to isolate himself from the mass of his fellows and withdraw into the circle of family and friends; with this little society formed to his taste, he gladly leaves the greater society to look after itself."[29] As we sought to exhibit an intimate connection between classical liberal individualism and the ambition of material gain in chapter 1, so Tocqueville perceives this same ambition as fueling *individualisme:* the "democratic taste for mate-rial well-being," he wrote in a draft of *Democracy in America*, "leads men to become absorbed in its pursuit or enjoyment."[30]

The resulting "habit" of not concerning oneself with anything that is common business is the "abandon[ment of] this care to the sole, clearly visible representative of common interests, which is the government."[31] It leads to increasingly centralized and more powerful government, which further discourages private efforts in a cycle of reinforcement that, if unchecked, will ultimately end in total "individual servitude."[32]

Yet Tocqueville regards the situation as rectifiable. It is so because *individualisme* is a misdirected *independance individuelle* that has been turned in upon itself by unconstrained material acquisitiveness. Of it-self, *independance individuelle* develops from "instinctual" *egoisme* to social interest through what Tocqueville variously called *egoisme intelligent* or *interet bien entendu*. In the face of prevailing seductions into *individualisme*, and most notably democracy's proffered opportunity of endless material gain, Tocqueville proposed to support the development of *independance individuelle* by encouraging the formation of communities, or *corps secondaires*. He believed that community was the context in which the ultimate identity of the good of the individual and the good of society could be recognized. In these tenets he stands closer to eudaimonistic individualism than to either classical liberal individualism or communitarianism.

In his widely read and discussed *The Culture of Narcissism*, Christopher Lasch contends that "the culture of competitive individualism" is dying, as attested by its deterioration into an approximation of a Hobbesian war of all against all, while at the same time the pursuit of happiness has devolved into "the dead end of a narcissistic preoccupation with the self."[33] Emblematic of the latter, according to Lasch, are psychology and psychotherapy, which both reflect and cultivate a self-preoccupation that has socially destructive consequences.

Earlier we proposed that critics of "individualism" are often found to use the term indiscriminately in apparent failure to notice important differences among various doctrines to which the term is applied, and this is particularly evident in Lasch. In a moment I will undertake to show that eudaimonistic individualism cannot reasonably be held to contain in itself the seed of narcissism, but neither, I think, can classical liberalism, which by its objectivizing and depersonalizing propensities (which we shall consider shortly) has had little tolerance for self-preoccupation. Indeed, we have sought to show that these propensities, together with the subjective/objective bifurcation upon which they are based, have had the debilitating consequence of rendering self-knowledge a dubious, if not a discredited enterprise. It is debilitating because, in the matter of persons' choices of their courses of life (including their traditions and communities), rightness is not decided by the courses of life described independently, but by the relationship between courses of life and persons. MacIntyre's depiction in *Whose Justice? Which Rationality?*[34] of the dilemma of relativism among traditions, for example, is only convincing because he, like the liberalism he attacks, ignores the function of self-knowledge. When self-knowledge is ignored, competing traditions are left to determine in themselves which among them most deserves human allegiance—and this they cannot do, for as MacIntyre shows, none of them affords access to independent truth. What rightly decides allegiance is the relationship between tradition and individual, and differences among traditions and among individuals are such that "right relationship" will not select the same tradition for all persons.

Eudaimonism attributes great importance to self-knowledge, not as an end in itself, but as instrumental to worthy living in the world. One's aim is to actualize objective value, and self-knowledge provides the answer to the question, "Which values are mine to actualize?" Narcissism is absorption in the self to the exclusion of the world, and a tendency to it is to be found in the preoccupation of second-rate romantic individualism with the cultivation of subjective sensibilities: a sunset is occasion for refinement of aesthetic discrimination; the good is occasion for enjoyment of feelings of moral approbation; evil is occasion for enjoyment of feelings of moral disapprobation; nature is occasion to inventory one's quasi-religious feelings, especially awe in the presence of the sublime, and reverence for the natural order. Such self-preoccupation drew from Carlyle a cold-water dousing: "Hang your sensibilities! Stop your snivelling complaints, and your equally snivelling raptures! Leave off your general emotional tomfoolerly, and get to WORK like men."[35]

Narcissism is a particularly egregious form of arrested development. As surely as human beings undergo development in their life-course, they are subject to developmental arrest at every stage, but narcissism is quite certainly pathology from eudaimonism's viewpoint no less than Lasch's. However, Lasch's proffered cure—renunciation of individualism—is the renunciation of the enterprise of self-knowledge which is the foundation of every person's moral responsibility of actualizing his or her potential worth in the community.

The fact that fulfillment of this basic moral responsibility rests in the first instance on individuals' initiatives gives eudaimonism an important plot of common ground with the liberal individualism from which we have on many points been concerned to distinguish it. The exercise of this initiative requires the protection of negative rights, that is, rights against unwarranted interference. In behalf of liberal individualism, Ronald Dworkin succeeds in demonstrating that a society in which no conception of the good is mandated, and disagreement about the character of the good life is accepted, is obliged to respect certain individual rights.[36] The difference is that for eudaimonism these rights, together with the liberties they protect, are conceived as instrumental goods, serving moral responsibility, not intrinsic goods that are logically prior to moral responsibility. Entailments of this distinction have been studied in the preceding chapter, but may be summarized here. The end of worthy, value-productive living means that the liberty to be incorporated is not formal liberty merely, but effective liberty. Accordingly basic human rights include "positive" rights as well as "negative." At the same time the indiscriminate proliferation of positive rights is curtailed by the limitations inherent in the individual responsibilities that rights serve.

Thus far in this chapter we have sought to show that eudaimonistic individualism is antagonistic neither to community nor to tradition, but on the contrary entails these two kinds of allegiances by individuals as constitutive of their individuality. But the individuality of which it is constitutive is a developmental outcome, not an *ab initio* given, and accordingly the tradition and community that are among its constituents are not the received tradition and community of one's birth (though they may be these as they have subsequently been chosen). Eudaimonistic individuality precludes the legislation of individuals' courses of life by tradition and community, either directly or by systematic restriction of possibilities. It endorses a society encompassing an extensive array of diverse communities among which individuals may choose, and a meta-tradition encompassing diverse traditions.

Is our country not just such a setting by virtue of its diversity of ethnic heritages and communities, its diversity of religions, its diversity of regional patterns of life, of family practices? But a moment's reflection yields a negative answer. The appropriate meta-tradition and society do not exist, for this diversity is not offered as possibilities for the choice of individuals in their self-directed living. On the contrary, most traditions and communities jealously try to preserve themselves by disparaging rivals and conditioning their young to lifelong fidelity. In this situation the developmental work of exploration toward self-discovery goes undone; and although defections are common enough, self-knowledge is lacking, and their motivation is largely negative—*against* the felt constraints of the enculturated pattern, rather than *for* the pattern (with its own constraints) that holds genuine prospect of self-fulfillment.

At the beginning of this chapter we spoke of a distinction between the inevitable impersonality of relations in society-at-large, and the active depersonalization of those relations. By "impersonal relations" we refer to relations among persons who appear to one another not as persons, that is, unified totalities that are ends in themselves, but rather as compartmented roles, offices, skills, and so forth. Relations in society-at-large are impersonal because they are utility relations, others appearing to each in but the aspect corresponding to the needs of each, and not for what they are in themselves. That we appear in this way to one another is dictated by the utility-relation, which will be compromised otherwise. The traffic policeman under whose direction we safely cross the street is an organization of roles, faculties, and interests, but if, for example, his apprehensions over his wife's suspected love affair, or his troubles with the Internal Revenue Service, intrude upon his direction of traffic, the utility relation is diminished.

Impersonal relations are a convenience whose necessity is the necessity of convenience. By contrast depersonalized relations are a norm that attacks the personhood of those engaging in them. According to Kant's imperative, we are obliged to regard those with whom we interact impersonally as persons nonetheless; but by depersonalization we are invited to regard those with whom we interact as nonpersons, and this progressively infects their, and our, self-conceptions. It does so, first, because depersonalization is at odds with the moral work of self-integration and the virtue of integrity. It comes easier to persons who are not integrated, and it encourages the compartmentalization of the self into unrelated roles. (Lately we hear mounting calls for "integrity" in business and government, for example, but what is meant is the "my station and its duties" rules-compliance of the businessman qua businessman and the office-holder qua office-holder. Integrity cannot be limited to a role, in disregard of the integration of the multiple roles of the individual. A compartmented integrity is a contradiction.)

But depersonalization infects self-conceptions most seriously in the early stages of the development of the individual, when the autonomous self is highly tentative and vulnerable and perceives itself as alone. In this condition the weight of depersonalized society thrown against the individual is an unequal contest. At the level of intermediate, interpersonal association, community can restore balance, but community itself requires in individuals a measure of the self-knowledge and self-direction that it serves to support. And depersonalization, by eroding the foundation of individuation, attacks the foundation of community. This recognition underlies Robert Nisbet's contention that "it is the liberal concentration upon the individual, rather than upon the associations in which the individual exists, that serves, paradoxical as it may seem, to itensify the processes that lead straight to increased governmental power."[37] The most fateful effect of early liberal individualism, according to Nisbet, was the breakdown of the traditional intermediate associations of patriarchal kinship, class, gild, and village community. Such associations were termed by Hobbes "worms in the bowels of the state."[38] Nisbet contends that "to weaken [intermediate associations] is to convert a culture into an atomized mass," and in this condition "the normal plurality of authorities and functions in society must be supplanted by a unity of authority and function arising from the monistic state."[39]

Can this be descriptive of the condition of people in the United States, who were recognized as long ago as Tocqueville to be compulsive "joiners," and are known today worldwide as such? We are joiners indeed, but on this score judgments by Tocqueville, as by Bellah, MacIntyre, and others, are telling. Identifying ourselves independently of our associations at bottom, or essentially, leaves us in only contingent relation to such subsequent associations as we form, and obstructs our self-identification *as* our associations. In eudaimonistic perspective, the piece of work that each individual is has its associations, that is, its community and tradition. They represent the natural line of growth of the self from interests that appeared initially (in self-discovery) to be its own exclusively, to inclusive interests, that is, from the exclusively conceived self of classical liberalism to the inclusive self of eudaimonism. This line of development is severed by the depersonalizing strategies of classical liberalism, which we shall now consider.

Classical liberalism began by conceiving of "personality" as partiality—bias in behalf of the self understood exclusively—and sought the advantages of objectivity of judgment through the depersonalization of judgment and judges. Locke's famous contention is that what above all distinguishes civil association from the state of nature is the disinterested judgment of cases of conflict by impartial judges.[40] This was extrapolated into a depersonalizing ideal on the supposition that objective truth appears identically to the rationality in all human beings, when such rationality is cleansed of coloration by "personality."

The principal depersonalizing devices of classical liberalism to be considered here are formalism, legalism, and technicism, or the "sovereignty of technique."

What is referred to as the "formalism" of classical liberalism is its practice of concerning itself with the definition of persons in lieu of their substance. It is this practice that causes liberalism to transform various hard-won developmental outcomes—such as freedom, individuality, rights—into postulates. As Michael Sandel observed in our previous citations, this is to take these matters as "article(s) of faith" rather than as "object(s) of continuing concern and attention." Defining them into human beings eliminates the problem of discovering their developmental conditions. But this problem is the cornerstone of any effort to generalize the opportunity—the effective opportunity, not the merely formal opportunity—of worthy, self-directed living. From its neglect of this problem it follows that classical liberalism serves to protect persons who already possess effective freedom, individuality, and rights, to the neglect of those who do not.

What is here meant by "legalism" is not just the reliance of a polity upon law, but the transformation of society and individuals into their reflections in the eyes of the law. Where legalism in modern life has had its most powerful depersonalizing effects is in the domain of moral theory and moral conduct. As we have had occasion to observe previously, the dominant modern mode of moral theory is the quasi-legal mode of formulating rules of conduct, and the dominant modern understanding of moral conduct is the quasi-legal mode of obedience to the rules that appertain to particular situations. As Edmund Pincoffs observes, the foundation of the modern mode is the "Hobbesian truism"[41] that in the absence of recognized rules and generally rule-abiding conduct, the lives of persons are unbearable. This sets morality together with law as institutions existing for the preservation of social order. If we recognize that the paramount interest of moral theory from classical Greece and Rome to modernity was the development of moral character, we are in a position to perceive that, by contrast, modern morality in its predominant form ignores the development of moral character other than that which is required to secure obedience to rules. This is the depersonalization of moral theory and moral conduct to which we refer.

The minimalist position of modern morality in respect to the development of moral character is a direct consequence of legalism. The interest of preserving social order requires the observance by (almost) everyone of rules that are understood and acknowledged by (almost) everyone. For this to be the case, the rules must be very simple and straightforward, and acting in accordance with them must require very little in the way of developed moral character. If they require very much in the way of developed moral character, then persons in whom such development is lacking will be unable to act according to the rules. The modern way of handling the occasional cases of persons who demand more of themselves than the rules require is by regarding such persons as "saints" or "heroes," and their conduct as "supererogatory."[42]

Highly influential rules-moralities have been generated from such principles as Hobbes's natural right to self-preservation, Locke's natural rights to life, liberty, and property, Kant's categorical imperative,

Bentham's "greatest happiness" principle, and Rawls's two principles of justice. By contrast to the derivative rules that govern various moral situations, the principles themselves are far from simple, especially in respect to their derivation and to the claims of authority that attend them. But in the prevailing belief, these are matters for philosophers and need not unsettle rule-abiding conduct.

In the rules-morality framework, when persons in a given moral situation act according to the governing rule, they act identically, and this feature is formulated as the "universalizability" requirement of moral conduct: the morally right act for me in any given moral circumstances would be right for any person in relevantly similar circumstances. The universalizability criterion is designed to thwart the native partiality of persons to themselves. But it has the additional effect of precluding from consideration objective differences among persons in levels of moral development. As a skilled swimmer can accomplish a deepwater rescue that a novice cannot, a morally more developed individual can be (morally) effective in some types of situations that cannot be ameliorated by individuals of lesser development. Modern rules morality cannot demand more of any of us that everyone can be expected to comply with, but for classical morality greater moral responsibility attends greater moral development—in a phrase, *noblesse oblige*. Where we are morally responsible, we are responsible to do our best, and the best of the morally more developed person is better than the best of the person of lesser development. Because the obligation of continued moral development applies to all persons at every level of achieved development, there is no room for the populist disclaimer that some few are "born heroes," whereas little should be expected of the rest of us.

In summary: the development of moral character is the development of personality and produces not uniformity but individuation. A developing person makes moral judgments according to different standards at different stages of his or her development. As noted above with the analogy of the swimmer, persons at different stages of moral development have different moral obligations. Moreover persons at the same stage of moral development will differ in their moral judgments of identical situations by virtue of their respective identification with different values, where "identification" means the personal commitment to actualize, defend, and conserve those values.

How, then, is it possible to achieve the agreement in moral judgments that social existence requires? In the first place, while persons at different stages of moral development have differing moral obligations, they nevertheless share some moral obligations, namely those that are codified by moral minimalism (and in many cases enacted into law): "Do not lie"; "Do not steal"; "Do not commit murder"; "Keep your promises"; and so forth. Second, they are agreed on the moral responsibility of all persons for continuous moral development. This entails respect for moral judgments different from one's own by persons at different levels of development. And finally, it entails a perspectivism that recognizes in every situation a variety of values-actualizing possibilities, with responsibilities apportioned according to the values-identifications of different individuals. It is the work of community to harmonize these diverse values-identifications on the Platonic presupposition of the inherent congeniality of aspects of the good; and it is the responsibility of individuals to recognize varieties of value and to respect both diverse values-identifications and different stages of moral development. The pluralism indicated here is nevertheless a pluralism in the matter of values and can agree in any situation upon the objective of maximizing the realization of compossible values that the situation affords.

The reduction to uniformity that is accomplished by legalism does not undertake this work but attempts to circumvent it by uniformity of standards the acceptance of which undermines the moral development of individuals and results in moral minimalism. Minimalist morality is a cramped room with a low ceiling and not much of a view. It is therefore not surprising that in modernity human aspirations have fled the confines of morality for the apparently limitless horizons afforded, for example, by the pursuit of scientific truth and the pursuit of material gain. I think we must recognize the quests for truth and for material gain as powerful innate human incentives. The mission of a contemporary eudaimonism is to restore the incentive to moral growth to its rightful place beside them.

Connection of the "sovereignty of technique," not with classical liberalism, but with the beginnings of modernity, has been insightfully delineated by Michael Oakeshott in his essay "Rationalism in Politics." But its intrinsic connection with classical liberalism will be established by recognizing that liberalism's "rules morality" is the sovereignty of technique in moral thought and moral life.

In Oakeshott's historical analysis, Machiavelli promotes the sovereignty of technique in the case of the princes to whom he offers advice, but it is Francis Bacon and Rene Descartes who together set technique on course for comprehensive sovereignty.

Briefly, technique is a set of rules that can be precisely formulated and learned by heart, and the sovereignty of technique rests on the supposition that the acquisition of knowledge, as well as its practical application, are entirely the province of technique. The supposition is mistaken, Oakeshott argues, because it ignores the indispensable kind of knowledge that is available only through the development of the character and understanding of the knower in the conduct of a practice.

What admirably suited the claims of sovereignty of technique to the rise of modernity is the supposition by persons who were seizing the new opportunities that they were casting off tradition and beginning afresh. They were, in Bacon's phrase, the "new men," to whom the past was nothing more than a repository of errors and follies (Bacon's "Idols") that were henceforth to be avoided. Lacking the understandings that only come through long training and service in a traditional practice, they were in need of a manual of instruction, a book—or in Oakeshott's term, "a crib."[43] As Bacon put it, "There remains but one course for the recovery of a sound and healthy condition—namely that the entire work of understanding be commenced afresh, and the mind itself be from the very outset not left to take its own course, but guided at every step."[44] The starting-point according to Bacon was the experience before every person's eyes, with a technique for analyzing and organizing it; for Descartes it was methodical doubt leading to indubitable truth, followed by deductive method arriving at certain knowledge of God and the world; for Locke it was the combination of deduction from self-evident truths in the moral sphere, and inductive arrival at probable truths in politics.

Depersonalization attends the sovereignty of technique under the norm of uniformity. Every person who learns and applies a technique does so (ideally) identically. Not only does what each person bring to the technique in terms of prior experience and developed character not count, it counts against him or her as part of the past that is a record of follies and errors that must be left behind. Moreover the supposition in which lay the great hope for technique—that whoever applies it arrives at identical results—means that no relevant development of character occurs through practice in the technique (though to be sure one learns to apply the technique well rather than badly), for character-development is a variable, and relevant character-development would produce relevantly different results. Protection for the doctrine of identical results has been afforded by the corollary conviction that differences of result are the products of "epistemic error."

Such was the perceived promise of technique that, as Oakeshott describes, modernity sped forward on the crest of its wave. Here we will confine ourselves to notice of three key outcomes. One of them is the previously considered transformation of moral theory and moral practice by the sovereignty of technique. It is particularly significant because it eliminated the resistance to depersonalization that was to be expected above all from moral theory in the classical mode, that is, as what we have termed morality of character.

Another is the transformation of philosophy by the sovereignty of technique, as it issued eventually in the Anglo-American sovereignty of the techniques of linguistic analysis beginning with G. E. Moore's *Principia Ethica* in 1903 and extending to mid-twentieth century. It was attended by the disparagement of the history and tradition of philosophy, in support of the claim by analytic philosophers to be the "new men" who set the discipline for the first time on a path leading to genuine results. The special significance here stems from the traditional definition of philosophy as love of wisdom. Such is the disparity between wisdom and technique that the dominance of analytic philosophy was strikingly attended by the disappearance of the term "wisdom" from the vocabularies of philosophers. Only now is it reappearing at the threshold, blinking its eyes like a child emerging from a dark room.

Bureaucracy represents the sovereignty of technique in organizational structure and management. Echoing MacIntyre and others, Bellah et al. observe that "the bureaucratic organization of the business corporation has been the dominant force in this century."[45] Clearly its influence has been pervasive, resulting in the bureaucratization of government and public administration, of trade unions, of the public school system, of universities, of special interest groups, of charities, of private schools, golf clubs, Kiwanis International, Lions Clubs, and perhaps even the family, in what has been aptly termed "organizational America."[46]

The irresistible attraction in bureaucratic organization and management, of course, is efficiency in production through effective management of means. Regarding the means that workers and managers alike represent, bureaucracy achieves efficiency by transforming them into tools of production through depersonalization. It is of the essence of bureaucratic organization that interactions are among roles and offices and not among persons. In his classical formulation, Max Weber's images are unmistakable. He says, for example, that bureaucratized law and public administration are "technically" superior to other forms, as "machine production is superior to non-mechanical methods."[47] He refers to bureaucracy as the "canonization of the abstractly imper-sonal."[48] And he argues that administrative efficiency, "with its appropri-ateness for capitalism," is "the more fully realized the more bureaucracy 'depersonalizes' itself, i.e., the more completely it succeeds in achieving the exclusion of love, hatred, and every personal, especially irrational and incalculable, feeling from the execution of official tasks."[49]

It may at first sight seem counterproductive that by contriving to exclude "every personal . . . feeling" bureaucracy excludes, for example, workers' love of the work and their pride in and loyalty to the organiza-tion. But this is "rationalized" (in a favored bureaucratic term) by a presupposition that is implicit in Weber's phrase "its appropriateness for capitalism." The underlying presupposition is that workers work only for their pay; and this presupposition is employed by management to justify its dedication exclusively to profit: profitable businesses give workers more of what they want. The consequent managerial philoso-phy has been crisply summarized by management theorist Neil W. Chamberlain:

Employees are being paid to produce, not to make themselves into better people. Corporations are purchasing employee time to make a return on it, not investing in employees to enrich their lives. Employees are human capital, and when capital is hired or leased, the objective is not to embellish it for its own sake but to use it for financial advantage.[50]

It is stating the obvious to say that philosophies of management of this type serve utterly to preclude the sense of community in their organizations. (They are opposed to every feature of the definition of community offered earlier.) A notable turn of the past decade is marked by the growing propensity to call into question the bureaucratic prem-ise that a sense of community in product-oriented organizations is coun-terproductive. Moreover just now two veteran management scholars, William G. Scott and David K. Hart, are forcefully arguing that the health of American organizations depends upon recovery by workers of the moral integrity that has been supposed by management to compro-mise organizational loyalty.[51] (Organizational loyalty has become an intense concern of management in the past two decades for reasons that will be considered in the next chapter.)

Our own contribution to this turn is reserved to the concluding chapter, in which we shall offer a eudaimonistic theory of organizational structure and management with the claim that it combines community and personal integrity with optimal productivity. Here, our contention is that bureaucratic organization violates the foundational ethical principle that persons must never be treated as means merely, but always also as ends in themselves.

To treat a person as an end in herself is at minimum to respect her moral responsibility for integrating the distinguishable aspects of her life into a coherent development. By exacting depersonalization in the workplace, bureaucratic management actively obstructs the exercise on the part of employees of their self-integrative responsibility. In so doing, it attacks the core of their personhood—their integrity—without which their personhood decomposes into unrelated faculties, desires, roles, and life-shaping choices. In an integrated life, faculties, desires, roles, and life-shaping choices complement one another and together contribute to realization of the image of fulfilled personhood that guides the individual's development. In this condition a person's every act is backed up by his or her total personhood. It is the responsibility of organizations and managers to respect this total personhood. It is not their responsibility to actively further it; on the contrary, to do so would be to disrespect the personhood of workers by attempting to usurp their self-responsibility. But it is the responsibility of organizations and managers to define themselves and their functions in ways that do not obstruct, but rather facilitate, workers' self-integrations. Depersonalization demands that what the work personally means to workers and managers alike, because this implicates other dimensions of their lives, be excluded from the workplace, whereas integrity forbids such "partitioning" of the self.

In this chapter we have sought to show that current attacks upon "individualism" by communitarians and traditionalists are in good part scattergun broadsides that fail to distinguish important differences among "individualisms." In particular, eudaimonistic individualism is hostile neither to community nor to tradition, but entails both. As the individual who manifests objective values is significantly unfulfilled without persons who appreciate and utilize those values, so the community deteriorates into meaningless usages without continuous revitalization by infusion of individual initiatives.

Normative individuation requires a supportive context. To reestablish the foundations of normative individuality in self-knowledge, self-identification, and self-responsibility, it is imperative to strengthen the "intermediate associations" that buffer individuals against the conditioning effects of impersonal association-at-large. In the next chapter we will address the questions of appropriate organizational structure and management. Here, we will close with an illustration of how community can be re-equipped to buffer individuals against depersonalization and encourage their moral growth as individuals.

The example to be offered directly obstructs the depersonalization through "legalism" that was considered earlier. It works to make legal recourse in cases of conflict a last resort by introducing a means of resolution *in situ*, that is, in the context in which the disputes arise. I am referring to San Francisco's Community Boards, begun in 1977 and now emulated in a dozen other cities.

Community Boards trains volunteers in case development, conciliation, outreach, follow-up, and related skills. Currently residents of twenty San Francisco neighborhoods are resolving conflicts through voluntary agreements reached at Community Boards panel hearings. Problems include harrassment, vandalism, property damage, theft, landlord-tenant disputes, family disputes, consumer grievances, and organizational conflicts. According to Community Boards founder and director, Raymond Schonholtz, "We are finding that in addition to conflict resolution, this work has a strong neighborhood-building aspect to it, and responds to people's interest in performing significant civic work at the neighborhood level."[52]

Community Boards supports the enlargement of the sympathetic identifications of individuals by rendering their extended sympathies efficacious. At the same time it buffers disputants from the depersonalizing effects of litigation that are especially pronounced when courts of law are—as they have increasingly become—the first resort. The closed doors of the courtroom effectively symbolize the radical disparity between the world in which the dispute occurred and the world in which it is legally resolved. When two contending neighbors, for example, decide to go to court, they face the immediate problem that the court will not recognize their dispute as they perceive it. The first purpose for which they must engage lawyers is to translate their conflict into terms acceptable to the court. But as expressed in the alien language of the law, the conflict is no longer recognizable by the disputants as theirs. In consequence, the forthcoming judicial decision is no resolution to the minds of the disputants; it returns them to their community (or their separate communities) bewildered, and often no less aggrieved than before. That this is no concern of the law is again symbolized by the closing of the courtroom doors at the conclusion of the case.

Similar dissatisfactions with legal resolution of conflicts (including, of course, their cost) are leading American businesses to first utilize the services of professional mediators. In *Mediate, Don't Litigate,* Peter Lovenheim reports that more than four hundred large corporations have signed agreements committing them to first try mediation before pursuing litigation in cases of dispute with other companies that have signed the agreement.[53] This, too, is an example of functioning "intermediate association."

There can be no doubt of the need for law and for judicial means for resolving conflict, nor can the impersonal proceedings of the courtroom be personalized, for to do so would destroy the efficacy of judicial settlement in its necessary status as the last resort. The function of Community Boards is not to undermine the law, but to prevent the reflexive effect of "legalism" by which the power of the law depersonalizes individuals in their own self-conceptions. But as we have seen, depersonalization works in multiple ways. The Community Boards example is offered to show how one of the ways depersonalization works can be countered. The strengthened community that normative individuality requires is to be sought by designing comparable instruments of community to counter each of the reflexive avenues of depersonalization.

Summarizing the theses of this chapter: eudaimonistic individualism is hostile neither to community nor to tradition, but is inherently connected to both. Unlike classical liberalism, which renders association contingent by conceiving of the individual as essentially independent of his or her associations, eudaimonism invests the individual's community-identification and tradition-identification with the same moral necessity that attends the individual's work of self-actualization. But to paraphrase Emerson, communities and traditions are the lengthened shadows of the individuals who comprise them; they exist, not to extinguish the individualities of their constituents, but to actualize the social implications of those individualities, thereby contributing to individuals' fulfillment.

CHAPTER SEVEN

Good Government

The theory of good government to be offered in this chapter is revisionist Platonism. I will argue that while *The Republic* contains a central error giving rise to a number of other errors, it remains the eudaimonistic paradigm of good government and good organizational management and the best model for these today. On the face of it it is hardly surprising that a book in eudaimonist political theory should find its paradigm in Plato, a father of the school. In Dewey's words,

No one could better express than did he the fact that a society is stably organized when each individual is doing that for which he has aptitude by nature in such a way as to be useful to others (or to contribute to the whole to which he belongs); and that it is the business of education to discover these aptitudes and progressively to train them for social use.[1]

But *The Republic* is presently in disesteem as the consequence of charges against it of authoritarianism and totalitarianism. I hope to show that they reflect mistakes of interpretation, to which some plausibility is lent by Plato's error. We will identify the error and propose a rectification that, I think, preserves the Platonic spirit, applying what we arrive at to current organizational management (including state government) and management theory. Then we will consider a classical liberal model of good government in the endeavor to disclose within it the telling deficiency that revisionist Platonism makes good.

But to clear the way it is first necessary to overturn the anarchistic

argument that advocacy of autonomy in individuals precludes all authority to forms of government external to individuals. For if this argument
were sound, eudaimonism would be political anarchism, and the no-
tions of good state government and good organizational management
would be contradictions in terms.

A well-known example of the argument is Robert Paul Wolff's contention that

> if all men have a continuing obligation to achieve the highest degree of auton-
> omy possible, then there would appear to be no state whose subjects have an
> obligation to obey its commands. Hence, the concept of a de jure legitimate
> state would appear to be vacuous, and philosophical anarchism would seem to
> be the only reasonable political belief for an enlightened man.[2]

The defect in this is that Wolff equates the obligation to achieve
autonomy with the achievement of it. The legitimacy of external government lies in the need for it. If we suppose that persons who have
achieved the highest degree of autonomy possible have no need of
external government, then external government lacks legitimacy with
respect to them. But this achievement by them is a development out of
their prior condition of dependence, understood as incapacity for self-
government, which is the need for and authorization of external government. Wolff's failure to acknowledge the implications of the fact that
individual self-government is a developmental outcome leads him to
mistakenly regard individual autonomy and external authority as mutually exclusive. Supposing it to be true that they cannot apply to the same
entity, at the same time, in the same respect, nevertheless they both can
and do apply to the individual human being who achieves autonomy,
representing opposite poles of the continuum of growth (dependence
to autonomy). In this analysis they apply to the individual not simultaneously but *seriatim*. But also, on the continuum of growth an individual may at a given time be autonomous in some respects and dependent
in others, in which case the terms apply simultaneously to the individual
but to distinguishable aspects of him or her. Finally, state government
regulates a society that is inclusive of persons from infancy to old age
and therefore encompasses all stages of development. Accordingly state
government is authorized by the need for it on the part of persons who
are incapable, or insufficiently capable, of self-government. Since such
need is perennial in a mixed populace, so likewise is the authority of
external government, and the question is not of its presence or absence,
but of better external government or worse. Good external government

is defined by Plato as government that "produce(s) in it men and women of the best type."[3] We shall now undertake to show that, consistent with his eudaemonistic ethical theory, *The Republic* understands persons "of the best type" to be those who develop morally from dependence to the autonomous actualization of their innate potential values. Since autonomy means self-direction it cannot be literally produced by the state, and we shall argue that the good state, Platonically conceived, is the state that *is conducive* to eudaimonic living by all persons. But to understand *The Republic* in this way requires that we refute the charges against it of authoritarianism and totalitarianism. We will deal with them in their highly influential presentation by Karl Popper in *The Open Society and Its Enemies*.

Popper's reading of *The Republic* as a prescription for the "unchallenged rule of one class"[4] is a basic misperception. True, Plato indeed believes that governing is properly the work of persons of a certain kind, but by no means is their governance unchallengeable. Plato expressly holds Rulers answerable by stipulating that they must depend for all of their utilities, including their food and shelter, upon voluntary provision by the citizenry.[5] By denying Rulers their needs, citizens unseat them from rule; by providing their needs, citizens retain them. What citizens judge is the quality of governance by Rulers, and especially in respect to Rulers' "first and chief" responsibility, which is to place citizens in the society according to the kind of work that each is by his or her nature best suited to do. Such placement is offered by Plato as the meaning of justice.

Popper rightly says that this conception of justice is "fundamentally different from our ordinary view"[6] and attributes the discrepancy to Plato's deceitful intention to "make propaganda for his totalitarian state by persuading the people that it was the 'just' state."[7] But in fact the discrepancy reflects the deep difference between the eudaimonistic and the modern conceptions of the human being, the former an essentially productive conception while the latter is essentially a recipient conception. As presented in chapter 5, classical ethics is responsibilities-based, beginning in the moral responsibility of every person to live the worthy life that is innately his or hers to live. Rights derive from responsibilities as entitlements to what a person needs in order to fulfill his or her basic moral responsibility. On the other hand modern moral thought begins with rights, from which it derives responsibilities, beginning with the responsibility to respect the rights of others.

Popper stresses the centrality to justice of the idea of equality, but supposes the latter to be absent in *The Republic,* whereas it is present in the meaning of proportional equality. The equality that Popper affirms is the formal equality of classical liberalism, that is, equality under the law on the ground of identical human rights. Proportional equality incorporates normative differences among individuals in accordance with the words with which Socrates begins his description of the Republic: ". . . it occurred to me . . . that no two people are born exactly alike. There are innate differences which fit them for different occupations."[8] Proportional productive equality obtains when A and B are alike doing the work for which each is by nature best suited, and proportional recipient equality obtains when A and B alike possess the particular goods and utilities to which each is entitled. In *The Republic,* for example, the education appropriate for future Rulers is different from the education appropriate for future craftsmen, but Rulers and craftsmen are equally entitled to the education appropriate to them.

The productive orientation of *The Republic* recognizes that what persons do is more important to their well-being than what they own. What is most important to well-being is the development of worthy character, and this must be achieved by each person for himself or herself; it cannot be conferred. By contrast recipient desires do not depend upon first-person agency for their gratification. My desire for a new car, for example, will be fully gratified if a benefactor makes me a present of one. And because they are not restricted by the inherent limitations of first-person agency, recipient desires are in principle limitless. The "perpetual desire of power after power that ceases only in death" which Hobbes posits as the "general inclination of all mankind"[9] is the expression of a recipient orientation (Hobbes regarded all utilities including material goods as "powers"). The in-principle limitlessness of recipiency is reflected in modern "consumerism" and the abandonment of the Greek principle of *sophrosune,* by which excess was condemned no less than deficiency.

To employ a developmental model: for a child the paramount question must be "What shall I receive?", but with adolescence the pressing question becomes "What shall I do?" In this light the exchange of a productive for a recipient orientation is quite evidently a regression.

In Plato's meanings, "justice" is inseparably connected to "happiness" (*eudaimonia*). Recognizing the central place of happiness in *The Republic,* Popper says, "There is no reason to doubt that one of [Plato's] most powerful motives was to win back happiness for the citizens."[10] But by supposing that Plato sought happiness in a reversion to "tribalism" to dispel the destructive forces of "democracy and individualism," Popper exhibits his failure to understand Plato's meaning of happiness. To correct this failure is to overturn Popper's charge of totalitarianism against *The Republic*, for happiness *in Plato's meaning* is possible only for individuals who are leading autonomous lives. *Eudaimonia* has a double meaning. Objectively it means living in accordance with one's *daimon*, and subjectively it is the feeling attendant upon such living. It implies autonomy because it requires self-knowledge, acting upon which is autonomous action, while failure to act upon the self-knowledge one possesses is invariably dysdaimonic or akrasic—manifesting the inner discord that is happiness's opposite. In Chapter XIV of *The Republic* Plato expects of every citizen the measure of wisdom that management of the self depends upon. This is knowledge of the good of the self, that is, self-knowledge. It is the autonomy and self-knowledge of citizens by which they are equipped to judge the performance of Rulers in the manner previously noted. Out of self-knowledge each individual can judge for himself or herself whether Rulers have in fact successfully performed their "first and chief" function of placing citizens according to the natures of each.

But beforehand lies Plato's central mistake. It is his assignment to Rulers of the work of identifying the innate natures of citizens of *The Republic* in their early childhood. Plato of course prescribes that Rulers shall themselves have received training designed to enable them to accomplish this. But by the combined findings of sociology and developmental psychology of the past 150 years, this work cannot be done. The reason is that persons in childhood are necessarily social products. Their dependence is an identity-dependence, requiring that their child-identities be conferred upon them by the adult community. These conferred identities overlie children's innate natures, which remain merely latent in childhood and are not discoverable there by adults, no matter how well-trained. In children of whatever age, the most that trained adults will be able to discern is enculturated beliefs, enculturated preferences and aversions, enculturated identities.

It is Plato's prescription that children be placed by Rulers and role-trained for adult life accordingly that lends a prima facie credence to charges against him of totalitarian intent—that is, of intent that the lives of citizens be controlled from beginning to end and in every dimension. But that this was not his intent has been shown above, by the demonstration that individual autonomy is a condition of both the *eudaimonia* Plato sought to generalize and of the justice that constitutes its generalization. On this understanding, Plato's reason for prescribing placement of children by Rulers is not far to seek.

For justice to prevail, persons must be so placed in society as to lead the kinds of productive lives that each is by his or her innate nature best suited to. This is determined by each individual's innate potentiality, or *daimon*. In order to live eudaimonically, according to Plato, a person must possess self-knowledge and be guided by it. But in the Hellenic understanding the great imperative, *Gnothi seauton*—"Know Thyself"—is to be addressed, not to children, but to persons in later life, specifically "when a young man's beard begins to grow" (and correspondingly for young women). There could be no question of leaving formal education to the beginning of adolescence. And Plato's conviction that education from the beginning should be in accordance with the innate natures of students led him to believe that it could be, through identification of these natures by Rulers trained to the task. On the supposition that such identification is possible, Plato regarded delay of tailored education until the emergence of self-knowledge as an intolerable waste of time that was, moreover, fraught with perils of developmental misdirection. But the supposition is mistaken.

To limn this "first and chief" work from the job descriptions of Rulers may seem to be an alteration so drastic as to render the outcome contra-Platonic. It entails that the education of children cannot be role-training, and this puts an end to the rigid censorship of influences upon children that Plato prescribed. True, his purpose in prescribing censorship will find a responsive chord in every parent; it was to ensure that children should be exposed exclusively to models of good moral growth for their emulation. But in the first place we are obliged by modern developmental knowledge to abandon the closed teleology on which Plato designed the education of children for a liberal, open-ended teleology whose ends require to be discovered through exploration. And this liberalism is inconsistent with the ambition to restrict children's exposure to good models exclusively—it is enough that good models be prominent.

And if identification of individuals according to their innate natures becomes possible only at adolescence, then to be true to the autonomy that distinguishes adolescence from childhood (termed by us "pre-individuated autonomy" in chapter 3), it must be self-identification. Then self-identification becomes the basis for the life-shaping choices that inaugurate adulthood. Chapter 3 was our attempt to identify facilitating conditions for self-discovery in adolescence.

This picture remains deeply Platonic in what it is meant to achieve: complementary interrelationship of self-directed, eudaimonic human lives on the foundation of (Platonic) justice. It departs from Plato on the means by which this end is to be achieved. Thanks to modern sociological and developmental knowledge we are positioned to recognize some of what Plato took to be means as in fact obstructions.

Plato supposed that individuals, having been initially placed and role-trained by Rulers, would in the course of their subsequent development arrive independently at the self-knowledge by which to judge their placement. Rulers adjudged unsuccessful at correct placement were to be unseated (as we saw) by citizens' withdrawal of Rulers' subsistence. Plato offers no details about the appropriate levels of success and failure for termination or retention of Rulers, nor does he make provision for negotiating disputes over placement. On these matters he avails himself of the Utopianist's prerogative of supposing perfect accomplishment of placements by Rulers, as subsequently confirmed by citizens upon their arrival at self-knowledge. For our part we have obviated the questions just noted by divesting Rulers of the work of placement. Our thesis is that placement and the self-discovery on which it is based are central aspects of the self-actualization that is primarily each individual's moral responsibility. But alike, government, workplace, community, school, and family must provide conducive contexts.

To conclude on *The Republic:* we have confuted the charge of totalitarian intent by showing that the "happiness" Plato sought to generalize was only possible, on his meaning, to autonomous individuals. Therefore his undeniable intent to universalize happiness was his intent to universalize individual autonomy. The same conclusion follows if we recognize that for Plato, Socrates was the supreme exemplar of worthy living, and that Plato designed *The Republic* to generalize the opportunity of Socratic moral excellence in its generalizable aspects. As we sought to show in chapter 4, the generalizable aspects are the moral virtues, beginning in the virtue of integrity as it issues from self-knowledge (a measure of wisdom). Socrates's integrity was the product of his discovery of the particular values that were innately his own, and his identification with them as the work of actualizing, conserving, and defending them. On the model of Socrates, Plato sought to generalize worthy living by providing the conditions to put as many persons as possible in touch with the values that are their own, to actualize, conserve, and defend.

We turn now to a consideration of some of the implications of *The Republic,* suitably revised, for contemporary government and organizational management.

A contemporary eudaimonism will, I think, be bound to accept Plato's thesis that managers are a distinct class of persons. This is so because Plato's criteria for good managers are demanding and as valid today as when he wrote. First, to be a good manager requires that one possess knowledge of the good of the social organization as a whole that one manages; and second, it requires that one identify one's own good with the good of the whole. Plato to the contrary notwithstanding, I think that more sorting is done by the second criterion than by the first. To be a productive member of a social organization requires at least a general notion of the good of the organization, and few persons are incapable of testing, refining, and concretizing this general notion, should they choose to do so, with the help of appropriate training. But the diversity of persons in their essential natures is such as to make it unreasonable to suppose that more than a few will experience their personal fulfillment by accepting the good of the whole as their personal good. Indeed, there is a diversity to be organized just because organization and management are not everyone's destiny and fulfillment. For many the unending challenge is to organize and manage the whole that is the self, in order to actualize, conserve, and defend the values that are particular to it. By virtue of the objectivity of the values they realize, such lives are no less social for foregoing management; and because the self-management of the individual is a form of government, neither are they shirking politics. Moreover their values are distinct from the values of management and require distinct forms of service. Rousseau's doctrine of the General Will makes qualified managers of all citizens by requiring (1) that they will the good of all, and (2) that they do so with the will of all.[11] But this would mean the loss to society of individuated values that can be realized only through wholehearted commitments by individuals to these values. What effective democracy requires, in state, community, or workplace, is not that everyone be managers, or be qualified to manage, but that everyone be capable of distinguishing better management from worse. And to be guided by good management does not compromise the autonomy and integrity of individuals, but is a manifestation of the division of labor that autonomy and integrity entail. In Spinoza's phrase, *Omnis determinatio est negatio:* to choose what one shall become is to choose not to become everything else that one might have sought to become instead. Each individual has need of what others become. Persons who choose not to become managers have need of them: they have reason to learn to distinguish better managers from worse and to welcome good managers.

Organizational management must be for the good of the social whole, which is necessarily inclusive of the goods of individuals who comprise the whole. Potential conflict appears in the recognition that by eudaimonism's equation of individuality with self-responsibility, it is individuals themselves who bear primary responsibility for their own well-being. Resolution lies in eudaimonism's recognition that effective, self-responsible individuality requires a conducive social setting. If we term both social engineering and the welfare state "maximal government," and the night-watchman state of classical liberalism "minimal government," then good government, eudaimonistically conceived, lies intermediate between them, as conducive government.

The welfare state is variously defined, but in any case sets off on the wrong foot by choice of the term. At bottom the true welfare of individuals is their moral character, which cannot be conferred by administrative distribution, but requires to be earned. In order to affirm this we must cease to speak of distributed "benefits" and concern ourselves with distribution of the non-self-suppliable conditions for the exercise of self-responsibility, with emphasis upon the conditions for the discovery by each individual of his or her self *as* a responsibility.

Management as social engineering found archetypal, microcosmic expression in our country in such "company towns" as Pullman, Illinois, and Kohler, Wisconsin.[12] It planned the civic life, the education, the architecture, the recreation, the cultural enrichment, the social and family patterns of worker-residents, and in so doing violated their integrity as individuals. This was so conspicuous as to throw such endeavors into disrepute, but today social engineering survives in more insidious form, as subjective conditioning of workers by management. Orthodox management theory presently is indebted to the combined work of Chester I. Barnard and Herbert Simon, which around 1950 brought it "as close as it had [come] before or has since to a legitimate paradigm of thought."[13] Arguing that molding employee motives and morals is a crucial responsibility of management, Barnard wrote that managers must shape "the conditions of behavior, including a conditioning of the individual by training, by the inculcation of attitudes, by the construction of incentives."[14] Supporting this Simon wrote that "the behavior of a rational person can be controlled . . . if the value and factual premises upon which he bases his decisions are specified for him."[15]

Such undertakings are the predictable projection of the relentless movement of modern management toward complete control. As rehearsed by Harry Braverman,[16] it began three centuries ago in the gathering of workers in a central workplace and the dictation of the hours of the workday; it moved to the supervision of workers for diligence, the enforcement of rules against distractions, the subdivision of labor into small, precisely repeatable operations (as in Adam Smith's classical description of pin-making),[17] setting of production minimums, redesign of the workplace to facilitate supervision, and the creation of cadres of quality-control monitors. In the first quarter of our century it arrived at the "scientific management" of Frederick W. Taylor, which sought total control of the work by breaking down every task into its elements and redesigning them. (The *Encyclopaedia Britannica*, 15th ed., credits Taylor's book, *The Princples of Scientific Management*, 1911, with having "influenced the development of virtually every country enjoying the benefits of modern industry.")

Although Braverman's outline is obviously simplified, no one will doubt that the progression it describes has in fact occurred. An immediate question it poses is why at every step workers were on the whole ready to accept new incursions by management for pay increases. The most satisfactory answer is that they had nothing to lose because they were engaged at alienated work already. This presupposes that most work in modernity has been alienated work. By the modern conception of the individual, alienation of worker from work is not a problem but a natural condition. Work is an unpleasant necessity that persons are obliged to undertake to meet needs whose gratification could in principle be conferred—and preferably conferred, for thus the requirement to work would be obviated. But what is in fact lost is the eudaimonistic recognition that the happiness and well-being of persons lies in doing the right work, that is, the work for which each is by nature best suited. By the modern understanding, persons so situated will be occasional oddities, leaving modern presuppositions unchallenged.

From a eudaimonistic standpoint, alienated work is at monumental social and individual cost, yet it has this last-ditch benefit, that it blocks management control from penetrating the private person of the worker—or appears to do so. The self of the worker can be preserved, apparently, by deliberate disidentification with the work in favor of identification with other dimensions of his or her life, such as family, avocations, religion, community.

But ultimately this resort could not be left standing by management, because the alienated worker does not invest the best of himself in his work. Accordingly management seeks to produce identification by manipulating the self-conceptions of workers. On one front this is reflected in the paradigm of orthodox management theory produced by Barnard and Simon. On another front, it appears in the subversion to management purposes of the "humanistic" work-reform initiatives of the 1950s through 1970s, as effected most prominently by Douglas MacGregor's "Theory Y" management. In the 1980s it arrived at the device of shaping lives by shaping "organizational culture." These initiatives are analyzed in William G. Scott and David K. Hart, *Organizational Values in America*. Their conclusion is:

As it now stands, humanistic techniques—such as OD, organizational transformation, and organizational imagination—are used to manipulate people into identifying with that mutant form of labor we call the modern job. The techniques of these applied versions of human development are packaged and marketed by a staggering number of management consultants.[18]

But another incursion of what Scott and Hart term the "organizational imperative" was calculated to penetrate still deeper into persons' self-conceptions because of its earlier entry into their life-histories. This was the conquest in the 1920s of the National Education Association, and thereby the system of public education in the United States, by the "scientific management" of Frederick W. Taylor and his followers.[19] It led the public education system to conceive of itself unapologetically as a business, turning out "products" for the "market." Primary and secondary teachers began to be trained in conceptions of "classroom management" mandating total control of students in the interest of efficiency as measured by students' test scores, whereas teachers themselves became subject to comparable management by school administrators.

Nevertheless it is unlikely that management theory and practice can ever become totally overt and public about its ambition to control the persons of workers (and students as future workers). This is because it is in principle bound by what John Rohr has called the American "regime values,"[20] centering in the right of individual self-determination. In this context, managerial conditioning of persons is recognizable as a form of the tyranny that Michael Walzer defines as the dominance of the values of a sphere of human experience outside that sphere.[21] By conditioning of persons to managerial norms, managerial responsibility projects itself into private life, usurping the responsibility of individuals for self-direction and self-management.

Scott and Hart are more explicit about totalitarian implications of the "organizational imperative."[22] When the sociological tenet that persons are "social products" is taken as the whole truth, without remainder, it represents total control of persons by social institutions. The modern organization translates this sociological tenet into a technology for creating the kind of persons the modern organization requires. The fact that persons acquiesce to the process does not represent endorsement of the controlling institutions by individuals, for true individuals—persons capable of leading self-directed lives on the basis of independent judgments—do not exist. Such endorsement by persons who are institutional products is but the institutions' self-endorsement.

Achievement of the moral virtue of integrity is central to every individual's self-responsibility because self-actualization demands it, and because it is the deep foundation of the basic honesty that social existence requires. Good management, as we are conceiving it, recognizes its obligation to respect this responsibility of individuals. Because integrity is an inclusive virtue, integrating all dimensions of the individual's life, respecting the individual's responsibility for this virtue is respect for the individual as an inclusive whole. This means that management cannot be indifferent to, or obstructive of, workers' commitments to family, friends, avocations, civic and religious commitments. And just as workers of integrity are whole persons within the workplace, so the workplace is a whole within the larger whole of community and nation and must promote and conserve the welfare of both. Workplace managers cannot coercively induce, or try to induce, the integrity either of the community or of workers, but must contribute to the former and provide a conducive setting for the latter. Both services will require active measures in some cases—for example, provision of a healthy and safe workplace, provision of preschool child care where needed, loan of management expertise to community ends—and elimination of obstructions in others, such as clean waste disposal, adjustment of production schedules, flex-time, elimination of involuntary overtime.

Just now what may be a new management paradigm is discernible in Max de Pree's *Leadership is an Art*.[23] It affirms the necessity to one another of healthy organizations and personal integrity of members, an integrity for which individuals themselves are responsible, and whose foundation lies outside the organization. De Pree recognizes that future productivity in the United States depends upon rediscovering the intrinsic rewards of work. For the past two decades the cost of American labor has by degrees been pricing American goods out of both foreign and domestic markets. Ironically this outcome reflects the success of organizational management at buying the compliance of workers with material rewards. On this path endless escalation of the requisite rewards was predictable by the long-recognized truth that material acquisitiveness has no intrinsic upper limit.

The warrant for identifying de Pree's management model as a new paradigm is its renunciation of one of the deep principles of the established models, namely that personal integrity in workers is at cost to company loyalty.

But the intrinsic rewards of work are only recoverable by a major effort to secure the matching of workers to the particular kinds of work that they as individuals experience as self-fulfilling. This entails the self-knowledge of workers, which implicates our patterns of education. It is not a matter of simply "plugging in" a new management theory in place of the old. Our intent in chapter 3 was to show that recovery of meaningful work mandates an overhaul of education from bottom to top.

It may be thought that the concept of conducive, noncoercive organizational management is applicable to voluntary organizations but not to the state. In response we shall endeavor to show, first, that state government can be noncoercively conducive to self-responsible, self-directed living by individuals; and second, that by an adequate conception of human beings good state government is required to be conducive government.

It is true that state government must be a monopoly of coercive power in respect to public safety, law enforcement, and national defense, but this makes state government inherently coercive only in respect to these functions, and we shall shortly show why good government cannot be limited to these functions. The more frequently presented case for inevitable coercion is that, thanks to the dependence of childhood, persons in the beginning of their lives are inevitably and involuntarily politicized by the institutional pattern of their society. And certainly it is true that in the dependent first stage of life, persons are social products. But this is merely inevitable, not coercive, for "coercion" by definition seeks to override individual self-determination, of which children are incapable. The capacity for self-determination makes its appearance only subsequent to childhood, and therefore whether the training of children is coercive or not can only be determined with reference to the kind of adolescence and subsequent life for which the child is being prepared. The education of children will be coercive if it constitutes a role-training for adult life that precludes to its recipients their eventual life-shaping choices. It will not be coercive if it does not preempt their subsequent choices. But we readily recognize that good childhood education cannot be defined merely in terms of noninterference with subsequent life-shaping choices. It must be actively directed to providing children with the personal resources—the knowledge and skills—that life-shaping choices require if they are to be soundly made. It must be conducive to subsequent sound choice.

Government-provided utilities for adults, such as public highways, waterways, airports—a public information service as a supplement and corrective to advertising, the National Youth Service proposed in chapter 3—are noncoercive if their use is optional. In the case of utilities whose use is unavoidable, such as law enforcement, public sanitation, and the regulation of food and drug manufacture and sale, their coercive nature is proportional to the lack of autonomy in the adult population and inversely proportional to its presence. This is because an autonomous adult is not determined by her circumstances, but by the meaning her circumstances have for her, and these meanings are self-determined. If "autonomy" meant absence of unchosen external circumstances it would be inapplicable to human beings, who are subject to such intractable natural conditions as the law of gravity and their own mortality. But autonomy here remains applicable because persons are capable of determining for themselves what such imposed conditions shall mean to them. (All human beings must die, but the history of thought is rich with alternative interpretations of the meaning that our mortality has for us while we live.) The implication for our thesis is that provision of unavoidable utilities does not per se constitute coercion by government in a society that effectively promotes the capacity for self-direction in individuals.

To be sure, provision of utilities by government requires taxation. But this is not of itself inimical to the autonomy and self-responsibility of individuals, for it is consistent with the social responsibility that follows from the inherently social nature of persons. On the eudaimonistic thesis, this social responsibility is fulfilled primarily by each individual's actualization of his or her own innate potential worth. But it is not thus exhausted, because some of the necessary conditions of self-actualizing living by individuals cannot be self-provided. Their necessity mandates their universal availability, which calls for institutionalized provision. To participate in such provision through taxation is but to return what one has received.

But does not conducive government violate the American regime-value of individual liberty, understood in Mill's phrase as the "freedom . . . of pursuing our own good in our own way"? The answer here proposed is that because both the discovery of one's own good and the capacities requisite to pursue it are developmental outcomes, they require a social setting that is conducive to such development. The reason that the minimal night-watchman state could ever have been conceived as the proper setting for the pursuit by individuals of their own good in their own way is that classical liberalism largely ignores the moral development of individuals. As we sought to show in chapter 1, it holds an essentially nondevelopmental conception of individuality and theorizes on the presupposition of the antecedent existence of such individuality. In Dewey's words, "The underlying philosophy and psychology of earlier liberalism led to a conception of individuality as something ready-made, already possessed, and needing only the removal of certain legal restrictions to come into full play. It was not conceived as a moving thing, something that is attained only by continuous growth."[24]

The spirit of "earlier liberalism" finds forceful expression today in such influential thinkers as F. A. Hayek, Karl Popper, the Robert Nozick of *Anarchy, State, and Utopia,* and Michael Oakeshott, and doubtless, as some partisans and critics alike contend, it emanates from the foundations of our political tradition to quietly pervade our thought and conduct from below. We will now undertake to show that its minimal, merely protective and procedural government is in fact obstructive of the freedom Mill describes and that we in the United States rightly prize. For its elegance and power, our chosen treatise in classical liberalism will be Michael Oakeshott's *On Human Conduct.*

The political theory of *On Human Conduct* (Parts II and III) centers in Oakeshott's comparison of what he holds to be the two paradigmatic forms of association in modernity, "collective enterprise association" and "civil association." The former is association of persons on the basis of common purpose, and Oakeshott acknowledges that it is and has always been the more prevalent of the two forms. Indeed, its prevalence poses the problem that most people, including some political theorists, "mistakenly think there is no alternative to it. Recognizing conduct *inter homines* as agents seeking satisfactions in the responses of others, they erroneously conclude that all durable human relationship must be enterprise relationship. They find it impossible to imagine association except in terms of a common purpose."[25]

What Oakeshott means by "civil association" is categorially different from common enterprise association. It is association in terms, not of common purpose, but of the agreement of associates to pursue their individual purposes according to accepted rules. In Oakeshott's words, "Civil associates are persons (*cives*) related to one another, not in terms of a substantive undertaking, but in terms of the common acknowledgment of the authority of civil (not instrumental) laws specifying conditions to be subscribed to in making choices and in performing self-chosen actions."[26]

A crucial difference between the two forms of association lies in the kind of freedom each affords. Civil association affords freedom to individuals to form their own purposes and pursue them. This freedom is denied in collective enterprise association by the common purposes that are the basis of the association. But the member of an enterprise association is free if "his situation is a choice of his own," and if "he can extricate himself from it by choosing to do so." To this Oakeshott adds, "For him to be associated in the performance of joint actions contingently related to a common purpose and not to have chosen his situation for himself and to be unable to extricate himself from it by revoking his choice, would be to have severed the link between belief and conduct which constitutes moral agency."[27]

Since moral agency is (by the argument of Part I of *On Human Conduct*) definitive of human beings, Oakeshott's basic thesis is that involuntary collective enterprise association constitutes dehumanization.

The final step in Oakeshott's argument is his contention that while the good state certainly can and will (by the principle of freedom of association) include voluntary collective enterprise associations, it cannot itself be a collective enterprise association because "a state, on any reading of its character, is a comprehensive, exclusive, and compulsory association."[28] Accordingly "the undertaking to impose this character upon a state . . . constitutes a moral enormity, and it is the attempt and not the deed which convicts it of moral enormity. And it matters not one jot whether this undertaking is that of one powerful ruler (or *coup d'etatiste*), or a few, or a majority."[29]

The rejoinder that provision for emigration renders association within the state voluntary will be branded naive by Oakeshott. By virtue of their dependence, children cannot emigrate by choice. And to be reared within a state that is a common enterprise association is to be conditioned in the common purpose(s) as one's own purpose(s), at an age when one is devoid of resources by which to resist. We acquire our initial beliefs and habits of conduct, Oakeshott says, "in the same way as we acquire our native language. There is no point in a child's life at which he can be said to begin to learn the language which is habitually spoken in his hearing; and there is no point in his life at which he can be said to begin to learn habits of behavior from the people constantly about him."[30] Oakeshott terms such conditioning "inevitable,"[31] and of course recognizes that it occurs in states having the character of civil association. But in their case he holds that because the state has no substantive purposes to be inculcated in individuals as qualifications of membership, they are free in later life to choose their own purposes on the condition that they pursue them according to the rules of their civil association.

Oakeshott insists that under civil association habits of conduct must be inculcated in children, and an immediate criticism of his political theory has been that the distinction between civil association and enterprise association breaks down because uniform habits of conduct inevitably embody collective, substantive purposes. I will not take up this issue, because what I am about to offer applies alike to both sides.

Supposing Oakeshott to be correct in contending for the reasons given that a state is involuntary association, and that involuntary collective enterprise association constitutes dehumanization and tyranny, yet there remains one collective purpose that may be institutionalized as a purpose of the state without either tyranny or dehumanization. It is the purpose of generalizing the opportunity of self-directed living among citizens by providing those of its necessary conditions that cannot be self-supplied by individuals—the conditions, we may say, of self-humanization. But our claim is stronger than that these necessary conditions can be provided without tyranny: it is that they must be provided if suppression of humankind is to be avoided. For unless they are provided the individual does not arrive at the strength of character by which to resist the influence upon him or her of the powerful shaping forces of society. To pit the tentative early intimations of normative individuality against the juggernaut of fully formed social forces is to insure the unchallengeable sovereignty of the latter and the abject conformity of the former.

If Oakeshott is mistaken to suppose that habits of conduct can be inculcated without implicit inculcation of substantive ends (as I think he is), this means that together with the beliefs and feelings that must come under review as the first step of self-identification, so also must habits of conduct. The fear that this will destroy the procedural framework that the sociality of self-directed individuals unquestionably requires is unwarranted. The review affords assessment of enculturated conventions of conduct to distinguish those that continue to serve the purpose of self-responsible living by individuals from those that obstruct it. The need for periodic review is implicit in the definition of conventions as collective habits, occasioning action without thought. Clearly it is useful in some situations to be able to act without thought, but just as clearly conventions that are never reviewed may lose their utility, sometimes becoming obstructions.

In concert with the classical liberal mode that it expresses, Oakeshott's purely procedural government presupposes ready-made individuals who are prepared to utilize it. What this mistake produces is sufficiently demonstrated by the history of classical liberalism as presented by Oakeshott himself. The extreme disorder of the late Middle Ages and early Renaissance (described in citations from Burckhardt, Huizinga, and Pocock in chapter 1) reflected the breakdown of feudal order in religion, politics, society, and morality. It effectively left rising numbers of individuals to their own devices, and classical liberalism endorsed the self-management of individuals in these circumstances. But as Oakeshott says,

> . . . there were some (perhaps many) who found themselves invited to make choices for themselves in matters of belief, language, conduct, occupation, relationships and engagements of all sorts, but who could not respond. The old certainties of belief, of understanding, of occupation, and of status were being dissolved not only for those who had some confidence in their ability to inhabit a world composed of autonomous individuals (or who had some determination to do so) but also for those who by circumstances or temperament had no such confidence or determination.[32]

Oakeshott terms those who could not or did not respond *individuals manques,* and says no more about them except to acknowledge (in a separately published essay) that they comprise the masses that were later to be organized by various collectivisms, including of course Marxist communism.[33] This reflects the ingrained propensity of classical liberalism to dismiss *individuals manques* as but a necessary cost that must be paid for the advantages that classical liberalism affords. But the cost is much too high to be thus regarded, for dismissed with it is the democratic character of individualism. If individualism is to be joined to democracy, the *individual manque* becomes the test case. How is he to be understood? What can be done to diminish his numbers? The credo of moral democracy is expressed by Ralph Barton Perry:

> In democracy it is not a question of giving room and authority to the genius that has already declared itself, and of sacrificing thereto the residual mass of

mediocrity, but one of tapping new sources, and discovering genius in obscure and unsuspected quarters. By giving light and air to the hitherto buried masses of mankind, democracy hopes to enrich human culture in the qualitative, and not merely in the quantitative sense.[34]

In fact *individuals manques* are not the necessary cost of individualism, but a gratuitous cost resulting from failure to investigate the developmental requirements of effective individuality. But it has been a purpose of this book to show that those who accepted classical liberalism's invitation also incurred great costs, for with it they accepted an economistic conception of self and society that has by its moral minimalism rendered invisible the large demands and rewards of worthy living.

Notes

Preface

1. Forceful advocacy of the classical mode of ethical theorizing over the modern is the purpose of Alasdair MacIntyre, *After Virtue* (Notre Dame: University of Notre Dame Press, 1981); Richard Taylor, *Ethics, Faith, and Reason* (Englewood Cliffs, N.J.: Prentice-Hall, 1985); and Edmund L. Pincoffs, *Quandaries and Virtues* (Lawrence: University Press of Kansas, 1986). Some favor for the classical mode appears in Bernard Williams, *Ethics and the Limits of Philosophy* (Cambridge: Harvard University Press, 1985), and Robert Nozick, *Philosophical Explanations* (Cambridge: Harvard University Press, 1981), pt. 5. My own *Personal Destinies* (Princeton: Princeton University Press, 1976) was, I think, the first book-length effort to demonstrate the continued viability today of eudaimonistic ethical theory; it is lately joined in this endeavor by John Kekes, *The Examined Life* (Lewisburg, Pa.: Bucknell University Press, 1988). It will be recognized that philosophical re-interest in "the virtues" has been mounting rapidly for more than a decade, beginning with Philippa Foot, *Virtues and Vices* (Berkeley, Los Angeles, London: University of California Press, 1978). Consolidation of this focus is afforded by Peter A. French, Theodore E. Uehling, Jr., and Howard K. Wettstein, eds., *Midwest Studies in Philosophy*, vol. XIII: *Ethical Theory: Character and Virtue* (Notre Dame: University of Notre Dame Press, 1988).

Opposition to the recent turn toward classical "virtues ethics" and away from modern "rules ethics" already takes a number of forms, of which I will here mention three.

In an article entitled "Human Flourishing, Ethics, and Liberty" (*Philosophy and Public Affairs* 12(4):307–322 (Fall 1983), Gilbert Harman contends that an ethics of "flourishing" (perfectionism) must be either a form of utilitarianism, or else centered in "imitation of excellence," which is deficient because it requires an antecedent idea of excellence that must be imported into the theory from somewhere else and is not justified by the theory. I have counterargued that eudaimonism's teleological tenet divorces it from utilitarianism, whereas its insistence upon individual autonomy precludes "imitation of excellence" (*Reason Papers*, no. 10, Spring 1985, pp. 101–105).

Kurt Baier argues that attention to moral virtues is appropriate within the mainstream ethics of today (Kantianism, utilitarianism, contractarianism), but goes awry when it mistakes itself for an alternative kind of ethics. In his terms, he supports "moderate" virtues ethics, but opposes "radical" virtues ethics. (See his essay, "Radical Virtue Ethics," in French et al., *Midwest Studies in Philosophy*, vol. XIII, pp. 126–135.) My counterargument is suggested in preceding pages of the preface of this book. Modern ethics, as rules ethics, can accommodate only the measure of moral character that rules-obedience requires. Because rules must be applicable alike to everyone, rules-obedience can demand only minimal development of moral character. By contrast virtues ethics is an ethics of ideals, and it is characteristic of ideals that they can enlist the full measure of human aspiration. To merely add virtues considerations within rules frameworks dilutes moral thought and moral life by eliminating the higher moral conduct and character that are outcomes of extended moral development in individuals.

Gisela Striker is a Greek scholar and friend of eudaimonism who nevertheless believes that it is not moral theory because it neglects "what we have learned to consider as the most fundamental question—the justification of moral decisions or the foundation of moral rules." (She appends her belief that eudaimonism is, however, incorrectly regarded as a rival to moral theory, and instead "we should probably see them as complementing one another.") But eudaimonism is teleological value-theory that lodges justification of moral decisions in the values they actualize, and it locates the foundation of moral rules in the development of moral character that it is their purpose to support. Striker appears to identify "moral theory" with modern rules morality, which prevents her from recognizing eudaimonism as an alternative mode of moral theory. In this light she regards Stoicism as an improvement upon eudaimonism because it considered morality and moral theory "to be a question of rules." See Gisela Striker, "Greek Ethics and Moral Theory," in Grethe B. Peterson, ed., *The Tanner Lectures on Human Values* (Salt Lake City: The University of Utah Press, and Cambridge: Cambridge University Press; 1988), vol. IX, pp. 183–202.

Introduction

---

1. My impression over the years has been that few Anglo-American scholars fully recognize the depth, subtlety, and richness of the Greek concept of Eros. A stunning exception is Anne Carson, *Eros, the Bittersweet* (Princeton: Princeton University Press, 1986).

In the myth, the interpretation I have offered of fire as spiritual fire, that is, Eros, gives the myth broader and deeper meaning than does the more common reading as literal fire. By the latter, Prometheus is the father of technology. But Eros is creativity, understood as apprehension and actualization of possibilities. Technology is an important mode of human creation, but the more profound role for creativity lies in the unfinished condition of humankind—human beings are obliged to fashion themselves: Eros equips them to do this. When Herakles unchains Prometheus in Shelley's *Prometheus Unbound*, it is love (Eros) that spreads over the world.

2. Behind the brief depiction of eudaimonism in the introduction of this book is my book-length treatment, *Personal Destinies* (Princeton: Princeton University Press, 1976). Today growing numbers of American philosophers are working in closely related, Greek-based "virtues ethics." I mention a number of them in the endnote to the preface.

3. Friedrich Nietzsche, *On the Genealogy of Morals*, trans. Walter Kaufmann (New York: Random House Vintage Books, 1969).

4. Henry D. Thoreau, *Walden*, ed. J. Lyndon Shanley (Princeton: Princeton University Press, 1971), p. 97.

5. See John Kekes, *Facing Evil* (Princeton: Princeton University Press, 1990). As I write, the book has yet to be published. I have read it in typescript and regrettably cannot supply page references.

6. W. F. R. Hardie, "The Final Good in Aristotle's Ethics," in *Aristotle*, ed. J. M. E. Moravcsik (New York: Doubleday, 1967), pp. 297–322.

7. A good analysis of kinds of individualism is Steven Lukes, *Individualism* (New York: Harper & Row, 1973).

8. Michael Oakeshott, *On Human Conduct* (London: Oxford University Press, 1975), pt. II.

9. Michael Oakeshott, "On Being Conservative," in *Rationalism in Politics* (Totowa, N.J.: Rowman & Littlefield, 1977), p. 188.

10. John Stuart Mill, *On Liberty* (Indianapolis: Bobbs-Merrill Library of Liberal Arts, 1956), p. 80.

11. John Dewey, *Reconstruction in Philosophy* (Boston: Beacon Press, 1957), p. 186.

Chapter One: Classical Liberalism

1. Aristotle, *Physics* IV, 223b–224a.

2. J. G. A. Pocock, *The Machiavellian Moment: Florentine Political Thought and the Atlantic Republican Tradition* (Princeton: Princeton University Press, 1975), e.g. p. 155.

3. Albert O. Hirschman, *The Passions and the Interests: Political Arguments for Capitalism Before Its Triumph* (Princeton: Princeton University Press, 1977), p. 11.

4. Francis Bacon, *Novum Organum* (London & New York: George Routledge & Sons, n.d.), p. 77.

5. *Ibid.*, p. 79.

6. Jacob Burckhardt, "The Civilization of the Renaissance in Italy," in *Western Political Heritage*, ed. William Y. Elliott and Neil A. McDonald (New York: Prentice-Hall, 1949), pp. 456, 452, 451.

7. Johan Huizinga, *The Waning of the Middle Ages*, trans. F. Hopman (London: Edward Arnold, 1924), pp. 9, 18, 19, 20.

8. Pocock, *Machiavellian Moment*, p. 165.

9. Bacon, *Novum Organum*, p. 18.

10. *Ibid.*, p. 6.

11. Thomas Hobbes, *English Works* (London: Molesworth, 1839), vol. 1, p. ix.

12. Peter Laslett, intro. to John Locke, *Two Treatises of Government*, rev. ed. (Cambridge: Cambridge University Press, 1963), p. 91.

13. John Dewey, *The Quest for Certainty* (New York: G. P. Putnam's Sons Capricorn Books, 1960), p. 35.

14. Eugenio Garin, *Italian Humanism: Philosophy and Civic Life in the Renaissance*, trans. Peter Munz (Oxford: Oxford University Press, 1965), p. 61.

15. Pocock, *Machiavellian Moment*, p. 160.

16. John Stuart Mill, *Considerations on Representative Government* (Indianapolis: Bobbs-Merrill Library of Liberal Arts, 1958), p. 98.

17. Niccolo Machiavelli, *The Prince*, trans. George Bull (London: Harmondsworth, 1961), p. 91.

18. See Quentin Skinner, *The Foundations of Modern Political Thought* (Cambridge: Cambridge University Press, 1978), vol. 2, pp. 114–123.

19. *Ibid.*, e.g. pp. 118, 179.

20. Niccolo Machiavelli, *The Discourses*, trans. Leslie J. Walker, ed. Bernard Crick (London: Harmondsworth, 1970), pp. 278–279.

21. Emile Durkheim, *Elementary Forms of the Religious Life*, trans. Joseph Ward Swain (Glencoe, Ill.: The Free Press, n.d.), e.g. pp. 230–231.

22. Pocock, *Machiavellian Moment*, p. 166.

23. *Ibid.*, p. 37.

24. *Ibid.*, pp. 38–42.

25. *Ibid.*, p. 162.

26. J. O. Urmson, "Saints and Heroes," in Joel Feinberg, ed., *Reason and Responsibility* (Belmont, Calif.: Wadsworth, 1985), p. 520.

27. Machiavelli, *The Prince*, p. 96.

28. Machiavelli, *Discourses*, pp. 97, 111–112.

29. Henry Osborn Taylor, *Thought and Expression in the Sixteenth Century* (New York: Macmillan, 1920), vol. 1, pp. 83, 93.

30. Giovanni Botero, *The Reason of State*, trans. P. J. and D. P. Waley (London: 1965), p. 41. Cited in Skinner, *Foundations of Modern Political Thought*, vol. 1, p. 249.

31. Aristotle, *Nichomachean Ethics*, 1102b.

32. Thomas Hobbes, *Leviathan* (Indianapolis: Bobbs Merrill Library of Liberal Arts, 1958), p. 86.

33. Jeremy Bentham, *The Rationale of Reward* (London: Hunt, 1825), p. 206.

34. Gregory S. Kavka, *Hobbesian Moral and Political Theory* (Princeton: Princeton University Press, 1986), p. 289.

35. *Ibid.,* pp. 46–51.

36. Thomas Hobbes, *Human Nature,* in Kavka, *Hobbesian Moral and Political Theory,* pp. 46–47.

37. Hobbes, *Leviathan,* p. 125.

38. *Ibid.,* pp. 80, 83.

39. Richard Taylor, *Ethics, Faith, and Reason* (Englewood Cliffs, N.J.: Prentice-Hall, 1985), p. 4.

40. Hobbes, *Leviathan,* ch. 14; Kavka, *Hobbesian Moral and Political Theory,* p. 345.

41. Kavka, *Hobbesian Moral and Political Theory,* p. 347.

42. *Ibid.,* p. 64.

43. *Ibid.,* p. 65.

44. *Ibid.,* pp. 66–67.

45. Hobbes, *Leviathan,* p. 86.

46. Aristotle, *Nichomachean Ethics,* 1168b.

47. Hobbes, *Leviathan,* p. 107.

48. Louis Dumont, *From Mandeville to Marx: The Genesis and Triumph of Economic Ideology* (Chicago: University of Chicago Press, 1977), p. 81.

49. R. H. Tawney, *Religion and the Rise of Capitalism* (New York: Harcourt, Brace & Co., 1926), pp. 179–180.

50. Hirschman, *The Passions and the Interests,* p. 37.

51. Adam Smith, *An Inquiry into the Nature and Causes of the Wealth of Nations,* ed. E. Cannan (New York: Random House Modern Library, 1937), p. 325.

52. Machiavelli, *Discourses,* p. 132.

53. Montesquieu, "Esprit des lois," cited in Hirschman, *The Passions and the Interests,* p. 60.

54. Tawney, *Religion and the Rise of Capitalism;* Max Weber, *The Protestant Ethic and the Spirit of Capitalism,* trans. Talcott Parsons (New York: Scribner's, 1958).

55. See F. B. Kaye, Commentary, Bernard Mandeville, *The Fable of the Bees: Or, Private Vices, Publick Benefits* (Oxford: Oxford University Press, 1924), pp. xxxix–cxi.

56. Smith, *Wealth of Nations,* bk. IV, ch. 2.

57. Mandeville, *The Fable of the Bees,* vol. 1, pp. 411–412.

58. Smith, *An Inquiry into the Nature and Causes of the Wealth of Nations,* Edwin Cannan text, abridged Richard E. Teichgraeber, III (New York: Modern Library, 1985), pp. 240–241.

59. John Locke, *The Second Treatise of Government,* ed. with intro. Thomas P. Peardon (Indianapolis: Bobbs-Merrill Library of Liberal Arts, 1952), ch. 5 "Of Property," p. 17.

60. *Ibid.,* pp. 19, 23.

61. *Ibid.,* p. 17.

62. *Ibid.*, p. 29.

63. C. B. MacPherson, *The Political Theory of Possessive Individualism, Hobbes to Locke* (London, New York: Oxford University Press, 1962), pp. 208–210 and *passim*.

64. Locke, *Second Treatise*, pp. 22–23.

65. MacPherson, *The Political Theory of Possessive Individualism*, p. 212.

66. Richard Ashcraft, *Locke's Two Treatises of Government* (London: Allen & Unwin, 1987). James Tully, *A Discourse on Property: John Locke and His Adversaries* (Cambridge: Cambridge University Press, 1980). John Dunn, *The Political Thought of John Locke* (Cambridge: Cambridge University Press, 1969).

67. Ashcraft, *Lockes's Two Treatises of Government*, p. 170.

68. *Ibid.*, pp. 127–128.

69. *Ibid.*, p. 135.

70. *Ibid.*, p. 127.

71. *Ibid.*, p. 134.

72. *Ibid.*, p. 136.

73. *Ibid.*, p. 132.

74. *Ibid.*, pp. 133–134.

75. Locke, *Second Treatise*, p. 29.

76. *Ibid.*, p. 29.

77. Ashcraft, *Locke's Two Treatises of Government*, p. 141.

78. *Ibid.*, p. 126.

79. *Ibid.*, pp. 141–142.

80. *Ibid.*, p. 146.

81. *Ibid.*, p. 147.

82. Hobbes, *Leviathan*, p. 79.

83. Tawney, *Religion and the Rise of Capitalism*, p. 185.

84. John Stuart Mill, *Utilitarianism* (Indianapolis: Bobbs-Merrill Library of Liberal Arts, 1957), p. 23.

85. Neil W. Chamberlain, *The Limits of Corporate Responsibility* (New York: Basic Books, 1973), p. 92.

86. Robert Nozick, *Philosophical Explanations* (Cambridge: Harvard University Press, 1981), pp. 436–444.

87. P. F. Strawson, "Social Morality and Individual Ideal," *Philosophy*, XXXVI (1961), p. 8.

88. See R. M. Hare, *Freedom and Reason* (Oxford: Oxford University Press, 1965), p. 176 and *passim*. In his subsequent *Moral Thinking*, Hare believes he solves the problem that fanaticism poses to his universal prescriptivism, but he retains the definition of the fanatic that is offered in *Freedom and Reason*, and it is the definition I am questioning.

89. This criticism is one of several directed against moralities centering in "the self-conscious pursuit of moral ideals" by Michael Oakeshott in "The Tower of Babel," *Rationalism in Politics* (Totowa, N.J.: Rowman & Littlefield, 1977), pp. 59–79.

90. Urmson, "Saints and Heroes," in Feinberg, ed., *Reason and Responsibility*, p. 517.

91. Nozick, *Philosophical Explanations*, p. 438.

Chapter Two: Individuality Reconceived

1. I borrow the term from C. B. Macpherson, *The Life and Times of Liberal Democracy* (London: Oxford University Press, 1977), ch. 3.

2. John Dewey, *Individualism Old and New* (New York: Minton, Balch & Co., 1930).

3. John Stuart Mill, *On Liberty*, ed. Currin V. Shields (Indianapolis & New York: Bobbs-Merrill Library of Liberal Arts, 1956), pp. 6, 68, 76.

4. *Ibid.*, p. 72.

5. *Ibid.*, p. 76.

6. *Ibid.*, p. 71.

7. John Stuart Mill, *Considerations on Representative Government*, ed. Currin V. Shields (Indianapolis & New York: Bobbs-Merrill Library of Liberal Arts, 1958), p. 25.

8. *Ibid.*, pp. 47–48.

9. *Ibid.*, p. 50.

10. *Ibid.*, p. 54.

11. *Ibid.*, p. 53.

12. *Ibid.*, pp. 54–55.

13. *Ibid.*, p. 86.

14. *Ibid.*, p. 180.

15. *Ibid.*, p. 58.

16. A detailed description of Hare's system is to be found in Dennis F. Thompson, *John Stuart Mill and Representative Government* (Princeton: Princeton University Press, 1976), pp. 102–103.

17. As presented in P. F. Lazarsfield, B. Berelson, and H. Gaudet, *The People's Choice* (New York: Duell, Sloan, & Pearce, 1954); B. Berelson, P. F. Lazarsfield, and W. McPhee, *Voting* (Chicago: University of Chicago Press, 1954); H. Campbell, G. Gurin, and W. E. Miller, *The Voter Decides* (Evansville: Row, Peterson & Co., 1954); M. Benney, A. P. Gray, and R. H. Pear, *How People Vote* (London: Routledge & Kegan Paul, 1956).

18. See Bernard Berelson, "Democratic Theory and Public Opinion," in H. Eulau, J. G. Eldersveld, and M. Janowitz, eds., *Political Behavior: A Reader in Theory and Research* (Glencoe, Ill.: The Free Press, 1956), pp. 107–115.

19. Herbert Tingsten, *Political Behavior* (London: P. S. King & Son, 1937), cited in Steven Lukes, "The New Democracy," in Lukes, *Essays in Social Theory* (London: Macmillan, 1977), pp. 46–47.

20. Macpherson, *The Life and Times of Liberal Democracy*, pp. 78–79.

21. Several of its illogicalities and insufficiencies are exposed by Steven Lukes in his "The New Democracy," *Essays in Social Theory*.

22. Dewey, *Individualism Old and New*, pp. 80–81.

23. John Dewey, *Liberalism and Social Action* (New York: G. P. Putnam's Sons, 1935), p. 34.

24. John Dewey, *Reconstruction in Philosophy*, enlarged edition (Boston: Beacon Press, 1957), p. 194.

25. Dewey, *Liberalism and Social Action*, p. 40.

· 26. John Dewey, *Democracy and Education* (New York: The Free Press, 1966), p. 122.

27. Dewey, *Liberalism and Social Action,* p. 31.

28. Dewey, *Democracy and Education,* p. 100.

29. *Ibid.,* pp. 102–103.

30. *Ibid.,* p. 154.

31. *Ibid.,* pp. 161–162.

32. *Ibid.,* p. 161.

33. *Ibid.,* p. 141.

34. John Dewey, *The Quest for Certainty* (New York: G. P. Putnam's Sons Capricorn Books, 1960), ch. 10.

35. A notable example is Alasdair MacIntyre, *After Virtue* (Notre Dame: University of Notre Dame Press, 1981), pp. 54–57.

36. Dewey, *Individualism Old and New,* p. 159.

Chapter Three: Implementation

1. John Stuart Mill, *On Liberty* (Indianapolis: Bobbs-Merrill Library of Liberal Arts, 1956). Mill credits the phrase to Heinrich von Humboldt.

2. Aristotle, *Rhetoric,* bk. II, ch. 12.

3. Shakespeare, *As You Like It,* Act 2, Scene 7.

4. Robert Louis Stevenson, "Letter to a Young Gentleman," in *Across the Plains* (New York: Scribner's, 1904). He develops the theme that "youth is wholly experimental."

5. James S. Coleman, "The School to Work Transition," in U.S. Congressional Budget Office, *The Teenage Employment Problem: What Are the Options?* (Washington, D.C.: U.S. Government Printing Office, 1976), pp. 35–40.

6. Margaret Mead, "A National Service System as a Solution to a Variety of National Problems," in *The Draft: A Handbook of Facts and Alternatives,* ed. Sol Tax (Chicago: University of Chicago Press, 1967), p. 105.

7. The National Commission on Excellence in Education, *A Nation at Risk: The Imperative for Educational Reform* (Washington, D.C.: U.S. Government Printing Office, 1983). William J. Bennett, *First Lessons: A Report on Elementary Education in America* (Washington, D.C.: U.S. Government Printing Office, 1986).

8. Carnegie Council Report, *Giving Youth a Better Chance: Options for Education, Work, and Service* (San Francisco: Jossey-Bass, 1979), pp. 94–95.

9. Willard Wirtz and the National Manpower Institute, *The Boundless Resource: A Prospectus for an Education-Work Policy* (Washington, D.C.: New Republic Books, 1975), p. 9.

10. Quoted in Michael W. Sherraden and Donald Eberley, *National Service: Social, Economic, and Military Impacts* (New York: Pergamon Press, 1981), p. 35.

11. William James, "The Moral Equivalent of War," in *Essays in Religion and Morality* (Cambridge: Harvard University Press, 1982), p. 172.

12. Quoted in Sherraden and Eberley, *National Service*, p. 35.

13. Estimate collated from surveys by governmental and private agencies, reported widely in national news media in September, 1982. See, e.g., *U.S. News and World Report*, Sept. 27, 1982, pp. 57–61.

14. Cited in Sherraden and Eberley, *National Service*, pp. 17, 164.

15. See Stephen J. Pyne, *Fire in America: A Cultural History of Wildland and Rural Fire* (Princeton: Princeton University Press, 1982).

16. Walter Shapiro, "The Gap Between Will and Wallet: Should Students Perform National Service to Pay for College?", *Time*, Feb. 6, 1989, p. 32.

17. *Ibid.*, p. 32.

18. Sherraden and Eberley, *National Service*, p. 166.

19. *Ibid.*, p. 147.

20. Mead, "A National Service System," p. 106.

21. Wirtz, *The Boundless Resource*, p. 64.

22. John Rawls, *A Theory of Justice* (Cambridge: Harvard University Press, 1971), p. 426.

23. Robert Goldmann, "Six Automobile Workers Abroad," in *American Workers Abroad*, ed. Robert Schrank (Cambridge: MIT Press, 1979), p. 42.

24. John W. Gardner, *Excellence* (New York: Harper & Row Perennial Library, 1961), p. 80.

25. Harold L. Hodgkinson, *All One System: Demographics of Education, Kindergarten through Graduate School* (Washington, D.C.: Institute for Educational Leadership, 1985), pt. 1, p. 3.

26. Barbara Kantrowitz and Pat Wingert, "How Kids Learn," *Newsweek*, April 17, 1989, pp. 50–57.

27. Nell Noddings, *Caring: A Feminine Approach to Ethics and Moral Education* (Berkeley, Los Angeles, London: University of California Press, 1984).

Chapter Four: Meaningful Work

1. See Stephen G. Salkever, "Virtue, Obligation, and Politics," *The American Political Science Review* 68(1):78–92 (Mar. 1974).

2. Aristotle, *Nichomachean Ethics*, 1105a,b.

3. *Ibid.*, 1127a 19–20, 27–28.

4. F. H. Bradley, *Ethical Studies*, cited in Peter Singer, *Practical Ethics* (Cambridge: Cambridge University Press, 1979), p. 209.

5. Robert Nozick, *Philosophical Explanations* (Cambridge: Harvard University Press, 1981), p. 410.

6. John Cowper Powys, *The Meaning of Culture* (New York: W. W. Norton, 1929), pp. 260–261.

7. Lester H. Hunt, "Courage and Principle," *Canadian Journal of Philosophy* 10(2):289 (June 1980).

8. Philippa Foot, *Virtues and Vices and Other Essays in Moral Philosophy* (Berkeley, Los Angeles, London: University of California Press, 1978), p. 129.

9. Arthur Schopenhauer, "On Genius," in *The World as Will and Idea*, trans. R. B. Haldane and J. Kemp (New York: Charles Scribner's Sons, 1948), vol. III, pp. 138–166; Ralph Waldo Emerson, "Gifts," in *Essays First and Second Series* (Boston: Houghton Mifflin, n.d.), pp. 154–159, second series.

10. Carol Gilligan, *In a Different Voice, Psychological Theory and Women's Development* (Cambridge: Harvard University Press, 1982), ch. 3, e.g. pp. 74, 85.

11. Henry D. Thoreau, *Journal*, gen. ed. John C. Broderick (Princeton: Princeton University Press, 1981), vol. 1, p. 222.

12. Ralph Waldo Emerson, *Self-Reliance* (Mount Vernon, N.Y.: Peter Pauper Press, 1967), p. 7.

13. Aristotle, *Nichomachean Ethics*, 1120a, 25–27.

14. See, e.g., Lester H. Hunt, "Generosity," *American Philosophical Quarterly* 12(3):241 (July 1975).

15. Emerson, *Self-Reliance*, p. 40.

16. Gilligan, *In a Different Voice*, e.g., p. 76.

17. E.g. Paul Friedlander, *Plato* (New York: Bollingen Series LIX, 1964), vol. 2, pp. 19–20, 26–28, and notes; Lester H. Hunt, "Generosity and the Diversity of the Virtues"; O. Gignon, "Studien zu Platons *Protagoras*," in *Phyllobia fur Peter von der Muhl* (Basel, 1946), p. 139 et seq.; D. Gallop, "Justice and Holiness in *Prot.* 330–331," *Phronesis* vol. 6, 1961, pp. 88–89.

18. Gregory Vlastos, "The Unity of the Virtues," in *Platonic Studies* (Princeton: Princeton University Press, 1973), p. 227.

19. *Ibid.*, pp. 227–228.

20. Plato, *Protagoras* 349d, 2–8.

Chapter Five: Responsibilities and Rights

1. A. I. Meldin, *Rights and Persons* (Oxford: Basil Blackwell, 1977), p. 231.

2. Robert Nozick, *Anarchy, State, and Utopia* (New York: Basic Books, 1974), p. 33.

3. Ronald Dworkin, *Taking Rights Seriously* (London: Duckworth, 1977), p. 181 and *passim*.

4. *Ibid.*, pp. xiv, 181.

5. Leo Strauss, *Natural Right and History* (Chicago: University of Chicago Press, 1953), p. 182.

6. H. L. A. Hart, "Between Utility and Rights," in *The Idea of Freedom*, ed. Alan Ryan (London: Oxford University Press, 1979), p. 77.

7. Jeremy Bentham, *Pannomial Fragments*, in *Works*, gen. sup. John Bowring (Edinburgh: 1834–1843), vol. III, p. 293.

8. J. M. E. McTaggart, *Studies in Hegelian Cosmology* (Cambridge: Cambridge University Press, 1918), p. 72.

9. Joel Feinberg, "The Nature and Value of Rights," in *Rights, Justice, and*

the Bounds of Liberty: Essays in Social Philosophy (Princeton: Princeton University Press, 1980), p. 151.

10. Wesley Newcomb Hohfeld, *Fundamental Legal Conceptions* (New Haven: Yale University Press, 1919)

11. I am indebted to George Mavrodes and Gilbert Harman for criticisms of an earlier version of my argument that rights derive from responsibilities by "ought implies can." Responsibility for the present version is, however, wholly mine.

12. H. J. McCloskey, "Rights," *Philosophical Quarterly*, 15(1965): 118.

13. Carl Wellman, *A Theory of Rights: Persons Under Laws, Institutions, and Morals* (Totowa, N.J.: Rowman & Allanheld, 1985), p. 105

14. *Ibid.*, p. 6.

15. *United Nations Bulletin*, vol. VI, no. 1 (January 1, 1949).

16. Bertrand de Jouvenel, *Sovereignty: An Inquiry Into the Political Good*, trans. J. F. Huntington (Chicago: University of Chicago Press, 1957), p. 261.

17. H. B. Acton, *The Morals of Markets* (London: Longman, 1971), p. 71.

18. Iredell Jenkins, *Social Order and the Limits of Law* (Princeton: Princeton University Press, 1980), p. 263.

19. Henry Shue, *Basic Rights: Subsistence, Affluence, and U. S. Foreign Policy* (Princeton: Princeton University Press, 1980), p. 19.

20. *Ibid.*, pp. 37–39.

21. Martin P. Golding, "Towards a Theory of Human Rights," *The Monist* 52(1968): 546.

22. Joel Feinberg, "Voluntary Euthanasia and the Inalienable Right to Life, *Philosophy and Public Affairs,* 7(2):105 (1978).

23. *Ibid.*, p. 105.

24. *Ibid.*, p. 105.

25. H. L. A. Hart, "Are There Any Natural Rights?" in *Rights,* ed. David Lyons (Belmont, Calif.: Wadsworth, 1979), pp. 14–25.

26. Shue, *Basic Rights,* pp. 73–74.

27. Harry Frankfurt, "Freedom of the Will and the Concept of a Person," *Journal of Philosophy* 68(Jan. 14, 1971): 5–20.

28. Isaiah Berlin, "Two Concepts of Liberty," in *Four Essays on Liberty* (London: Oxford University Press, 1969).

29. See the discussion of "dominant end" versus "inclusive end" interpretations in chapter 4.

30. R. Avery, G. Elliehausen, G. Canner, and T. Gustafson, "Survey of Consumer Finances, 1983: Second Report," *Federal Reserve Bulletin* 70 (December 1984): 865. Cited in D. W. Haslett, "Is Inheritance Justified?" *Philosophy and Public Affairs* 15(2):123–124 (Spring 1986).

31. John Locke, *The Second Treatise of Civil Government* (Indianapolis: Bobbs-Merrill Library of Liberal Arts, 1952), p. 17.

32. Nozick, *Anarchy, State, and Utopia,* p. 57.

33. Ralph Waldo Emerson, *Self-Reliance,* (Mt. Vernon, N.Y.: Peter Pauper Press, 1967), p. 7.

34. Abraham Maslow, in conversations, 1963–1964.

35. House of Commons speech, date unknown: *Oxford English Dictionary of*

Quotations (1966). Cited in Tibor R. Machan, *Individuals and Their Rights* (Peru, Ill.: Open Court Press, 1989).

36. Examples of extended lists are to be found in Edmund L. Pincoffs, *Quandaries and Virtues* (Lawrence: University Press of Kansas, 1986).

37. Jane English, "Abortion and the Concept of a Person," in *Social Ethics: Morality and Social Policy*, ed. Thomas A. Mappes and Jane S. Zembaty (New York: McGraw-Hill, 1987), p. 36.

38. Locke, *Second Treatise*, p. 19.

Chapter Six: Community as the Sociality

1. A useful study of varieties of individualism is Steven Lukes, *Individualism* (Oxford: Blackwell, 1973).

2. Immanuel Kant, *Foundations of the Metaphysics of Morals*, trans. Lewis White Beck (Indianapolis: Bobbs-Merrill Library of Liberal Arts, 1959), p. 47.

3. Robert N. Bellah, Richard Madsen, William M. Sullivan, Ann Swindler, Steven M. Tipton, *Habits of the Heart: Individualism and Commitment in American Life* (Berkeley, Los Angeles, London: University of California Press, 1985), p. 107.

4. *Ibid.*, p. 114.

5. Alasdair MacIntyre, *Whose Justice? Which Rationality?* (Notre Dame: University of Notre Dame Press, 1988), p. 367.

6. Erik H. Erikson, *Childhood and Society*, 2d ed. (New York: W. W. Norton, 1963), pp. 262–263.

7. Michael J. Sandel, *Liberalism and the Limits of Justice* (Cambridge: Cambridge University Press, 1982).

8. Sandel, *Liberalism and the Limits of Justice*, p. 175.

9. *Ibid.*, p. 183.

10. *Ibid.*, p. 152.

11. Martin Buber, *I and Thou*, trans. Walter Kaufmann (New York: Charles Scribner's Sons, 1970).

12. E.g., "Thus the time of human life is formed into an abundance of actuality; and although human life *cannot and ought not to overcome the It-relation*, it then becomes so permeated by relation that this gains a radiant and penetrating constancy in it." Buber, *I and Thou*, p. 163, my emphasis.

13. Jean-Paul Sartre, *Being and Nothingness*, trans. Hazel E. Barnes (New York: Philosophical Library, 1956), p. 568.

14. MacIntyre, *Whose Justice? Which Rationality?*, p. 383.

15. Michael Walzer, *Spheres of Justice: A Defense of Pluralism and Equality* (New York: Basic Books, 1983), p. 30.

16. Bellah et al., *Habits of the Heart*, pp. 65–71.

17. Walzer, *Spheres of Justice*, ch. 2, "Membership," e.g. p. 51.

18. An insightful discussion of Rousseau's concepts of "denaturing" and "second nature" appears in Roger D. Masters, *The Political Philosophy of Rous-*

seau (Princeton: Princeton University Press, 1968), pp. 297–299. Rousseau's *promeneur solitaire,* exemplified in Emile, undergoes no such denaturing, but is presented by Rousseau as a rare exception.

19. Jean Jacques Rousseau, *The Social Contract,* in *Social Contract,* ed. Ernest Barker (New York: Oxford University Press Galaxy Books, 1962), p. 180.

20. Rousseau, *The Social Contract.* Because it is clearer, I have used Manheim's translation, in Emil Durkheim, *Montesquieu and Rousseau* (Ann Arbor: University of Michigan Press, 1960), p. 105. Barker reads ". . . the general will, if it be deserving of its name, must be general, not in its origins only, but in its objects, applicable to all as well as operated by all . . ." *Social Contract,* p. 196.

21. Durkheim, *Montesquieu and Rousseau,* p. 112.

22. Jose Ortega y Gasset, *Man and People,* trans. Willard Trask (New York: W. W. Norton, 1957), p. 174.

23. Ralph Waldo Emerson, *Self-Reliance* (Mt. Vernon, N.Y.: Peter Pauper Press, 1967), p. 13.

24. *Ibid.,* p. 40.

25. C. B. MacPherson, *The Life and Times of Liberal Democracy* (Oxford: Oxford University Press, 1977), p. 43.

26. Philip Eliot Slater, *The Pursuit of Loneliness: American Culture at the Breaking Point,* rev. ed. (Boston: Beacon Press, 1976), p. 11. Carol Gilligan, *In a Different Voice: Psychological Theory and Women's Development* (Cambridge: Harvard University Press, 1982), p. 142. Christopher Lasch, *The Culture of Narcissism: American Life in an Age of Diminishing Expectations* (New York: W. W. Norton, 1978), p. xv.

27. Alexis de Tocqueville, *Democracy in America,* ed. J. P. Mayer, trans. George Lawrence (Garden City, N.Y.: Doubleday Anchor Books, 1969).

28. Christopher Lasch, *The Culture of Narcissism: American Life in an Age of Diminishing Expectations* (New York: W. W. Norton, 1978).

29. Tocqueville, *Democracy in America,* p. 506.

30. Cited in James T. Schleifer, *The Making of Tocqueville's Democracy in America* (Chapel Hill: University of North Carolina Press, 1980), pp. 250–251.

31. *Ibid.,* p. 253.

32. Tocqueville, *Democracy,* p. 676.

33. Lasch, *The Culture of Narcissism,* p. xv.

34. MacIntyre, *Whose Justice? Which Rationality?,* e.g., and notably, ch. XX, "Contested Justices, Contested Rationalities."

35. Cited in William James, "The Dilemma of Determinism," in *The Will to Believe and Other Essays in Popular Philosophy,* ed. Fredson Bowers (Cambridge: Harvard University Press, 1979), p. 134.

36. This is a central intent of Dworkin's major works, including *Taking Rights Seriously* (London: 1977) and *A Matter of Principle* (Cambridge: Harvard University Press, 1985).

37. Robert Nisbet, *Community and Power* (formerly *The Quest for Community*) (New York: Oxford University Press Galaxy Books, 1962), p. 256.

38. *Ibid.,* p. 134 (cited).

39. *Ibid.,* pp. 219–220.

40. John Locke, *The Second Treatise of Government,* ed. Thomas P. Peardon

(Indianapolis: Bobbs-Merrill Library of Liberal Arts, 1952), p. 50 ". . . the end of civil society being to avoid and remedy these inconveniences of the state of nature which necessarily follow from every man being judge in his own case, by setting up a known authority to which everyone of that society may appeal upon any injury received or controversy that may arise, and which everyone of the society ought to obey."

41. Edmund L. Pincoffs, *Quandaries and Virtues: Against Reductivism in Ethics* (Lawrence: University Press of Kansas, 1986), p. 58.

42. J. O. Urmson, "Saints and Heroes," in *Reason and Responsibility*, ed. Joel Feinberg (Belmont, Calif.: Wadsworth, 1985), pp. 515–522.

43. Michael Oakeshott, "Rationalism in Politics," in *Rationalism in Politics and Other Essays* (Totowa, N.J.: Rowman & Littlefield, 1977), p. 24.

44. Francis Bacon, *Novum Organum,* cited in Oakeshott, *Rationalism in Politics,* p. 14.

45. Bellah et al., *Habits of the Heart,* p. 45.

46. The term and its underlying thesis have considerable currency in social thought and criticism. With express indebtedness to William H. Whyte, Jr., *The Organization Man* (New York: Simon & Schuster, 1956), it first appears, I believe, in William G. Scott and David K. Hart, *Organizational America* (Boston: Houghton Mifflin, 1979). The thesis of the book is: "The modern organization . . . has produced vast transformation of the traditional American value system. We term this new value system, and the new society it has produced, respectively 'the organizational imperative' and organizational America" (p. 2).

47. *From Max Weber: Essays in Sociology,* ed. and trans. H. H. Gerth and C. Wright Mills (London: Oxford University Press Galaxy Books, 1946), p. 214.

48. *Ibid.,* pp. 219–220.

49. *Max Weber on Law in Economy and Society,* ed. Max Rheinstein, trans. Max Rheinstein and Edward Shils (Cambridge: Harvard University Press, 1954), p. 351.

50. Neil W. Chamberlain, *The Limits of Corporate Responsibility* (New York: Basic Books, 1973), p. 92. My thanks to David K. Hart for this reference.

51. William G. Scott and David K. Hart, *Organizational Values in America* (New Brunswick, N.J.: Transaction Publishers, 1989).

52. Correspondence, Raymond Schonholtz.

53. Peter Lovenheim, *Mediate, Don't Litigate* (New York: McGraw-Hill, 1989).

Chapter Seven: Good Government

1. John Dewey, *Democracy and Education* (New York: The Free Press, 1966), p. 88.

2. Robert Paul Wolff, *In Defense of Anarchism* (New York: Harper & Row, 1970), p. 19.

3. Plato, *The Republic,* 456.

4. Karl Popper, *The Open Society and Its Enemies,* 5th ed. (London: Routledge & Kegan Paul, 1966), vol. I, pp. 90–91.

5. Plato, *The Republic,* 416.

6. Popper, *The Open Society and Its Enemies,* p. 90.

7. *Ibid.,* p. 92.

8. Plato, *The Republic,* 369.

9. Thomas Hobbes, *Leviathan* (Indianapolis: Bobbs-Merrill Library of Liberal Arts, 1958), p. 86.

10. Popper, *The Open Society and Its Enemies,* p. 171.

11. Jean-Jacques Rousseau, *The Social Contract,* in *Social Contract,* ed. Ernest Barker (New York: Oxford University Press, 1962), p. 196. In the composite translation used by Barker, Rousseau's prescription for the General Will reads: ". . . the general will, if it be deserving of its name, must be general, not in its origins only, but in its objects, applicable to all as well as operated *by* all . . ."

12. A description of Pullman, Illinois, appears in Michael Walzer, *Spheres of Justice* (New York: Basic Books, 1983), pp. 295–299. Kohler, Wisconsin, is described in Walter H. Uphoff, *Kohler On Strike: Thirty Years of Conflict* (Boston: Beacon Press, 1966), ch. 1, "The 'Model Village'—Dreams, Realities and Myths."

13. William G. Scott, "The Concentric Circles of Management Thought," in *Papers in the Ethics of Administration,* ed. N. Dale Wright (Albany: State University of New York Press, 1988), p. 28.

14. Chester I. Barnard, *The Functions of the Executive* (Cambridge: Harvard University Press, 1938), p. 15.

15. Herbert A. Simon, *Administrative Behavior* (New York: Macmillan, 1954) p. 223.

16. Harry Braverman, *Labor and Monopoly Capital, The Degradation of Work in the Twentieth Century* (New York: Monthly Review Press, 1974), p. 90.

17. Adam Smith, *An Inquiry into the Nature and Causes of the Wealth of Nations,* ed. Richard F. Teichgraeber, III (New York: Modern Library, 1985), pp. 6–7.

18. William G. Scott and David K. Hart, *Organizational Values in America* (New Brunswick, N.J.: Transaction Publishers, 1989), p. 117. McGregor's influential treatment of Theory Y is Douglas McGregor, *The Human Side of Enterprise* (New York: McGraw-Hill, 1959.)

19. Raymond E. Callahan, *Education and the Cult of Efficiency: A Study of the Social Forces that Have Shaped the Administration of the Public Schools* (Chicago: University of Chicago Press, 1962).

20. John Rohr, *Ethics for Bureaucrats* (New York: Marcel Dekker, 1978).

21. Walzer, *Spheres of Justice,* pp. 17–20.

22. Scott and Hart, *Organizational Values in America,* pp. 97, 147–150.

23. Max De Pree, *Leadership is an Art* (New York: Doubleday, 1989).

24. John Dewey, *Liberalism and Social Action* (New York: G. P. Putnam's Sons Perigee Books, 1980), p. 39.

25. Michael Oakeshott, *On Human Conduct* (London: Oxford University Press, 1975), p. 118.

26. *Ibid.,* p. 313.

27. *Ibid.,* pp. 157–158.

28. *Ibid.,* p. 242.

29. Michael Oakeshott, "On Misunderstanding Human Conduct: A Reply to My Critics," in *Political Theory* 4(3):367 (Aug. 1976).

30. Michael Oakeshott, "The Tower of Babel," in *Rationalism in Politics and Other Essays* (Totowa, N.J.: Rowman and Littlefield, 1977), p. 62.

31. *Ibid.,* p. 62.

32. Oakeshott, *On Human Conduct,* p. 275.

33. Michael Oakeshott, "The Masses in Representative Democracy," in *American Conservative Thought in the Twentieth Century,* ed. William F. Buckley, ed. (New York: Bobbs-Merrill, 1970).

34. Ralph Barton Perry, *Puritanism and Democracy* (New York: Harper Torchbooks, 1944), p. 453.

Index

Designer:	U.C. Press Staff
Compositor:	Huron Valley Graphics
Text:	10/13 Galliard
Display:	Galliard
Printer:	Maple-Vail Book Mfg. Group
Binder:	Maple-Vail Book Mfg. Group